Building Inclusive Cities

Building on a growing movement within developing countries in Latin America, Africa and Asia–Pacific, as well as Europe and North America, this book documents cutting-edge practice and builds theory around a rights-based approach to women's safety in the context of poverty reduction and social inclusion. Drawing upon two decades of research and grass-roots action on safer cities for women and everyone, this book is about the right to an inclusive city. The first part of the book describes the challenges that women face regarding access to essential services, housing security, liveability and mobility. The second part of the book critically examines programmes, projects and ideas that are working to make cities safer. *Building Inclusive Cities* takes a cross-cultural learning perspective from action research occurring throughout the world and translates this research into theoretical conceptualizations to inform the literature on planning and urban management in both developing and developed countries. This book is intended to inspire both thought and action.

Carolyn Whitzman is Associate Professor in Urban Planning at the University of Melbourne. She is the author of *The Handbook of Community Safety, Gender, and Violence Prevention* (Earthscan, 2008) and has authored and contributed to several leading texts on safe cities.

Crystal Legacy is a Research Associate at the City Futures Research Centre at the University of New South Wales, Sydney. Crystal completed her PhD in urban planning from the University of Melbourne in 2010.

Caroline Andrew is the Director of the Centre on Governance, University of Ottawa, and is currently Chair of the Board of Women in Cities International. Her research interests are in the relationships between community-based equity-seeking groups and municipal governments.

Fran Klodawsky is Professor in the Department of Geography and Environmental Studies at Carleton University, Ottawa. Her feminist geographic research and writing have focused on the intersections of identity, housing and homelessness, governance and social inequalities.

Margaret Shaw is a sociologist and criminologist who works as an independent consultant and is currently a Fellow and former Director of Analysis and Exchange for the International Centre for the Prevention of Crime in Montreal. She is a board member of Women in Cities International.

Kalpana Viswanath is an expert on gender and urban safety and has led the Gender Inclusive Cities Programme of Women in Cities International. She is also Senior Advisor to the Safe Cities Programme of Jagori in Delhi.

Building Inclusive Cities

Women's safety and the right to the city

Edited by
Carolyn Whitzman
Crystal Legacy
Caroline Andrew
Fran Klodawsky
Margaret Shaw
Kalpana Viswanath

Routledge
Taylor & Francis Group
LONDON AND NEW YORK

earthscan
from Routledge

First published 2013
by Routledge
2 Park Square, Milton Park, Abingdon, Oxon, OX14 4RN

Simultaneously published in the USA and Canada
by Routledge
711 Third Avenue, New York, NY 10017

Routledge is an imprint of the Taylor & Francis Group, an informa business

© 2013 selection and editorial material, Carolyn Whitzman, Crystal Legacy, Caroline Andrew, Fran Klodawsky, Margaret Shaw and Kalpana Viswanath; individual chapters, the contributors.

The right of Carolyn Whitzman, Crystal Legacy, Caroline Andrew, Fran Klodawsky, Margaret Shaw and Kalpana Viswanath to be identified as authors of the editorial material, and of the individual authors as authors of their contributions, has been asserted in accordance with sections 77 and 78 of the Copyright, Designs and Patents Act 1988.

All rights reserved. No part of this book may be reprinted or reproduced or utilised in any form or by any electronic, mechanical, or other means, now known or hereafter invented, including photocopying and recording, or in any information storage or retrieval system, without permission in writing from the publishers.

Trademark notice: Product or corporate names may be trademarks or registered trademarks, and are used only for identification and explanation without intent to infringe.

British Library Cataloguing in Publication Data
A catalogue record for this book is available from the British Library

Library of Congress Cataloging-in-Publication Data
Building inclusive cities: women's safety and the right to the city/
edited by Carolyn Whitzman . . . [et al.].
  p. cm.
Includes bibliographical references and index.
1. City planning – Social aspects. 2. Women – Crimes against.
3. Women – Violence against. I. Whitzman, Carolyn.
HT166.B817 2013
307.1'216 – dc23
2012007716

ISBN: 978-0-415-62815-0 (hbk)
ISBN: 978-0-415-62816-7 (pbk)
ISBN: 978-0-203-10069-1 (ebk)

Typeset in Sabon and Gill Sans by
Florence Production Ltd, Stoodleigh, Devon

Printed and bound in Great Britain by the MPG Books Group

Contents

List of figures vii
List of tables viii
Notes on contributors ix
Acknowledgements xii
List of abbreviations xiv

1 Introduction: challenges, opportunities and tools 1
MARGARET SHAW, CAROLINE ANDREW, CAROLYN WHITZMAN,
FRAN KLODAWSKY, KALPANA VISWANATH AND CRYSTAL LEGACY

PART I
Challenges and opportunities 17

2 Gendered livelihoods and inclusive cities 19
FRAN KLODAWSKY

3 Women's safety and everyday mobility 35
CAROLYN WHITZMAN

4 Migrant women's safety: framing, policies, and practices 53
SARA ORTIZ ESCALANTE AND ELIZABETH L. SWEET

PART II
Interventions 73

5 Gender Inclusive Cities Programme: implementing change for women's safety 75
KALPANA VISWANATH

6 The role of partnerships in creating inclusive cities   90
CAROLINE ANDREW AND CRYSTAL LEGACY

7 What it looks like when it's fixed: collaboration towards a shared vision of city safety   103
BARBARA HOLTMANN

8 Safe access to basic infrastructure: more than pipes and taps   117
PRABHA KHOSLA AND SUNEETA DHAR

PART III
Tools   141

9 From gender mainstreaming to intersectionality: advances in achieving inclusive and safe cities   143
ANITA LACEY, REBECCA MILLER, DORY REEVES AND YARDENA TANKEL

10 Safer discursive space: artistic interventions and online action research   162
MELANIE LAMBRICK

11 How do we evaluate the safety of women?   184
MARGARET SHAW

12 Conclusion: women's safety and the right to the city   201
FRAN KLODAWSKY, CAROLYN WHITZMAN, CRYSTAL LEGACY, CAROLINE ANDREW, MARGARET SHAW AND KALPANA VISWANATH

Index   208

Figures

2.1	Warwick Junction: internationally recognized gender-sensitive land-use planning	28
4.1	Casa Segura's (Safe Home) street theater performance to raise awareness about the intersection of gender-based violence, patriarchy, and class struggle (Chicago, Illinois, 2006)	64
4.2	Multiple factors that should be considered when developing approaches to safe cities for migrant women and girls	67
5.1	Participating cities, populations and partners	77
5.2	Factors causing women to feel unsafe	82
7.1	Breaking the cycle of violence	109
7.2	Safe community of opportunity	111
7.3	Department of Education	113
7.4	A safe city for women	114
8.1	Conceptual modes of infrastructure for everyday life	120
8.2	Map of Delhi and the National Capital Region, showing Bawana and Bhalswa	125
8.3	Woman in a community toilet complex	127
8.4	Muddy streets in all seasons	129
8.5	Girls fetching water from a water tanker in Bhalswa	130
8.6	Man cleaning the drain outside his home, Bhalswa	132
8.7	Woman cooking outside her home on her 'veranda' over the drain, Bawana	132
10.1	Defaced woman figure in Rosario, Argentina	169
10.2	Several recovered women figures in Rosario, Argentina	169
10.3	Y R U LOOKING AT ME, *Blank Noise* action heroes	178
10.4	'Mohini. Age 19. A stranger rubbed himself against me', *Blank Noise* action heroes	179

Tables

2.1	Informal employment as percentage of non-agricultural employment in selected regions and countries, various years (1995–2000)	21
5.1	Types of harassment faced by survey respondents in the past year (%)	81
5.2	Women's responses to sexual harassment (%)	83
8.1	Prevailing wage rates, 2 January 2008	134
8.2	Bawana: the opportunity costs for water from public standpipes	135
8.3	Bawana: the opportunity costs of water without the provision of public water	135
8.4	Bhalswa: the opportunity costs of tanker supply	135
8.5	Bhalswa: the opportunity costs of pumps pumping leachate	135

Notes on contributors

Caroline Andrew is the Director of the Centre on Governance, University of Ottawa, Canada. Her research interests are the relationships between community-based equity-seeking groups and municipal governments, particularly focusing on the intersections of gender and immigration status. Caroline is currently Chair of the Board of Women in Cities International (WICI).

Suneeta Dhar is the Director of Jagori, a women's resource centre based in Delhi. She has worked on women's rights with national and international agencies, including the UN. She is a core group member of the South Asian Network of Gender Activists and Trainers (SANGAT) and a Founding Director of the South Asia Women's Fund.

Barbara Holtmann has a Master's in Management (Public and Development Management) from University of Witwatersrand and a Ph.D. (Management of Technology and Innovation) from the Da Vinci Institute. Her book, *What it Looks Like When its Fixed*, describes her methodology for transforming complex, fragile social systems. She is the VP of the International Centre for Prevention of Crime (ICPC) and serves on the board of Women in Cities International (WICI).

Prabha Khosla is an urban planner. For over fifteen years she has worked on issues of urban sustainability, urban environments, democratizing local governance, water and sanitation, and training and capacity building. She has authored numerous articles and papers. Her latest training manuals are: *A Training Package: Improving Gender Equality & Grassroots Participation through Good Land Governance* (2010) and *Gender in Local Government: A Sourcebook for Trainers* (2008), both published by UN-HABITAT.

Fran Klodawsky is Professor in the Department of Geography and Environmental Studies at Carleton University in Ottawa, Canada. Fran's feminist geographic research and writing has focused on the intersections of identity, housing and homelessness, governance, and social inequalities. Currently, she is preparing a manuscript about feminist urban-based community organizing that will draw in part on the in-depth examination of two case-study organizations.

Anita Lacey is a Senior Lecturer in International Relations. She is also a committed activist, and her research and activism intersect. She has published on the governance of global poverty (with Suzan Ilcan), resistances to neoliberal globalization, asylum and identity, NGOs and voluntarism, protest, and gendered protest spaces.

Melanie Lambrick is an artist and researcher. She holds a Master's of Urban Planning from McGill University and has a Bachelor of Fine Arts – Visual Art/Bachelor of Arts – Political Science from the University of Victoria. She worked for several years with WICI in Montreal, Canada.

Crystal Legacy is a Research Associate at the City Futures Research Centre at the University of New South Wales, Sydney. Crystal completed her Ph.D. in Urban Planning at the University of Melbourne in 2010, before commencing a post-doctoral researcher position at the University of Melbourne, which included development of this edited book manuscript. She is the co-author of the online Urban Safety Toolkit for Asia–Pacific (UN-HABITAT, 2010).

Rebecca Miller is a Foreign Expert at the Institute for Population and Social Research at Mahidol University in Thailand. She has worked for academic institutions, as well as governmental, intergovernmental, and nongovernmental organizations in fourteen countries. Her fifteen years of research and professional work have focused primarily on gender and human rights, social protection, gender-based violence, irregular migration, and crime prevention.

Sara Ortiz Escalante is a researcher and consultant on gender, urban planning, women's safety, and migrant women. She is part of Col·lectiu Punt 6, a group of feminist planners and activists. She holds a Sociology degree from the Autonomous University of Barcelona, a Diploma on Gender Relations from the National Autonomous University of Mexico, and a Master in Urban Planning from the University of Illinois at Urbana-Champaign.

Dory Reeves is a chartered town planner and Professor of Planning in the School of Architecture and Planning at the University of Auckland in New Zealand. She is also the focal point for the partnership with UN-HABITAT and has participated in the World Urban Forums in Nanjing and Rio.

Margaret Shaw Ph.D. is a sociologist and criminologist who works as an independent consultant and is currently a Fellow at the International

Centre for the Prevention of Crime (ICPC) in Montreal, Canada. From 1999 until 2011 she was Director of Analysis and Exchange at ICPC. She is a board member of WICI. She has worked for the Home Office in Britain, taught at Concordia University, Montreal, and undertaken extensive research, including on gender, women's imprisonment, evaluation and crime prevention.

Elizabeth L. Sweet is a Visiting Assistant Professor at Temple University in the Department of Geography and Urban Studies. Her scholarship examines the role of planning and policy in the production and reproduction of social, economic, and spatial inequalities through the lens of gender, race, immigration, citizenship, and violence.

Yardena Tankel is a researcher at the Centre for Development Studies, the University of Auckland, New Zealand. She has researched and published in the areas of women's (in)security in cities, women's social activism and the right to the city, and local and transnational urban feminisms.

Kalpana Viswanath is an expert on gender and urban safety and has led the Gender Inclusive Cities Programme (GICP) of WICI. She is also Senior Advisor to the Safe Cities Programme of Jagori, UN Women, and the Delhi government. She has published in many journals and magazines on the issues of women's safety, right to the city, and related issues.

Carolyn Whitzman is Associate Professor in Urban Planning at the University of Melbourne. She is the author of *Suburb, Slum, Urban Village: Transformations in a Toronto Neighbourhood 1875–2002* (2009) and *The Handbook of Community Safety, Gender, and Violence Prevention: Practical Planning Tools* (2008), and the co-author of *Safe Cities: Guidelines for Planning, Design, and Management* (1994).

Acknowledgements

This book arose from conversations and inspiring presentations at the Third International Conference on Women's Safety, in Delhi, India, November 2010. The conference's theme was 'Building Inclusive Cities', and we have used that title for our book as well. The editors would like to thank the staff of Women in Cities International and Jagori, who organized the conference and who also managed the Gender Inclusive Cities Programme. These organizations, and many others working to prevent violence and create more inclusive cities, have informed and inspired us to share their contributions and activities with a much wider audience.

The University of Melbourne provided monetary support, as did Carolyn Whitzman's research budget, to hire Crystal Legacy to coordinate this book. Crystal's tireless organizational management skills were a key factor in getting this book completed relatively quickly and easily. For her work in reminding all authors of chapter deadlines, providing editorial support for multiple drafts of chapters, arranging copyright for illustrations, and multitudinous other matters, many thanks!

Carolyn Whitzman would like to thank, as always, her husband David Hunt and children Simon Hunt and Molly Hunt, for their encouragement, love, and support. Fran Klodawsky thanks the three men whose lives are most closely intertwined with hers – husband Aron, and sons Noah and Gabriel – for inspiring her to write clearly and compassionately about how women and men do and might learn to live well together. Kalpana Viswanath would like to acknowledge the entire GICP team at WICI and the four partners (Jagori, ICNIC-T, ICIWF, and CISCSA) for their inspiring work and commitment to creating safer communities and cities. Caroline Andrew and Margaret Shaw would like to thank the entire WICI team and our four partners in the *Together for Women's Safety Project*, Women of the Dawn, the Centre des ainés, Catholic Crosscultural Services and Action des femmes handicapées, and all the women who participated with such energy and commitment in the creation of inclusive and safe communities. Crystal Legacy would like to thank her loving partner Andrew Harris and family, particularly her parents Darlene and Kenneth Legacy and her brother Brandon for their continual encouragement and love.

Every effort has been made to contact and acknowledge copyright owners. If any material has been included without permission, the publishers offer their apologies. The publishers would be pleased to have any errors or omissions brought to their attention so that corrections may be published at later printing.

Abbreviations

AFHM	Action des Femmes Handicappées (Montréal)
ASSOTSI	Associação dos Operadores e Trabalahdores do Sector Informal
CAFSU	Centre d'action sur femmes et sécurite urbain (Women's Action centre on Urban Safety)
CBGA	Centre for Budget and Governance Accountability
CCTV	closed-circuit television
CEMR	Council of European Municipalities and Regions
CRP	Crime Reduction Programme
CTCs	community toilets complexes
DTC	Delhi Transport Corporation
ECLAC	Economic Commission for Latin America and the Caribbean
EQIAs	equality-impact assessments
GBV	gender-based violence
GIAs	Gender-Impact Assessments
GICP	Gender Inclusive Cities Programme
GRBIs	gender-responsive budget initiatives
ICIWF	International Centre of the Independent Women's Forum
ICNIC-T	International Centre for Network and Information on Crime – Tanzania
ICPC	International Centre for the Prevention of Crime
IDRC	International Development Research Centre
ILO	International Labor Organization
IOM	International Organization for Migration
IVAWS	International Violence Against Women Survey
JJ	Jhuggi Jhopri
METRAC	Metro Toronto Action Committee on Public Violence Against Women and Children
MPD	master plan for Delhi
NGOs	non-government organizations
NSSO	National Sample Survey Organization
OECD	Organization for Economic Cooperation and Development
PUKAR	Partnerships for Urban Knowledge and Research

RMH	Women and Habitat Network
SANGAT	South Asian Network of Gender Activists and Trainers
SAPS	South African Police Service
SCGP	Safe Cities Free of Violence against Women and Girls Global Programme
SEWU	Self-Help Women's Union
SHRF	Shan Human Rights Foundation
SPT	Strathclyde Passenger Transport
SWAN	Shan Women's Action Network
TCPO	Town and Country Planning Office
UCLG	United Cities and Local Governments
UNODC	United Nations Office on Drugs and Crime
VAW	violence against women
WAV	Women Against Violence
WEJ	Women for Economic Justice
WHO	World Health Organization
WICI	Women in Cities International
WLB	Women's League of Burma
WSA	Women's Safety Audit

Chapter 1

Introduction

Challenges, opportunities and tools[1]

*Margaret Shaw, Caroline Andrew,
Carolyn Whitzman, Fran Klodawsky,
Kalpana Viswanath and Crystal Legacy*

The movement to increase the safety of women in cities has been growing over the past fifteen to twenty years in many regions of the world. It involves a surprisingly varied range of people, of all ages, backgrounds, races and cultures, in large and small cities, and working in communities, organizations and governments. They have been very creative and innovative, exchanged ideas, and in turn been inspired by other groups, individuals and organizations. The concept of a safe city for women has become more sophisticated and tangible, to encompass much more than just the absence of violence in women's lives. It has become more cross-disciplinary. The Third International Conference on Women's Safety: Building Inclusive Cities, which took place in New Delhi India in November 2011, marks the significance of this growth and movement and formed the inspiration for this book. As the Background Paper for that conference puts it:

> The Third International Conference on Women's Safety provides an important opportunity to assess some of the current and emerging trends, achievements and challenges in building safe and inclusive cities for women and girls. It is grounded in *a systemic rights-based approach to women's safety that recognizes diversity*. It emphasizes the need to work towards more equitable access to the opportunities cities can offer, regardless of age, gender, race, religion, sexual orientation, immigrant status, disability or any other factor, for all city dwellers, and it strongly reaffirms that solutions introduced by women to enhance safety will make cities safer for all.
> (WICI and Jagori, 2010, p. 1)

The Delhi conference was the third in a series spanning the past decade, concerned with the growth in knowledge and networks about how to increase the safety of women and make more visible the role of women in this work. The First International Women's Safety Seminar, 'Making the links', was held in Montreal, Canada, in 2002.[2] The second conference, entitled 'Safer Cities', was held in Bogota, Colombia, in 2004.[3] All three conferences have resulted in Declarations on women's safety that have helped to set the agenda for national and local governments, international organizations, community-based women's groups and civil society in general.

The Delhi conference brought together a wide range of people, from forty-five countries and eighty-one cities, to consider how women and girls can live more equitable and fulfilling lives in the face of some rapidly changing patterns of life across the globe. These changing patterns include increasing urbanization, the growing migration of women to cities, and environmental disasters and climate change. Globalization and technological changes are impacting lives in both positive and negative ways, and, as always, their impact on women and girls differs from that on men and boys in some very significant ways.

The themes of the conference are also reflected in the new vision for UN Women, as outlined by Michelle Bachelet, the first Executive Director, in January 2011 (see Box below).

UN Women's New Vision

UN Women's new vision and 100-day action plan includes five main thematic areas:[4]

1. *Expanding women's voice, leadership and participation,* working with partners to close the gaps in women's leadership and participation in different sectors and to demonstrate the benefits of such leadership for society as a whole.
2. *Ending violence against women* by enabling states to set up the mechanisms needed to formulate and enforce laws, policies and services that protect women and girls, promote the involvement of men and boys, and prevent violence.
3. *Strengthening implementation of the women, peace and security agenda,* through women's full participation in conflict resolution and peace processes, gender-responsive early-warning, protection from sexual violence and redress for its survivors in accordance with UN resolutions.
4. *Enhancing women's economic empowerment* is particularly important in the context of global economic and environmental crises. UN Women will work with governments and multilateral partners to ensure the full realization of women's economic security and rights, including productive assets and full social protection.
5. *Making gender-equality priorities central to national, local and sectoral planning and budgeting,* working with partners, UN Women will support national capacities in evidence-based planning, budgeting and statistics.

These priorities resonate strongly with the themes of the conference and the overall movement to increase women's security and inclusion in cities: the combination of women's leadership and voice; the importance of anti-violence work; and the focus on making sure that gender equality is seen as central to the issues of planning and budgeting across all levels of government.

This chapter provides a broad overview of some of the main global trends that are affecting women's and girls' lives, the implications of which are discussed in more detail in the subsequent chapters of the book. They can be seen as challenges, but equally as opportunities that can be exploited to further greater equality and access to the benefits of healthy urban life. Before exploring these, however, it is necessary to consider what we mean by the safety of women and girls.

Defining some terms: what do we mean by women's safety and other concepts used in this book?

Defining terms is always important, even though not everyone is always in agreement about precise wording. This may apply to some of the authors in this book, and the following definitions are not intended to trump their own understandings but simply to encourage discussion and dialogue. Concepts and understandings also change over time. What is more important is to set down some of the key concepts that are currently being used around the world, to help understand trends and action, and to frame problems and perhaps solutions. In many cases, but not all, they are grounded in internationally agreed upon definitions.

Two of the most important are violence against women and gender-based violence. The 1993 Declaration on the Elimination of Violence Against Women was the first international human-rights instrument exclusively to address the issue of violence against women (VAW). It defines it in Article 1 as:

> Any act of gender-based violence that results in, or is likely to result in, physical, sexual or psychological harm or suffering to women, including threats of such acts, coercion or arbitrary deprivation of liberty, whether occurring in public or private life.[5]

This definition has formed the basis for an enormous amount of action internationally, but has tended to be understood and acted upon primarily in relation to violence occurring in intimate or family settings – in private space.

To reflect the fact that violence against women results from an imbalance of power between women and men, and that women are subjected to it because of their gender, the term *gender-based violence* (GBV) in the definition has also come to be used widely at the international level over the past decade. The 1995 Fourth World Conference on Women (Beijing) recognized the elimination of gender-based violence as central to gender equality and the empowerment of women.[6]

As suggested above, in many countries, much of the work to eliminate violence against women focused initially on private or intimate violence. The fact that women were also at risk of violence and felt insecure about their safety in their daily lives outside the home and in public spaces remained unarticulated in policy terms. In part, this has reflected notions of women's culpability in inviting violence, that they 'asked for it' or should have stayed at home, that they were somehow less respectable than 'other' women. Government advice in the 1980s and 1990s tended to place the burden of responsibility on women themselves in terms of how they dressed and when and where they went out. More recently, the disappearance of women from city spaces has been ignored or downplayed by police and governments, as is demonstrated by the numbers of missing and murdered Aboriginal women in Canada, or the femicide which has occurred in Mexican or Central American cities (Native Women's Association of Canada, 2010; Prieto-Carrón *et al.*, 2007, p. 35).

Thus, the concept of *women's safety* grew out of this recognition that women have just as much right to go out and to use public spaces as men, and that their lives should not be restricted by fear or actual violence. It has been defined as involving 'strategies, practices and policies with the goal of reducing gender-based violence and women's fear or insecurity of violence' (Shaw and Capobianco, 2004, p. 5; Shaw and Andrew, 2005). In practice, strategies around women's safety focus on what can be done at the community and local level to increase their safety, and on the responsibilities of city governments and other sectors to take action, rather than blaming individual women.

What is useful about the concept of women's safety is that it offers a positive paradigm that places more focus on communities and the role of cities, and encourages practical initiatives that help create safer cities. It underlines that there is a continuum between private and public violence that requires us to work on both (Sweet and Ortiz Escalante, 2010; Shaw, 2009). However, the concept of safety has, over the past few years, come to be seen as being about more than just violence: it has expanded to include freedom from poverty, financial security and autonomy, and having a sense of self-worth, as they are all inextricably linked (Falu and Segovia, 2008; Lambrick and Travers, 2008). The full diversity of women and the importance of intersectionality have been central to the movement for the creation of safer cities for women. Economic, physical and environmental security are all key, as are an absence of exploitation, exclusion and injustice (Moser, 2004; Falu and Segovia, 2008).

Two other concepts that are especially relevant to building safe cities for women are gender mainstreaming and the right to the city. *Gender mainstreaming* was defined by the UN in 1997:

> Mainstreaming a gender perspective is the process of assessing the implications for women and men of any planned action, including legislation, policies or programmes, in all areas and at all levels. . . . The ultimate goal is to achieve gender equality.[7]

Gender mainstreaming initially had a difficult history. For some governments and policymakers, it was interpreted to mean that there was no longer a need to allocate specific funds and resources for women's issues. The result was often a cutting of resources for women's departments and committees, and a loss of focus on women's issues in policies and practice. More recently, however, there has been renewed attention to what gender mainstreaming means and requires, together with the development of tools that help to ensure that it is happening. These include gender auditing and gender budgeting, which are discussed elsewhere in this book. In relation to women's safety, gender mainstreaming aims to ensure that both women's and men's safety issues are separately taken into account at all levels of government and in all policies and interventions developed. This ranges from the routine collection of data on women's and men's concerns to the inclusion of women's voices in policy and strategy development (Moser, 2008).[8]

What is often forgotten is that gender includes not just women and girls but also men and boys. One of the important developments in recent years has been the recognition that increasing the safety of women requires considerable work to change culturally accepted attitudes about women, including acceptance of violence and exploitation. A number of programmes and networks have begun to emerge around the world that place an emphasis on the need to change the cultural acceptance of violence, and offer alternative lifestyle choices to men and boys.

A more recent concept is that of the *right to the city*, which builds on the 1948 Universal Declaration of Human Rights among other international declarations. As set out in the World Charter on the Right to the City in 2004–5, the notion of the right to the city is concerned with the right of all individuals living in cities to liberty, freedom and the benefits of city life. It stresses transparency, equity and efficiency in the administration of cities, participation and respect in local democratic decision-making, recognition of diversity in economic, social and cultural life, and the reduction of poverty, social exclusion and urban violence (Brown and Kristiansen, 2009).[9] The Charter has been endorsed by a number of countries and cities as a valuable normative framework that protects all types of human rights and fosters social inclusion in cities. This includes issues around urban development or renewal and the use of public and private space (Brown, 2010, p. 6). Expanding this still further, women's right to the city is seen as including:

- access to safe and healthy land and housing;
- the prevention of homelessness and forced evictions;

- access to essential services (water, sewage, waste disposal, roads, power etc.);
- access to other public services (health care, education, recreation etc.);
- the ability to move around the city in safety;
- access to safe and non-exploitative jobs and income.

Examples of cities or countries that have incorporated the notion of the right to the city include Brazil's City Statute (2001), the Civic and Citizens' Pact (2003) adopted by the city of Dakar, Senegal, the City of Montreal's Charter of Rights and Responsibilities (2006) and Ecuador's new Constitution (2008), which all recognize the right to the city (UN-HABITAT, 2010). It has also been adapted to the concerns of girls in cities with an eight-point call to action on 'Girls' rights to the city' (Plan International, 2010, p. 91). The 'right to the city' also incorporates a perspective, from the writings of Henri Lefebvre and more recent authors, about the importance of the political mobilization of urban citizens to actualize their rights to the city. In this way, the right to the city for women and girls is actively linked to the voice and active participation of women and girls in building safer and more inclusive cities (Lefebvre, 1968; Purcell, 2008).

The concepts of gender equality, women's safety and the 'right to the city' are all inextricably linked. Women's lack of safety is a serious obstacle to achieving gender equality. It curtails their mobility and ability to participate fully and freely as citizens in their communities. Women's 'right to the city' includes the right to live free from violence and fear, in more equitable, democratic and inclusive cities (Falu, 2010, p. 16). It recognizes that all women and girls have the right to participate and be a part of the decision-making process in local governance and urban planning. These concepts are also very closely linked to an intersectional analysis and the importance of considering the full diversity of women and girls. Intersectionality is discussed at greater length elsewhere in this volume, but it is also central to our whole understanding of the issue of the safety of women in cities.

So, what are the challenges?

We know from studies across the world that, in spite of many years of work, violence against women continues to be widespread both in public and private settings. To some extent, part of this increase relates to greater willingness to report violence against women, and thus rates of reporting are increasing, which is in itself a positive trend. However, we know that violence against women is still very much under-reported and is increasing, for example, in situations of war and conflict, and in relation to femicide. A number of recent international studies have demonstrated the widespread impacts of violence against women.

In 2005, the World Health Organization (WHO) collected information on intimate male violence against partners in ten countries.[10] Their multi-country study on women's health and domestic violence against women found that the proportion of women who had experienced physical or sexual violence, or both, in their lifetime ranged from 15 per cent to 71 per cent, with most countries recording between 29 per cent and 62 per cent. The study emphasizes, not only the damaging public-health impacts of such violence, but also the very strong persistence of gendered roles and expectations, which act as powerful constraints on change. In some countries, as many as 50–90 per cent of women felt that it was acceptable for a man to beat his wife in certain circumstances.

The *International Violence Against Women Survey* (IVAWS) is a victimization survey that has so far been adapted and used in eleven countries (Johnson *et al.*, 2008).[11] It looks at both intimate violence *and* violence perpetrated by men other than partners, and so this includes violence in public spaces. The findings from nine countries show that violence against women was prevalent in every country studied, and among all age and socio-economic groups of women:

- In the majority of countries studied, between 35 per cent and 60 per cent of women experienced physical or sexual violence from some man, since the age of sixteen.
- In most countries, between 22 per cent and 40 per cent of women have been physically or sexually assaulted by an intimate partner.
- Between 10 per cent and 31 per cent of women have been sexually assaulted by a man other than an intimate partner.
- Although physical violence tends to predominate in relationships with intimate partners, when other men are the perpetrators, sexual violence tends to occur with the same or greater frequency as physical violence.

Apart from these studies, there is a fast-growing documentation of violence against women in situations of war and conflict, and of femicide across a number of societies, including Canada, where some 600 Aboriginal women have gone missing or been murdered over the past twenty years (Native Women's Association of Canada, 2010). Concern about the extent of femicide in the Latin American and Caribbean region has led to heightened monitoring in Honduras, El Salvador, Nicaragua and Costa Rica, organized by *Red Feminista* (Prieto-Carrón *et al.*, 2007). Over 2,000 young women have been reported murdered since 2001 in Guatemala, and the deaths of many women have gone uninvestigated in border cities such as Cuidad Juarez in Mexico (Beltran and Freeman, 2007). The 2011 report of a Mexican parliamentary committee in collaboration with UN Women and the National Institute for Women documents the extent and growth of femicide in the country from 1985 to 2009.[12]

What are the current trends facing women and girls living in, or moving to, cities and urban spaces? They include, not only issues of safety in public spaces, but also access to essential services, to housing security, liveability and mobility. Violence against women is not declining, but there are four major trends affecting women's lives that will increase in likelihood in the coming years: increasing urbanization; increasing rural–urban migration; increasing polarization of wealth and poverty; and environmental and climate change. There are also changes in technology and international communications that are having significant impacts on the lives of women and girls. Each of these affects all other aspects of daily life – access to housing, water and sanitation, education, health and employment.

Increasing urbanization

Since 2007, the majority of the world's population is now living in cities, and cities are rapidly growing in size. Much of this is the result of an increasing rate of rural–urban migration around the world. Dispossession of lands, forced evictions, wars and conflicts, and lack of employment opportunities are some of the factors contributing to this development (UN-HABITAT, 2008). These trends will continue into the near future, with most of the expected growth in cities in developing countries, especially Africa and Asia. UN-HABITAT suggests it will be concentrated in a few countries, including China, India, the Congo, Nigeria, Bangladesh, Indonesia, Pakistan and the Philippines. The number of megacities with populations of 10 million or more is also growing, and fifteen of the twenty such cities are in developing countries (UN-HABITAT, 2009b, 2010).

The problem for cities is that, when urban growth happens so quickly, it can overwhelm the capacities of city governments to provide basic infrastructure such as housing, roads, water and sewage disposal. It means that government services such as transport, access to work and credit, health, education, social services or policing are inadequate and overstretched. Yet, many cities do not see their responsibilities as including provision for all their citizens. New residents often live in poverty in informal, peri-urban, underserviced settlements and are excluded from most of the benefits of city life, as well as safety and the rule of law. The polarization between incomes and quality of life for those living in cities is also increasing. In contrast to informal settlements, the urban rich (and some middle-income residents) are increasingly able to live in gated communities, guarded by private security, and enjoy high-quality services and access to public spaces. In informal settlements, female-headed households tend to predominate, and women are often victims of discrimination and abuse as well as violence.[13] City governments in many of these new megacities are increasingly orienting their priorities to becoming world-class cities and giving priority to these directions, rather than to increasing access to services for the urban poor (Abdelhalim and Shehayeb, 2011). Forced eviction of informal settlements is a common occurrence in many urban areas, often for reasons such as tourism or private land sales, which bring little or no benefits to the poor populations that are evicted (Menon Sen and Bhan, 2008).

Migration

Closely related to the rapid growth in cities and urban areas is the issue of migration. It may seem obvious – something that has been happening for centuries – but in fact both the 'idea' of migrating and patterns of migration are changing quite dramatically in the twenty-first century.

There are many factors that are both pulling and pushing people to leave their country for another, or to travel to urban areas within their own country. People are pulled by the prospects of a better quality of life and economic conditions, and pushed by poor living or environmental conditions, poverty and lack of opportunities, as well as because of conflict, discrimination or war.

Globalization has had many impacts on job opportunities and people's willingness to take risks to change their lives. One of the major changes taking place in migration patterns has been the increase in women migrants – what has been termed the *feminization of migration* (Castles and Miller, 2003; INSTRAW, 2007; Caritas Internationalis, 2010).[14] Increasing numbers of women are migrating – and without their families, as was more common in the past – to jobs in domestic work and health and care-giving in other countries. This is having serious consequences for their overall safety and for their own families of origin. The International Organization for Migration (IOM) estimates that, currently, the number of international migrants is between 175 million and 190.6 million, and women constitute 50 per cent of those migrants who are working, especially in developed countries (Global Migration Group, 2008). Many of the jobs to which women migrate are poorly paid and in unregulated sectors, so that their working and living conditions are neither good nor safe.

Although many women may choose to migrate, forced migration also has differential causes and impacts on women and men. People may be forced to leave their homes because of natural disasters, forced evictions, displacement from traditional lands, armed conflict or war. Some women may be escaping domestic abuse or forced-marriage practices, or become the victims of human trafficking unwittingly (Ehrenreich and Hoschild, 2003; Kedir and Admasachew, 2010). Displaced and refugee women are at high risk of sexual violence and of being trafficked. There are widespread reports of gender-based and sexual violence against women and girls in camps for refugees and displaced persons, as well as sexual violence against men and boys (UNHCR, 2003).

Although labour trafficking affects both men and women, women and girls are especially vulnerable to human trafficking for sexual purposes. In some cases, what may appear to be migration for a legitimate job turns into trafficking on arrival in the destination country, when women are forced into prostitution to pay back costs. Accurate information on the extent of human trafficking is very difficult to obtain, and estimates vary depending on the sources of data examined. The International Labour Organization estimates that labour trafficking exceeds trafficking for sexual purposes. Some 12.3 billion people worldwide were estimated, in 2009, to be in some form of forced labour or bondage, 8.1 million outside the sex industry and 4.2 million within it, and 57 per cent of those in forced labour were women and girls (ILO, 2009; US Department of State, 2010). UNODC's 2009 *Global Report on Trafficking in Persons* estimates that 75 per cent of trafficking is for the purposes of sexual exploitation and predominantly targets women and girls (UNODC, 2009). Of sixty-one countries collecting information in 2006, 66 per cent of victims identified were women and 13 per cent girls, with men and boys accounting for 12 per cent and 9 per cent, respectively. It also notes, however, that 30 per cent of traffickers are themselves women (UNODC, 2009).

Many of the initiatives to counter trafficking in relation to border controls and punitive sanctions have been contentious, with some arguing that it has led to the criminalization of migrants or has pushed a larger proportion of forced migrants into the hands of traffickers, but has had limited impact on the social and economic causes of the trade (Doucey, 2010).

The environment and climate change

Environmental disasters and climate change are already having a significant impact on the daily lives and safety of urban populations. Climate change is expected increasingly to affect access to water and food in cities, and hundreds of millions of people will be vulnerable to coastal flooding and related natural disasters such as tsunamis and bushfires. This, in turn, may encourage more rural populations to migrate to urban areas. As with many other trends, the changes are likely to affect some people more than others. The poorest people in the poorest countries will suffer the impacts of climate change the most, although they will have done the least to affect the earth's climate. UN-HABITAT reports, for example, that four out of every ten non-permanent houses in the developing world are now located in areas threatened by floods, landslides and other natural disasters (UN-HABITAT, 2009a).

Again, women are significantly affected, and in different ways from men and boys. The scarcity of water supplies and of sanitation has become a significant problem facing growing urban settlements and is widespread in South East Asian and Sub-Saharan African countries. As women and girls are traditionally the main water collectors, female members of households face time-limited access to water, and are at risk of violence and harassment when they go to collect it. Lack of sanitation and limited access to toilets can be degrading and physically dangerous for women and girls (Jagori, 2010). Time spent on accessing water and sanitation often results in reduced time available to attend school or travel to work. Furthermore, in many countries, women are primarily responsible for all forms of waste disposal (Reeves *et al.*, 2009).

Why don't we think in terms of opportunities?

Thus, the lives of women and girls in cities, particularly those doubly or triply marginalized through poverty, indigenity and/or disability as well as their gender, are significantly affected by all these changes taking place across the world. Yet the effects of migration and urbanization are not all bad, and moving to cities can have some very positive effects on people's lives. Cities can offer many social, economic and political opportunities to girls and women that are not available elsewhere (Giddings and Hovroka, 2010). In Botswana, for example, urban youth accept a wider range of women's and men's social roles than is the case among their rural peers. In South Korea, there is evidence to indicate that industrialization and urbanization have contributed to a decline in the cultural preference of sons over daughters, although the reverse appears to be the case in India (Chung and Das Gupta, 2007; Jha, 2011).

It is common to talk about challenges, but less common to think in terms of the opportunities that cities and city life offer, in addition to the improvements in the quality of people's lives. It is in placing women and girls as active and important participants in decision-making around urban futures that we can focus on the opportunities, not just the challenges.

This book looks at some of these opportunities in terms of the major resources that can be drawn on, the strategies, tools and practices that have been developed, and at some of the ways in which positive changes in the lives of women can be made, sustained and built upon. Focusing on the tools and strategies available also supports this perspective of looking at opportunities rather than dwelling only on marginalization and/or simply on women as victims.

By looking at the principal strategies and tools for improving women's safety, we are making clear the dimension of women's agency and keeping our focus on the potential for meaningful participation in the governance of the city. Strategies and tools include:

- good governance and civil-society engagement with local governments;
- strong women's networks and partnerships;
- gender mainstreaming;
- gender budgeting;
- gendered urban planning – environment, housing and transport;
- grass-roots academies and local-to-local dialogues;
- women's safety audits and other participatory approaches;
- use of art and culture to change attitudes and behaviour;
- changing the attitudes and behaviours of men and boys;
- specific strategies and tools that involve girls.

What this book documents

We have chosen to divide this book into three main parts, which incorporate the main themes. Part I deals with challenges and opportunities. This theme focuses in detail on some of the challenges women face in public space regarding access to essential services, housing security, liveability and mobility. Chapters 2 and 3 discuss home–life balances on two levels – the neighbourhood and the city – and bring some fresh light to these issues. Chapter 4 looks at the global level, and the increasingly important area of women's migration, and some of the policy and practice issues that reflect on women's safety. However, while outlining such challenges, the aim is to highlight the opportunities that exist to intervene and increase the power of women to take control of their lives, something that can better be understood when the problems are framed through a gender mainstreaming approach. The chapters demonstrate the common contexts of poverty and social exclusion and the importance of working to reduce them and create cities that are socially inclusive to enable women and girls to access their rights to the city. Thinking in terms of opportunities allows the full variety of forms of women's participation and of women's urban activism to be seen as central and as actions to be looked for, understood and supported.

Part II – on interventions – provides an important opportunity to highlight some of the very creative and innovative ways in which women's access to safe and equitable cities is being furthered in projects developed over the past five years. It looks at four action projects or programmes that have used a variety of participatory techniques to examine the ways in which women's safety is compromised in a range of different settings, and how grass-roots and women's organizations have been able to support community empowerment to begin to make changes and interact with governments and institutions. Chapter 5 outlines the final outcomes of the three-year Gender Inclusive Cities Programme, a highly innovative project rooted in the use of the participatory women's safety audit, which has been developed with local organizations and communities in four cities in different regions of the world, funded by the UN Trust Fund. Chapter 6 is concerned with one of the crucial characteristics of contemporary intervention, that of building and sustaining partnerships. Chapter 7 outlines a participatory methodology that is rooted in the development of a vision for a safe community and utilizes modern systems-theory techniques to help communities understand the complexity of causal factors, what needs to be done and who is to be involved in working towards that collective vision. It talks about the exchange of knowledge that happens through peer-to-peer learning, which is a technique used to understand people's unique experiences of space. Chapter 8 presents the findings of another innovative study using women's safety audits to explore women's access to water and sanitation, one of the central aspects of women's and girls lives that reflects the gendered nature of daily life in disadvantaged communities.

The final part of the book, entitled 'Tools', looks at three very significant concerns in the advancement of work on the safety of women and the right to the city: the issues of gender mainstreaming and intersectionality; maximizing the opportunities offered by contemporary communications and ways of capitalizing on them to promote women's safety; and the ongoing debates about the evaluation of programmes and how we can evaluate knowledge around women's safety once it is created. Although in part pragmatic, this section expands on the different ways in which women's safety and building inclusive cities have been explored theoretically in the literature.

Notes

1 This chapter draws extensively on the WICI and Jagori (2010) Background Paper for the Delhi conference on Building Inclusive Cities for Women and Girls, Montreal and New Delhi. The authors would like to thank WICI, who produced the paper, for allowing them to do so, and to acknowledge the work of Laura Capobianco who drafted an initial reference document. They would also like to thank Melanie Lambrick for her very helpful comments on the chapter.
2 The event was organized by the Centre d'action sur femmes et sécurite urbain (Women's Action centre on Urban Safety- CAFSU), with support from the City of Montreal, UN-HABITAT, the Huairou Commission and the International Centre for the Prevention of Crime, and brought together 160 stakeholders, from twenty-seven countries.
3 Organized by the City of Bogota, Politica de infancia y adolscencia, Cuidadas mas seguras, with support from the UN-HABITAT, UNIFEM and UNDP, it brought together 300 delegates from seventeen countries, including stakeholders from grass-roots and community organizations, national and local governments, gender experts, police, international women's networks and donors.
4 See www.unwomen.org/about-us/executive-director. In the consultations on UN Women's first strategic plan, ending violence against women received the most universal support of all the focus areas, and capacity building for national governments and civil society, opening space for dialogue and gender mainstreaming were the most strongly supported programme strategies. There was also strong support for evidence-based advocacy and programming, including data collection and analysis and research.
5 Declaration on the Elimination of Violence against Women General Assembly (Article 1), December 1993.
6 The Beijing Declaration and the Platform for Action: Fourth World Conference on Women: Beijing, China: 4–15 September 1995 (DPI/1766/Wom), paras. 114–16.
7 Report of the Economic and Social Council for 1997 A/52/3 Commonwealth Secretariat (2009).
8 See www.crime-prevention-intl.org
9 See www.env-health.org
10 The countries included were Bangladesh, Brazil, Ethiopia, Japan, Peru, Namibia, Samoa, Serbia and Montenegro, Thailand and the United Republic of Tanzania.
11 The countries include Australia, Costa Rica, the Czech Republic, Denmark, Greece, Hong Kong, Italy, Mozambique, the Philippines, Poland and Switzerland.
12 *Feminicido en Mexico. Aproximaciones, tendencias y cambios 1985–2009.* UN Women, Instituto Nacional de los Mujeres, Mexico, y Comision Especial Camera de Diputados (2011).

13 See, for example, UN-HABITAT and OHCHR (2005), p. 178; Chaturvedi (2010).
14 See also Report of the UN Special Rapporteur on trafficking in persons (2010) (A/65/288) para. 22 on the feminization of migration.

References

Abdelhalim, K. and Shehayeb, D. (2011). 'Crime prevention and urban development: the case of Greater Cairo'. In Shaw, M. and Carli, V. (eds) *Practical Approaches to Urban Crime Prevention*. Montreal: ICPC & UNODC.

Beltran, A. and Freeman, L. (2007). *Hidden in Plain Sight. Violence Against Women in Mexico and Guatemala*. Washington: WOLA.

Brown, A. (2010). e-Debate 1: Taking forward the Right to the City. Report to UN-HABITAT, e-Debate Moderator, Alison Brown, February 2010. Retrieved on 5 October 2010, from: www.unhabitat.org/downloads/docs/Dialogue1.pdf

Brown, A. and Kristiansen, A. (2009). *Urban Policies and the Right to the City*. Nairobi and Paris: UN-HABITAT and UNESCO.

Caritas Internationalis (2010). *The Female Face of Migration*. Background Paper for the Senegal Conference, November.

Castles, S. and Miller, M.J. (2003). *The Age of Migration*. New York: The Guilford Press.

Chaturvedi, B. (ed.) (2010). *Finding Delhi: Loss and Renewal in the Megacity*. New Delhi: Penguin Viking.

Chung, W. and Das Gupta, M. (2007). 'The decline of son preference in South Korea: the roles of development and public policy'. *Population and Development Review*, 33(4): 757–83.

Doucey, M. (2010). 'Gender and human security in the Haitian–Dominican border zone'. GCST *New Voices Series*, no. 8, November. Santiago: Global Consortium on Security Transformation.

Ehrenreich, B. and Hoschild, A.R. (eds) (2003). *Global Women: Nannies, Maids, and Sex Workers in the New Economy*. New York: Metropolitan Books.

Falu, A. (ed.) (2010). *Women in the City. On Violence and Rights*. Santiago: Women and Habitat Network of Latin America. Ediciones SUR.

Falu, A. and Segovia, O. (eds) (2008). *Living Together: Cities Free From Violence Against Women*. Santiago: Women and Habitat Network of Latin America. Ediciones SUR.

Giddings, C. and Hovroka, A. (2010). 'Place, ideological mobility and youth negotiations of gender identities in urban Botswana'. *Gender, Place and Culture*, 17(2): 211–29.

Global Migration Group (2008). *International Migration and Human Rights. Challenges and Opportunities on the Threshold of the 60th Anniversary of the Universal Declaration of Human Rights*. New York: United Nations.

ILO (2009). *Cost of Coercion. Global Report on Forced Labour*. International Labour Conference Report of the 98th Session, 2009. Geneva: International Labour Organization.

INSTRAW (2007). *Gender, Remittances and Development: The Feminization of Migration*. San Domingo: INSTRAW.

Jagori (2010). *A Handbook on Women's Safety Audits in Low-Income Urban Neighbourhoods. A Focus on Essential Services*. New Delhi: Jagori and Women in Cities International.

Jha, P., Kesler, M.A., Kumar, R., Ram, F., Ram, U., Aleksandrowicz, L., Bassani, D.G., Chandra, S. and Banthia, J.K. (2011). 'Trends in selective abortions of girls in India'. *The Lancet*, early online publication, 24 May 2011.

Johnson, H., Ollus, N. and Nevala, S. (2008). *Violence Against Women: An International Perspective*. New York: Springer.

Kedir, A. and Admasachew, L. (2010). 'Violence against women in Ethiopia'. *Gender, Place, Culture*, 17(4): 437–52.

Lambrick, M. and Travers, K. (2008). *Women's Safety Audits: What Works Where?* Nairobi: UN-HABITAT and WICI.

Lefebvre, H. (1968). *Le droit à la ville*. Paris: Anthropos.

Menon Sen, K. and Bhan, G. (2008). *Swept off the Map. Surviving Eviction and Resettlement in New Delhi*. Delhi: Yoda Press.

Moser, C. (2004). 'Urban violence and insecurity: an introductory roadmap'. *Environment and Urbanization*, 16(2): 3–16.

Moser, C. (2008). 'Safety, gender mainstreaming and gender-based programmes', in Proceedings of the 8th ICPC Colloquium, Queretaro, Mexico, 12–14 November.

Native Women's Association of Canada (2010). *What Their Stories Tell Us: Research Findings From the Sisters in Spirit Initiative*. Ottawa: Native Women's Association of Canada.

Plan International (2010). *Because I'm a Girl. The State of the World's Girls 2010. Digital and Urban Frontiers: Girls in a Changing Landscape*. London: Plan International.

Prieto-Carrón, M., Thomson, M. and Macdonald, M. (2007). 'No more killings! Women respond to Femicides in Central America'. *Gender & Development*, 15(1).

Purcell, M. (2008). *Recapturing Democracy*. New York: Routledge.

Reeves, D., Parfitt, B. and Archer, C. (2009). 'Global trends in gender and urban planning'. In UN-HABITAT, *Global Report on Human Settlements 2009*. London: Earthscan.

Shaw, M. (2009). 'An international overview of violence against women: trends, perspectives and lessons for Latin America and the Caribbean'. Consultancy study commissioned by Inter-American Development Bank.

Shaw, M. and Andrew, C. (2005). 'Engendering crime prevention: international developments and the Canadian experience'. *Canadian Journal of Criminology and Criminal Justice*, 47(2): 293–316.

Shaw, M. and Capobianco, L. (2004). *Developing Trust: International Approaches to Women's Safety*. Montreal: International Centre for the Prevention of Crime.

Shaw, M. and Carli, V. (eds) (2011). *Practical Approaches to Urban Crime Prevention*. Proceedings of the Workshop held at the 12th UN Congress on Crime Prevention and Criminal Justice, Salvador Brazil 12–19 April 2010. Montreal: ICPC and UNODC.

Sweet, E. and Ortiz Escalante, S. (2010). 'Planning responds to gender violence: evidence from Spain, Mexico, and the United States'. *Urban Studies*, 47(10): 2129–47.

UN-HABITAT (2008). *The State of the World's Cities 2008/2009*. Nairobi: UN-HABITAT.

UN-HABITAT (2009a). *Global Report on Human Settlements 2009*. London: Earthscan, p. 5.

UN-HABITAT (2009b). *The State of the World's Cities 2008/2009: Harmonious Cities*. Nairobi: UN-HABITAT.

UN-HABITAT (2010). *State of the World Cities 2010/2011: Bridging the Urban Divide*. Kenya: UN-HABITAT.

UN-HABITAT and OHCHR (2005). *Indigenous People's Right to Adequate Housing: A Global Overview*. Nairobi: UN-HABITAT & OHCHR.

UNHCR (2003). *Sexual and Gender-based Violence against Refugees, Returnees and Internally Displaced Persons*. Geneva: UNHCR.

UNODC (2009). *Global Report of Trafficking in Persons*. Vienna: UN GIFT.

US Department of State (2010). *Trafficking in Persons Report*, 10th Edition. Washington DC: US Department of State.

WHO (2005). *Multi-country Study on Women's Health and Domestic Violence against Women: Summary Report of Initial Results on Prevalence, Health Outcomes and Women's Responses*. Geneva: WHO.

WICI and Jagori (2010). 'Conference background paper'. Third International Conference on Women's Safety: Building Inclusive Cities, New Delhi, 22–24 November 2010. Montreal and New Delhi: Women in Cities International and Jagori.

Part I
Challenges and opportunities

Chapter 2

Gendered livelihoods and inclusive cities

Fran Klodawsky

The rationale for this chapter is a growing recognition that 'increasing women's access to jobs and to economic self-sufficiency can help to reduce the high numbers of women living in poverty', at the same time as women's vulnerability to violence also may be mitigated (Women in Cities International and Jagori, 2010, p. 26). It is widely acknowledged that dramatic changes are currently underway in cities, but the implications for women's and girls' access to livelihoods and improved quality of life, free of violence for themselves and their households, remain to be explored. Approaching these questions through the lens of gender mainstreaming in an urban context is a new approach, and one of potential value in helping to shape programmes and policies that are pro-poor and promote more inclusive cities.

The goal of this chapter is to assess current knowledge about the challenges and opportunities that women and girls in cities of the Global South face when they engage in paid work and other livelihood and provisioning strategies in the public realm. As well as work for wages in the formal sphere, such activities might include: informal or unregulated market exchange for daily necessities such as food; making and selling other products and services; and other diverse market transactions. Although it is vital to acknowledge that women's and girls' involvement in these activities captures a tremendous diversity, it is equally necessary to highlight structural factors that have differential and sometimes extremely disturbing implications for many women and girls and the households they head, compared with their male peers.

This chapter is organized into three sections. In the first two, the focus is on challenges related to gendered livelihoods in cities. I begin with a discussion of what is known about the gendered dynamics of urbanization and livelihoods and particularly the growing significance of informality in relation to both labour markets and urban settlements. The second section casts a spotlight on empirical city- and neighbourhood-level research about the implications of these trends for particular groups of women. The concept of *space–time feasibility* is drawn upon to highlight the growing difficulties that many women and girls face in trying to combine income-generating activities with myriad other responsibilities. The third and final section of this chapter shifts to a discussion of opportunities and presents an important case study of how women street traders have drawn on diverse collective strategies, at multiple scales, to address livelihood-related challenges in Durban, South Africa.

Urban informality

The 2006 World Urban Forum marked an important moment in highlighting both the growing global significance of cities and an alarming acceleration in the 'urbanization of poverty', most especially in the Global South (Tibaijuka, 2006; Watson, 2009). Recent research suggests that new, globally integrated approaches to investment and finance have contributed to increasingly divergent outcomes among urban residents in the realms of occupation, income, safety, social roles and access to land, housing and services. Put very simply, while some urban residents and households have benefited greatly from these shifts, there also are disturbing indicators of greater deprivation among many who are already marginalized, particularly within low- and medium-income countries.

Informalization as a concept has often been linked to such trends. It is a contested, umbrella term that has been linked to both labour-market and human-settlement dynamics. *Informal* has been associated with the wide variety of legal livelihood activities that are not formally recognized or regulated by any state institution (Snyder, 2005; Wick, 2010). According to the Organization for Economic Cooperation and Development (OECD), 'of the 3 billion paid employees working throughout the world today, 1.8 billion (i.e. 60 per cent) are informal' (Jutting and DeLaiglesia, 2009). UN-HABITAT has reported that, in the late 1990s, among non-agricultural workers in Africa, Asia and Latin America, the proportions of those working in informal employment were 72 per cent, 65 per cent and 51 per cent, respectively (Neto *et al.*, 2007) (See Table 2.1). Although informal work is not always badly paid or exploitative, there is considerable evidence that women in the informal sector tend to earn less than men and are concentrated in its less lucrative, secure and appealing sectors (Chen, 2010; Skinner, 2008; Wick, 2010).

Moreover, the informalization of paid employment and other livelihood activities is a growing feature of the global economy and is intricately related to policies of liberalization, privatization and deregulation. Gender-disaggregated studies of the relations between these macro-level policies and place-based impacts are highlighting how already existing class-, place- and gender-based inequalities tend to be exacerbated as a result. In Mexico, for example, the downsizing of the state and loss of public-sector employment have been linked to a general trend towards more poorly paid and precarious

Table 2.1 Informal employment as percentage of non-agricultural employment in selected regions and countries, various years (1995–2000)

Region and country	Informal employment as % of non-agricultural employment
Sub-Saharan Africa	72
Benin	93
Kenya	72
South Africa	70
Asia	65
India	83
Indonesia	78
Thailand	51
Latin America	51
Brazil	60
Mexico	55
Peru	54

Source: UN-HABITAT (2006)

work in the informal sector. Biles' recent in-depth examination of gender-disaggregated employment change among a representative sample of households in Mérida, Mexico, revealed two important insights. First, he found that 'self-employment in Mérida is significantly more pervasive, less likely to be voluntary, and paid considerably less' than had previously been reported for Mexico overall. Second, he revealed that women's and men's experiences were quite different, with women's involvement less likely to be voluntary and linked to strategies to 'supplement household incomes', but also that, among women, there was a 'bimodal' pattern, with younger and more highly educated women more likely to be better paid workers in the formal sector (Biles, 2008, p. 544).

Informal also has been used to refer to human-settlement growth, primarily at the periphery of large cities in some low- and medium-income countries. Roy (2005) has made a persuasive case against mainstream understandings that these settlements are occurring because state planning efforts have been unsuccessful or lacking. Rather, she has argued that,

> informality is not a separate sector but rather a series of transactions that connect different economies and spaces to one another ... [and is a] complex continuum of legality and illegality, where squatter settlements formed through land invasion and self-help housing can exist alongside upscale informal subdivisions formed through legal ownership and market transaction but in violation of land use regulations.
> (Roy, 2005, p. 149)

Within this framework, she has highlighted how, in the case of Calcutta, gendered norms about the relations between households, states, markets and communities are deployed in ways that have particularly adverse effects on those who are already disadvantaged.

Scholars such as Roy and AlSayyed (2004) and Weinstein and Ren (2009) have contributed to a growing understanding of how and why privatization and the withdrawal of funds from the public sector contribute to both the informalization of labour markets and the informalization of human settlements. For example, Weinstein and Ren (2009), writing about Mumbai and Shanghai, documented growing pressures on governments, operating at 'multiple geopolitical scales', 'to attract capital investment, and to position their cities as global ones' (p. 408). Others, such as Miraftab (2010), de Koning (2009), Erman and Turkyilmaz (2008), Falu (2010) and Rainero (2010), are explicit about the gendered impacts of such trends. For example Miraftab (2010), whose empirical focus is privatized waste-management practices in South African cities, notes that, 'in the Global South, neoliberal budget cuts and cash-strapped local governments privatize the provision of basic municipal services ... by moving the public responsibilities for urban and neighbourhood development to the private sphere of women's free work' (2010, p. 646). De Koning's (2009) research is distinctive in its focus on Cairo's upper-middle-class professionals, but her conclusions are somewhat similar in revealing a growing disconnect between their lives – at work, home and play – and the majority. Erman and Turkyilmaz (2008) link growing income and social polarization in the context of urban redevelopment in Istanbul to economic liberalization policies directed at local governments. A prominent outcome has been the growing likelihood of displacement to less desirable, and more violent, locations within the city on the part of the most vulnerable households.

From the perspective of Latin America, Falu (2010) analyses how 'cities are re-valued as "motors of change"', with the result being growing divides between 'the "new centralities" that are defined by urban concentrations of wealth ... [and] peripheral areas ... characterized by the sprawl of impoverished territories' (2010, p. 20). She connects these trends to gendered experiences of growing violence and insecurity, with adverse impacts on women's sense of citizenship, right to public space and, thus, access to livelihoods (p. 24). Rainero's (2010) observations, based on research in five cities of the Southern Cone – Montevideo, Uruguay; Asunción, Paraguay; Mendoza and Rosario, Argentina; and Talca, Chile – further specify the links between gendered violence and livelihoods: 'The main difference between women and men is that women modify their daily routines, where they circulate and at what time, whereas men do not' (Rainero 2010, p. 169). Both Falu and Rainero contribute numerous insights into the manner in which 'violence' is framed to blame victims and to shift the spotlight away from root causes.

Falu (2010) also highlights an important connection with livelihoods: 'women go out to work, often having to navigate areas that turn into real traps for their integrity, or are perceived as such' (Falu, 2010, p. 24). A particularly disturbing example of what Falu discusses is the femicide detailed by Sweet and Escalante (2010) in the border city of Ciudad Juárez, Mexico, the home of numerous assembly plants known as *maquiladoras* (see also Wright, 2004). As they note: 'The economic exploitation in Ciudad Juárez has coincided with extraordinary violence, of unfathomable proportions, against women' (Sweet and Escalante, 2010, p. 2138). Equally disturbing is the extent to which neither employers nor state officials accept any responsibility for these murders. Indeed, several scholars have 'explored a possible relationship between neo-liberal policies and the femicide in that the low value placed on women workers by the global economy made their annihilation acceptable' (Sweet and Escalante, 2010, p. 2139).

The connections that these authors make, including the link between economic liberalization and structural gendered violence, are a vital framework for the discussion to follow. Informalization is a growing trend, both in relation to labour markets and to human settlements. Its implications are multiple and multidimensional. Among others, Meagher (2010) has noted that, in the context of Sub-Saharan Africa, 84 per cent of women, but only 63 per cent of men, work in the informal sector, and that the result has been 'an intensification rather than a reversal of gender disparities in income, economic opportunity and burdens of reproductive labour . . . [with] . . . gender disparity in income . . . [being] higher in the informal economy than in the formal economy'. Chant (2010) provides particularly compelling evidence of such intensification through her comparative research in Gambia, the Philippines and Costa Rica. Although she found 'no consistent quantitative or qualitative evidence to support a generalized tendency to a "feminisation of income poverty"', she did identify a trend towards a 'feminisation' of responsibility and/or obligation (Chant, 2010, pp. 113–14; see also Moser, 2010).

This research on the intersection of gender and informalization reinforces Roy's (2003) assertion that, 'social reproduction . . . is located not in a single institution but rather in how the boundaries between state, household, economy, and community are contested' (Roy, 2003, p. 18). In other words, systematic distinctions in men's and women's lives are understood to be complex outcomes of multilayered interactions within and between households, communities and states. This understanding of gender has profound implications for conceptualizing and deriving policy innovations that might support the building of safer, more inclusive cities. Adding an urban, sociospatial lens to the analyses detailed above can highlight how the built environment, in interaction with these other elements, can both reinforce and challenge problematic trends in gender justice and economic justice. Broadly speaking, adding such a lens helps to highlight the ways in which space–time feasibility and its contextual characteristics, as well as concerns about safety, have differential impacts on women's and men's lives, at both the urban and the neighbourhood scale.

Space–time feasibility

According to Kwan (1999), space–time feasibility measures accessibility in a manner that is somewhat distinct from 'locational proximity'. Rather than focusing only on a certain type of trip, such as commuting between home and work, space–time feasibility opens up mobility studies, traditionally focused on work–home commuting patterns, to examinations of the full diversity of trips that women and men undertake on a daily basis, as well as the myriad factors that influence how and why trips take place. Linking this idea to the socio-spatial implications of a 'feminisation of responsibility' as identified by Chant (2010), as well as the structural gender violence and fear of violence concerns discussed by Falu (2010), Rainero (2010) and Sweet and Escalante (2010), it is reasonable to expect a trend among some women, more so than among men, to confront increasingly complex space–time arrangements in order to meet multiple obligations and cultural/social pressures. Intra-urban and regional gender-sensitive mobility studies from Cameron, South Africa, India and Thailand provide important insights into how urban land use and settlement patterns are implicated in both contributing to and alleviating these pressures.

For example, Fonchingong's (2005) research with women traders in Limbe, Cameroon, highlighted the manner in which labour-intensive domestic responsibilities, such as 'child care, farming, shopping, cooking, fetching water, and fuel wood collection', profoundly shaped the strategies that women utilize for adding paid employment to their already busy days. He found that their growing involvement in informal employment activities was less a means of advancing status and more a way of coping with deteriorating economic conditions. The flexibility offered by informal-sector activities, such as street trading, piecework done in the home and domestic work for others, was attractive because such activities supported women's efforts to balance many competing demands, particularly when they offered income-generating opportunities 'close to home'. Unfortunately, however, the elevated interest in working in these sectors contributed to the extremely low rates of compensation on offer (see also Heintz, 2010).

Sen's (2010) research revealed additional losses to such women, including the limits on 'women's choice of compatible income-earning opportunities, their ability to take time off for government programmes, social exchanges or minimal leisure, and their possibilities for acknowledging their own needs for rest, recuperation or healthcare' (Sen, 2010, p. 102). Her observations were reinforced by Floro and Pichetpongsa's (2010) research with Thai home-based women workers, who revealed that, despite considerable economic benefits, home-based work 'tends to reinforce the invisibility of women's work and allows for its intensification' (Floro and Pichetpongsa, 2010, pp. 7–8). Sen (2010) also noted the negative impacts of these pressures on daughters, particularly in South East Asia, where they are typically the first to be called upon to help with domestic tasks, often to the detriment of furthering their education (p. 103). Ironically though, as she also observed, in some contexts, women's 'successes' in managing all of these competing demands have been used to justify policies that promote further state downsizing and decentralization (p. 103).

In Delhi, Menon-Sen and Bhan (2008) documented the negative impacts on former residents of the centrally located slum of Yamuna Pushta when they were forcibly moved to the outlying informal settlement of Bawana. Among female domestic workers, a higher proportion became unemployed, given that 'Bawana is around 10 kilometres away from the nearest middle-class colony, buses are infrequent and earnings from domestic work are barely enough to cover the costs of the daily commute' (p. 63). Even more surprising though, was the authors' finding that many more women 'commuted more than 50 kilometres daily to work as housemaids for the families who employed them when they were in Pushta' (Menon-Sen and Bhan, 2008, p. 63). The reasons given had to do with greater 'flexibility' and safety:

> All the women we interviewed said that they preferred domestic work to working in a factory, mainly because of the support in the form of salary advances and interest-free loans given by employers in times of need. Regular payment of wages, festival gifts and a safe working environment were also mentioned as advantages of working with 'good households'.
>
> (p. 65)

Their reasons suggest survival under such circumstances is a finely calibrated dance of being able to match needs and resources, in a severely restricted field of 'opportunities'. Menon-Sen and Bhan's (2008) research highlights the role that land-use planning and governance more generally can play in influencing space–time feasibility. However, other authors highlight additional considerations, such as changing discourses and practices of safety and security, as well as gendered cultural attitudes and mores.

Kantor's (2009) research in Lucknow, India, and Erman and Turkyilmaz's (2008) Istanbul-based investigation provide insights about space–time feasibility that are complementary to those discussed above. In both of these studies, the focus is on interactions between gendered cultural norms about women's public visibility and their involvement in money-generating activities. In contrast to the other articles discussed here, there is a greater focus on mobility at the household and neighbourhood scales. Both studies highlight the need also to focus on cultural norms about mobility when considering land use and governance interventions to promote women's economic autonomy.

Kantor's (2009) longitudinal and mixed-methods examination of households across twelve slum communities in Lucknow sought to learn more about the circumstances under which women became involved in the informal labour market, both within and outside the home. Kantor's findings emphasized the extent to which participation in livelihood activities was first and foremost the result of 'push' factors tied to basic household survival needs. Questions of how to become involved revolved around husbands' and wives' understanding of what was culturally appropriate and seemly. Kantor summarized this insight from focus group discussions: 'Women should only work if reproductive tasks are complete, and ideally would work in the home to balance reproductive and productive work' (2009, p. 196). She also documented the extent to which such strategies contributed to lower wages and less ability to use work as a means of escaping poverty.

Erman and Turkyilmaz's (2008) in-depth research with rural migrant women, who lived in one of Istanbul's most marginalized (and dangerous) slums, reported similar conclusions with regard to cultural traditions and motivations to engage in livelihood activities. But they also offered two additional insights. The first had to do with the small number of women who did work outside the home. As one of the few means by which such women established connections outside their own communities, the authors reported instances where such connections had opened up additional opportunities:

> For example, a woman (40 years old) who worked as a cleaning woman for a middle-class family not only earned money to support her family, but also through this middle-class family was able to find a scholarship for her daughter, who was a university student in a small city.
> (2008, p. 1771)

The second insight had to do with the significance of a neighbourhood community centre where women's concerns about domestic violence, for example, were validated and where activities focused on boosting women's self-esteem.

Until now, this section's focus on space–time feasibility has been considered primarily from the perspective of individual women in the context of their households and communities. Complementary to this body of work are Brown (2006) and colleagues' investigations of street trading and the street economy as significant and highly visible aspects of the informal economy, where women are the majority but also are disproportionately involved in its least lucrative and attractive elements. The relevance of Brown's (Brown, 2006; Brown *et al.*, 2010) work to this chapter is particularly about the contradictions that are generated when city officials try to 'beautify' their cities in accordance with modern land-use planning guidelines. As Brown notes:

> Few modern-day urban management policies recognize the economic importance of urban public space to the poor . . . Planning policies result

in a polarized city, with the poor increasingly segregated in low-income ghettos and excluded from the central city and civic realm. Modern developments such as highways, shopping malls or gated communities can result in progressive erosion of urban public space available to the poor.

(2006, p. 11)

The shift of poor Delhi citizens from Yamuna Pushta to Bawana, as documented by Menon-Sen and Bhan (2008), is intricately linked to the dilemmas exposed by Brown (2006). For women, it typically means greater travel times and more challenges in how they manage competing demands, including personal-safety concerns and cultural pressures in their already very complicated lives.

The Commonwealth Secretariat's Discussion Paper on *Gender in Planning and Urban Development* (Malaza et al., 2009) acknowledges both the fact that street trading is a problem for many planners, insofar as it 'causes congestion and breaches planning regulations', but also that it is 'vital to the livelihoods of many poor people, especially women ... traders' and that when such markets are relocated to areas 'that may offer better facilities ... they are often not well located and so undermine incomes' (Malaza et al., 2009, p. 6). The best-known pro-poor response to this dilemma is the Warwick Junction urban-renewal project in Durban, South Africa, as will be discussed below.

Urban livelihoods and opportunities for building inclusive cities

Until now, the focus has been on the formidable and growing challenges that many women and girls face, alone and in households, in their search for sustainable livelihoods that avoid bodily or social risk. In this final section, the focus is on innovations conducive to promoting sustainable economic activity in the context of inclusive cities, and the lessons to be derived from their examination. The example of Durban, South Africa's positive accommodations of and support for women street traders, will be highlighted. The planning innovations that occurred in Warwick Junction between the mid 1990s and 2003 included improvements in public transportation, street lighting, positive environmental changes geared to street-trading activities, land-use planning readjustments and dedicated markets for specialized products, such as traditional medicines (Skinner, 2008, p. 234) (see Figure 2.1). How these improvements came about and what insights might be generalized to other contexts offer important lessons about circumstances that make it more or less likely for pro-poor regulatory and land-use innovations to be accepted and, indeed, encouraged.

Warwick Junction is a notable example of an internationally recognized urban-renewal project, developed through state–community collaboration,

28 F. Klodawsky

Figure 2.1 Warwick Junction: internationally recognized gender-sensitive land-use planning
© Gerald Botha: 'Working in Warwick: including street traders in urban plans'

that resulted in well-documented and widespread benefits to street traders, including greater economic security and safer working conditions (Malaza *et al.*, 2009; see also Lund and Skinner, 2004). Skinner (2008) has traced the history of Durban's municipal government's engagement with street traders between the 1920s and 2007 and, in so doing, has highlighted what distinguished periods of greater willingness on the part of local governments to engage with community organizations, from periods where such engagement was regarded as inappropriate, unattractive and/or counterproductive. Her research reinforces arguments about the potential benefits of an inclusive and participatory approach to planning that acknowledges and accommodates the diverse goals and concerns of myriad stakeholders (Skinner, 2008, p. 235).

Skinner describes a confluence of national and local, economic, political and social circumstances during which Durban's municipal government 'accepted street trading as contributing to the local economy and thus a reality that does not have to be transformed into something it is not' (2008, p. 239). Moreover, this engagement included 'consultation between traders and council officials, institutional innovation in the form of area-based management, collective action among street traders, and a political moment that combined with a well-resourced local authority' (2008, p. 239). She also traces the negative changes that have taken place since these innovations were implemented. She notes that 'The first signs that there was a significant shift . . . appeared in mid-2004', when 'the Metro Police, without warning, removed traders' goods at various intersections throughout the central business district and the neighbouring middle-class suburbs' (2008, p. 237). Her analysis raises questions about the impact of the May 2004 announcement that South Africa would host the 2010 Soccer World Cup. She also notes the strong reaction from organizations such as the Self-Help Women's Union (SEWU) and StreetNet International among others: 'StreetNet has increasingly become a significant lobbying force for an alternative approach . . . It has launched, partly in response to South Africa's winning the Soccer World Cup bid, a "World Cities for All" campaign' (2008, p. 239). Skinner's (2008) conclusions are noteworthy in terms of generalizing from this example to the larger project of building more inclusive cities: 'it shows the livelihood activities of street traders to be critically shaped by a complex interplay of national and local government policy approaches, combined with pressure from both formal business and collective action among street traders' (Skinner, 2008, p. 228).

The role of collective action is particularly pertinent to the opportunities under consideration here. Skinner (2008) and Lindell (2009) both highlight the considerable impacts that such actions can have on African street traders' negotiations with governmental authorities. A key element of Warwick Junction's land-use planning and governance successes has been attributed to the approach to consultation and, tied to this factor, the role of SEWU. This organization was launched in Durban in 1994 and was inspired by a somewhat similar movement in India (Kapoor, 2007). Skinner (2008) describes this approach by drawing on the words of the person who was SEWU's secretary-general at the time:

> 'The manner in which informal traders and other key stakeholders were engaged was qualitatively different from the type of consultation that is more often seen when project managers try to secure buy-in from stakeholders.' . . . 'The Council afforded informal traders the opportunity to participate on a sustained and continuous basis in negotiations about their needs and priorities . . . in a low key way, often on an issue-by-issue basis.'
> (Skinner, 2008, p. 235)

Devenish and Skinner (2006) also emphasize the importance of SEWU for ensuring the explicit incorporation of women's needs, given that gender-blind organizations were also significant players in the process, but far less likely to pay attention to women's specific concerns.

Hanson's (2009) review of 'programs of governmental and nongovernmental organizations and women's grassroots actions that are aimed at building women's skills, confidence, and business networks', in Botswana, India, Peru and the United States, reinforces the argument that women-centred networks, both large and small, are significant. Drawing upon four sets of research having to do with women and entrepreneurship, she highlights how, across a variety of contexts and characteristics, networks helped women enhance the impact of their own individual efforts, both for themselves and their communities. Her analysis particularly identified the importance of programmes that 'directly seek to change women's identities – from identities rooted in the status quo, accepting of subordination and feelings of helplessness, to identities rooted in having some degree of control over resources and the ability to change one's future' (Hanson, 2009, p. 257).

From a somewhat different but complementary perspective, Erman and Turkyilmaz's (2008) investigation of the situations of marginalized, rural female migrants, living in a particularly violent squatter settlement in Istanbul, revealed both the potential impact and limited reach of neighbourhood-level initiatives. They reported on a community centre's success in becoming a source of help for local women escaping domestic violence and as a place where skills were developed and self-confidence was nurtured. But, the authors also noted that the community centre and related NGO initiatives operated in the context of inadequate resources and time-limited project funds. This prevented it from reaching out and working with local women over a period of time adequate to address long-lasting cycles of patriarchal control, gendered violence and feelings of helplessness.

Networks and associations that include both women and men can also be influential in making improvements to the lives of both female and male workers in the informal economy. Lindell's (2009) account of the work of Associação dos Operadores e Trabalahdores do Sector Informal (ASSOTSI) [Association of Workers and Operators of the Informal Sector], in Maputo, Mozambique, documents how a local organization was established to support informal street vendors in reaction to the hostility of local state officials. She also notes that these organizing efforts became especially effective once that local organization had become part of a 'global network of associations and unions of street and market vendors, StreetNet International ... [which] grew out of the realization of the insufficiency of organizing at the local level and of the need to work internationally' (2009, p. 130). Among other benefits, ASSOTSI used its newly acquired knowledge of Durban's street traders' more favourable relationship with their own local council (through an exchange of members with a similar group from South Africa) to challenge existing local government–community relations in Maputo. Unfortunately though, both Brown *et al.* (2010) and Lindell (2011) have also noted that gender politics has played a problematic role in these mixed-sex organizations, with women more likely to be silenced or restricted in voice and presence.

Conclusions

The goal of this chapter has been to highlight the myriad ways in which the patterns and dynamics of gendered urban livelihoods have important implications for building inclusive, safe cities and promoting the right to the city in the Global South. As the opening section of this chapter argues, macroeconomic and political trends are driving shifts in how women and men, and girls and boys, generate income to support themselves and their households. More often than not, the outcomes tend to result in adverse gendered effects, particularly for those at the margins. The role of 'informalization', both in terms of livelihoods and urban redevelopment, was highlighted as having particularly negative impacts for many. Links were made to trends that accelerate loss of access to livelihoods that are both economically sustainable and that allow women to maintain dignified control over their bodies and their social positions within communities.

The chapter has also highlighted the potential for both governments and community organizations to have significant impacts on the circumstances that promote the right to the city via inclusive land-use and social-development planning. However, the extent to which such innovations, even under the best of circumstances, can make a difference to women's and men's experiences of living well in cities of the Global South depends significantly on macroeconomic and political trends, at least as much as sensitivity to local contexts and cultures. Chazan and Whiteside's (2007) examination of the differentiated impacts of AIDS on women and men street traders in Warwick Junction is a sobering reminder of the limits of local and/or built-environment initiatives. Their observations about the particularly negative impacts of AIDS on older women's burden of care highlight the need for gender mainstreaming to consider both macro- and micro-level processes that have impacts on people's daily lives and livelihoods in cities.

References

Biles, J. (2008) 'Informal work and livelihoods in Mexico: getting by or getting ahead?', *The Professional Geographer*, vol. 60, no. 4, pp. 541–55.

Brown, A. (2006) 'Challenging street livelihoods', in A. Brown (ed.), *Contested Space: Street Trading, Public Space, and Livelihoods in Developing Cities*, ITDG Publishing, Warwickshire, UK, pp. 3–16.

Brown, A., Lyons, M. and Dankoco, I. (2010) 'Street traders and the emerging spaces for urban voice and citizenship in African cities', *Urban Studies*, vol. 47, no. 3, pp. 666–83.

Chant, S. (2010) 'Towards a (re)conceptualisation of the "feminisation of poverty": reflections on gender-differentiated poverty from The Gambia, Philippines and Costa Rica', in S. Chant (ed.), *The International Handbook of Gender and Poverty: Concepts, Research, Policy*, Edward Elgar, Cheltenham, UK, pp. 111–16.

Chazan, M. and Whiteside, A. (2007) 'The making of vulnerabilities: understanding the differentiated effects of HIV and AIDS among street traders in Warwick

Junction, Durban, South Africa', *African Journal of AIDS Research*, vol. 6, pp. 165–73.
Chen, M. (2010) 'Informality, poverty and gender: evidence from the Global South', in S. Chant (ed.), *The International Handbook of Gender and Poverty: Concepts, Research, Policy*, Edward Elgar, Cheltenham, UK, pp. 463–71.
de Koning, A. (2009) *Global Dreams: Class, Gender and Public Space in Cosmopolitan Cairo*, The American University of Cairo Press, Cairo.
Devenish, A. and Skinner, C. (2006) 'Collective action in the informal economy: the case of the Self-Employed Women's Union, 1994–2004', in R. Ballard, A. Habib and I. Valodia (eds), *Voices of Protest: Social Movements in Post-Apartheid South Africa*, Pietermaritzburg, University of KwaZulu-Natal Press, pp. 255–78.
Erman, T. and Turkyilmaz, S. (2008) 'Neighborhood effects and women's agency regarding poverty and patriarchy in a Turkish slum', *Environment and Planning A*, vol. 40, pp. 1760–76.
Falu, A. (2010) 'Violence and discrimination in cities', in A. Falu (ed.), *Women in the City: On Violence and Rights*. Translated from the original: *Mujeres en la ciudad. De violencias y derechos*, by Georgia Marman and Paulina Matta, with the collaboration of Dr Rod Burgess and Alan Cahoon. Women and Habitat Network of Latin American/Ediciones S.U.R., Santiago de Chile, pp. 15–38.
Floro, M. and Pichetpongsa, A. (2010) 'Gender, work intensity, and well-being of Thai home-based workers', *Feminist Economics*, vol. 16, no. 3, pp. 5–44.
Fonchingong, C. (2005) 'Negotiating livelihoods beyond Beijing: the burden of women food vendors in the informal economy of Limbe, Cameroon', *International Social Science Journal*, vol. 57, no. 2, pp. 243–53.
Hanson, S. (2009) 'Changing places through women's entrepreneurship', *Economic Geography*, vol. 5, no. 3, pp. 245–67.
Heintz, J. (2010) 'Women's employment, economic risk and poverty', in S. Chant (ed.), *The International Handbook of Gender and Poverty: Concepts, Research, Policy*, Edward Elgar, Cheltenham, UK, pp. 434–9.
Jutting, J. and DeLaiglesia, J. (2009) 'Is informal normal? Towards more and better jobs in developing countries', OECD, available at: www.oecd.org/dev/poverty/employment, accessed 7 February 2011.
Kantor, P. (2009) 'Women's exclusion and unfavorable inclusion in informal employment in Lucknow, India: barriers to voice and livelihood security', *World Development*, vol. 37, no. 1, pp. 194–207.
Kapoor, A. (2007) 'The SEWA way: shaping another future for informal labour', *Futures*, vol. 39, pp. 554–68.
Kwan, M. (1999) 'Gender and individual access to urban opportunities: a study using space–time measures', *Professional Geographer*, vol. 51, no. 2, pp. 210–27.
Lindell, I. (2009) '"Glocal" movements: place struggles and transnational organizing by informal workers', *Geografiska Annaler: Series B, Human Geography*, vol. 91, no. 2, pp. 123–36.
Lindell, I. (2011) 'The contested spatialities of transnational activism: gendered gatekeeping and gender struggles in an African association of informal workers', *Global Networks*, vol. 11, no. 2, pp. 222–41.
Lund, F. and Skinner, C. (2004) 'Integrating the informal economy in urban planning and governance: a case study of the process of policy development in Durban, South Africa', *International Development Planning Review*, vol. 26, no. 4, pp. 431–56.

Malaza, N., Todes, A. and Williamson, A. (2009) *Gender in Planning and Urban Development*, Commonwealth Secretariat, London.

Meagher, K. (2010) 'The empowerment trap: gender, poverty and the informal economy in Sub-Saharan Africa', in S. Chant (ed.), *The International Handbook of Gender and Poverty: Concepts, Research, Policy*, Edward Elgar, Cheltenham, UK, pp. 472–7.

Menon-Sen, K. and Bhan, G. (2008) *Swept Off the Map: Surviving Eviction and Resettlement in Delhi*, Yoda Press, New Delhi.

Miraftab, F. (2010) 'Contradictions in the gender–poverty nexus: reflections on the privatisation of social reproduction and urban informality in South African townships', in S. Chant (ed.), *The International Handbook of Gender and Poverty: Concepts, Research, Policy*, Edward Elgar, Cheltenham, UK, pp. 644–8.

Moser, C. (2010) 'Safety, gender mainstreaming and gender-based programmes', in A. Falu (ed.), *Women in the City: On Violence and Rights*. Translated from the original: *Mujeres en la ciudad. De violencias y derechos*, by Georgia Marman and Paulina Matta, with the collaboration of Dr Rod Burgess and Alan Cahoon. Women and Habitat Network of Latin American/Ediciones S.U.R., Santiago de Chile, pp. 77–98.

Neto, F., Ha, Y. and Weliwita, A. (2007) 'The urban informal economy – new policy approaches', *Habitat Debate*, vol. 13, no. 2, pp. 4–5.

Rainero, L. (2010) 'A contribution to the debate on the city, public space and safety from a feminist perspective', in A. Falu (ed.), *Women in the City: On Violence and Rights*. Translated from the original: *Mujeres en la ciudad. De violencias y derechos*, by Georgia Marman and Paulina Matta, with the collaboration of Dr Rod Burgess and Alan Cahoon. Women and Habitat Network of Latin American/Ediciones S.U.R., Santiago de Chile, pp. 165–74.

Roy, A. (2003) *City Requiem. Calcutta: Gender and the Politics of Poverty*, University of Minnesota Press, Minneapolis, MD.

Roy, A. (2005) 'Urban informality: toward an epistemology of planning', *Journal of the American Planning Association*, vol. 71, no. 2, pp. 147–57.

Roy, A. and AlSayyed, N. (2004) *Urban Informality: Transnational Perspectives from the Middle East, Latin America and South Asia*, Lexington Books, Lanham, MD.

Sen, G. (2010) 'Poor households or poor women: is there a difference?', in S. Chant (ed.), *The International Handbook of Gender and Poverty: Concepts, Research, Policy*, Edward Elgar, Cheltenham, UK, pp. 101–4.

Skinner, C. (2008) 'The struggle for the streets: processes of exclusion and inclusion of street traders in Durban, South Africa', *Development Southern Africa*, vol. 25, no. 2, pp. 227–42.

Snyder, K. (2005) 'Gender segregation in the hidden labour force: looking at the relationship between formal and informal economies', in M. Texler Segal and V. Demos (eds), *Gender Realities: Local and Global*, Advances in Gender Research, vol. 9, Elsevier, Amsterdam, pp. 1–27.

Sweet, E. and Escalante, S. (2010) 'Planning responds to gender violence: evidence from Spain, Mexico and the United States', *Urban Studies*, vol. 47, no. 10, pp. 2129–47.

Tibaijuka, A. (2006) 'Introduction by Executive Director of UN-HABITAT', *State of the World's Cities 2006/07*, available at: www.unhabitat.org/documents/media_centre/sowcr2006/SOWCR_ED.pdf, accessed 7 February 2011.

UN-HABITAT (2006) *Innovative Policies for the Urban Informal Economy*, UN-HABITAT, Nairobi, Kenya.

Watson, V. (2009) '"The planned city sweeps the poor away ...": urban planning and 21st century urbanisation', *Planning in Progress*, vol. 72, pp. 151–93.

Weinstein, L. and Ren, X. (2009) 'The changing right to the city: urban renewal and housing rights in globalizing Shanghai and Mumbai', *City and Community*, vol. 8, no. 4, pp. 407–32.

Wick, I. (2010) *Women Working in the Shadows: The Informal Economy and Export Processing Zones*, Institut Für Ökonomie und Ökumene Süd, Evanglisch-Lutherische Kirche in Bayern, Siegburg/Munich.

Women in Cities International and Jagori (2010) *Third International Conference on Women's Safety: Building Inclusive Cities Conference Background Paper*, available at: www.femmesetvilles.org/english/sets_en/set_downloads_en.htm, accessed 7 February 2011.

Wright, M. (2004) 'From protests to politics: sex work, women's worth, and Ciudad Juarez modernity', *Annals of the Association of American Geographers*, vol. 94, no. 2, pp. 369–86.

Chapter 3

Women's safety and everyday mobility

Carolyn Whitzman

> Walk very very slowly. Walk without your phone. Walk without your eyes fixed to the ground. Walk in the middle of the pavement. Walk with your chin a little raised ... Walk without your hands clenched. Walk smiling. Walk smiling. Walk smiling.
> (Blank Noise Collective, 'Step by step guide to unapologetic walking' poster, 2008)

Introduction

Accessible, affordable and safe transportation options are essential for women and men living in cities. Access from one's home to a range of employment, education, leisure, health and social services is a precondition for attaining a decent standard of living and enjoying adequate health and well-being. Research on women's transport needs has found that gender-based violence and fear of violence are barriers to accessing transport options, and particularly active and sustainable transport options, such as walking, cycling and using public transport. Concerns about safety thus act as a barrier to physical mobility – getting around – and social mobility – the ability to access essential services that might improve life prospects (Morales, 2010, p. 6, citing UK Social Exclusion Unit, 2002; see also Law, 1999; Peters, 2001; Loukaitou-Sideris and Fink, 2009). The right to mobility is considered fundamental to Western ideas of citizenship (Cresswell, 2010), and the notion of mobility as a basic right stretches back to Hegel: 'It is a violation of my natural essential freedom not to be able to go where I please ... my personality is wounded by such experiences, because my most immediate identity rests in my body' (in Benard and Schlaffer, 1984, p. 395).

However, there is also a problem with over-emphasizing mobility and safety as simplistic goals. Transport innovations, over the past century, have often been seen as mechanisms to overcome barriers to almost limitless space (Urry, 2004). A credo of unlimited automobility, characterized by growing dependence on the speed of motorized vehicles, has led to traffic accidents becoming one of the leading causes of death and disability worldwide

(Murray and Lopez, 1996), and transportation being a major contributor to greenhouse-gas emissions (Newman and Kenworthy, 1999). Increasingly long commuting times between workplaces and homes disadvantage lower-income individuals without equal access to cars and reinforce the tendency towards extremely socially segregated cities (Silbaugh, 2007; Rojas *et al.*, 2008). A right to absolute mobility may lead to unexpected and undesirable environmental, health and social-equity impacts.

Safety should also not be conceptualized as a simple goal. From initial nineteenth-century concerns about 'the promiscuity of the crowd', urban-planning responses have often emphasized exclusion of 'women and children, along with other disruptive elements – the working class, the poor, and minorities' from the public realm, usually with the rhetoric that it is for their own good (Wilson, 1991, p. 6). A modern equivalent can be seen in women-only transport services and in the lingering attitudes that women require safety in the form of protectionism, whether that is closed-circuit television (CCTV) or increased policing. Part of women's right to the city is the right to undertake risk in the pursuit of urban citizenship, and part of the experience of any truly libratory city is encounter with strangers, including strangers who make others feel uncomfortable.

This chapter navigates between unconscionable extremes – forced immobility and forced mobility, patriarchal protectionism and gender-based violence – to outline transport-based interventions that seek to realize women's right to the city. A case study of Bogota will illustrate the balance between increasing mobility and increasing access, as a result of policies that were not explicitly about gender, but integrated an understanding of differential access to public space.

Transport and mobility reconsidered

Transport, put simply, is the process of getting things or people from one place to another. An underlying assumption of the term *transport* is therefore that it meets needs that cannot be provided without movement or physical mobility (Zielinski, 1995, p. 137). The terms *transportation disadvantage* and *transport captive*, referring to a gender gap in access to private motorized vehicles, provide further implicit assumptions of a norm that unfettered movement is necessary for full economic and social citizenship (Zielinski, 1995, p. 137, citing Wekerle and Rutherford, 1987). Mobility thus has a positive connotation of the freedom to roam and to pursue action. But mobility can be involuntary and stressful, even when it is not insecure or dangerous (Jarvis *et al.*, 2009, p. 158), and it may be possible to bypass transport needs by providing nearby goods and services – by privileging 'access over excess' (Zielinski, 1995, p. 131).

One of the basic starting points of any analysis of gender and transport is that women tend to have daily patterns of activity that are more complex than men, owing to roles that incorporate domestic chores and caregiving for children and elderly relatives, as well as paid work (Duchene, 2011, p. 7). These different needs have been ignored by most mainstream transportation research and theory. As McDowell (1993, p. 166) colourfully puts it: 'The gangs, the urban crowds, the *flâneurs*, the political activists, even the stolid figures of urban commuters were never encumbered by a baby, a stroller and the week's shopping.'

Productive, paid work and reproductive, unpaid work in maintaining home and family are increasingly separated physically. In the United States, Silbaugh (2007) provides examples of how a 15-minute meeting with an elderly parent's physical therapist or a child's teacher can absorb half a workday if it requires an additional round trip, particularly by public transport in non-peak hours. More women in the paid workforce, particularly in service-sector jobs, means more commuting to shopping malls, airports and other people's homes (if you are a maid or a health-care homeworker, for instance), often at non-peak times. This paid work can create the need to buy and maintain a car, simply because distances are too long to walk or cycle, and the public-transport service is inadequate. At the same time, paid work at home presents its own problems. Predominantly female garment or telephone-service workers, in the United States and elsewhere, are often poorly paid, hidden from unions and occupational health and safety checks, and isolated from other workers (Silbaugh, 2007, p. 35).

Much of the literature on women's transport has a simplistic focus on a choice between private car and public transport to access sprawling cities. It is only with recent literature on healthy communities, and an increasing focus on developing countries, that walking and cycling have received consideration as transport modes. Yet, internationally, walking is still the most common form of transportation for women and men and is a feature of most journeys (Duchene, 2011). Walking is also the healthiest, least expensive and most environmentally sustainable mode of travel, closely followed by cycling (Loukaitou-Sideris, 2004). Internationally, women are less likely than men to have access to motorized transport, but are also less likely to have access to bicycles or other intermediate transport such as scooters, are more likely to depend on public transport for longer-distance trips, and are equally likely to walk for transport (Peters, 2001, p. 11). In the United Kingdom, where women are more likely to walk than men (and men with company cars are least likely to walk), walking is considered the least safe way to travel (DfT, 1999, pp. 4–8).

Law (1999), in a review of the previous twenty years of feminist research on gender differences in transport, criticizes this literature on three main fronts. First, by replicating the mainstream emphasis on journey to work, albeit adding in more complex trip chaining related to care-giving, feminist literature neglects journeys for leisure and pleasure, as well as the latent demand of journeys that were not made. Second, the divide between largely qualitative research on constraints caused by fear of violence and quantitative research on women's actual travel patterns tends to result in the urban-transport literature being under-conceptualized as either an economic-development/public-health issue or a rights issue, but not both at the same time. Third, although there is some consideration of differences between women on the basis of class and ethnicity, there has been limited inclusion of literature from disability studies and also literature from less developed countries, which might enrich an understanding of difference, exclusion, access and justice. As a corrective, Law proposes a framework that explicitly adds the construction of subject identities through experiences of transport to more traditional, quantitative research on division of labour and activities and access to resources. Law (1999, p. 568) also differentiates between geographic and temporal scales in thinking about transport, using the term 'daily mobility' to differentiate between everyday, short-term and repetitive flows on the one hand, and travel or migration on the other hand.

One consequence of violence and insecurity in relation to transport options is *forced immobility*. Isha L'Isha, a feminist collective based in Haifa, Israel, provide one example of this in their survey of Jewish and Palestinian Israelis during the second Lebanese war. Eighty per cent of women in the northern part of Israel were left isolated in their homes:

> Most of these women did not choose to stay at home. They were forced to do so due to difficulties in mobility, responsibility to their children and other relatives who for assorted reasons could not leave the region, fear of losing their jobs, and primarily the inability to afford the high costs of travelling and living outside their homes for a long period with their families.
>
> (Dayif *et al.*, 2007, p. 19)

Immobility in this instance is the consequence of intersections between identities, location, culture, experiences, income, transport options and a combination of individual and institutional violence.

An equal and opposite aspect is *forced mobility*, caused when functions that are taken for granted in some places are absent in others. Because of inadequate water and sanitation infrastructure in low-income communities, many essential functions such as defecation and accessing water require long, risky trips (see Khosla and Dhar in this volume). In India, women lined up with pots waiting for water, and men and children relieving themselves in public, are commonplace sights. Less visible, but no less omnipresent, are women and girls who can only perform these latter functions under cover of darkness, after 10 p.m. or at 4 a.m., facing the threat of harassment or violence (Jarvis *et al.*, 2009, p. 129). The World Bank estimates that 'if the average distance to the moon is 384,400 km, South African women walk a distance equivalent to the moon and back 16 times a day just to fetch water' (in Duchene, 2011, p. 10).

To summarize, when applying a gendered lens to transport and mobility, it is important to consider choice in relation to both daily and occasional activities. It is also important to include walking as well as public transport and private motorized vehicles. Furthermore, solutions might be found in reconceptualizing the relationships between destinations such as places of residence, workplaces, shops and services, as well as through improving the journey itself.

Women's safety and transport reconsidered

Another basic starting point of literature on gender and transport is the difference that personal safety makes in both choice and experience of transport. Many surveys show that, whereas men prioritize speed and, to some extent, cost in their travel decisions, women prioritize safety. In Lima, Peru, men said that 'speed' was their top public-transport priority, whereas women put 'safety' as their top priority (Peters, 2001, p. 18). A poll of public-transport users in Toronto, Canada, in 1986 found that 45 per cent of women felt unsafe using services after dark, as compared with 13 per cent of men (in Whitzman, 2002, p. 102).

Although more violence takes place in homes and other parts of the private sphere, a constant stream of both fictional and media representations of violence in and around public transport and in multi-storey parking lots and garages may have some impact on feelings of safety (Loukaitou-Sideris, 2004, p. 105). More to the point, constant and iterative experiences of harassment and violence, including staring, groping, remarks and stalking, as well as assault, influence women's perceptions. More than 80 per cent of women say they were sexually harassed on public transport over the previous year, according to a survey in Delhi, India, by Jagori in 2009, and more than 62 per cent say they have been sexually harassed over the last year on streets. These experiences took place during the day as well as at night (WICI, 2010). A study by Delhi police in 2004 showed that almost 45 per cent of reported cases of molestation occurred on public buses, and another 25 per cent on the roadside (Bhattacharya, 2009).

These problems should not be characterized as belonging to 'less developed' cities. A New York City Subway Safety Survey of almost 2,000 women in 2007 found that two-thirds of women reported past experiences of sexual harassment, and one in ten reported sexual assault on trains (Loukaitou-Sideris *et al.*, 2008, p. 30). According to a survey of women in Edinburgh, Scotland, in 1998, 43 per cent said they had been harassed by rude or abusive comments on the street, and nearly one in five had been followed by strangers (DfT, 1999, p. 6).

Gender appears to be the most consistent factor in concerns around safety, although the intersections of age, racialization, income, sexual orientation, prior victimization and disability are factors as well (DfT, 1999; Loukaitou-Sideris *et al.*, 2008; WICI, 2010). An example of intersections between gender and other aspects of identity lies in the experiences of older women and those with disabilities, where fears about personal security blend with fear of falling and a more general sense of physical vulnerability to both bicycles and motorized traffic (DfT, 1999, pp. 4–5; see also Phadke, 2010, p. 4).

Given this reality of violence and insecurity, a common reaction by authorities is to offer increased 'protection' in the form of CCTV, more policing and, particularly in the case of public transport, separate facilities for women. Loukaitou-Sideris and Fink (2009, p. 565), in their survey of US public-transport safety initiatives, report that, although increased uniformed-police presence in transit stations was rated very effective, CCTV appears to have little impact on feelings of safety.

A plethora of international cities have introduced women-only transport services, to address cultural taboos against the mingling of the sexes as well as security concerns. Mumbai, Tokyo, Manila, Mexico City, Rio de Janeiro and Seoul are some of the cities with women-only train carriages. Women-only buses have been introduced in Thailand, United Arab Emirates, Indonesia, Brazil, Mexico, Pakistan and India. Women-only taxi companies have been established in the United Kingdom, Mexico, Russia, India, Dubai and Iran (Loukaitou-Sideris *et al.*, 2008; WICI and Jagori, 2010; Duchene, 2011). Peters (2001, p. 19) says that the Mexican City train experiment appears to have been met with some customer satisfaction, as did a similar programme in Pune, India. In Tokyo, reported cases of 'lewd behaviour' decreased by 3 per cent one year after women-only subway cars expanded in 2004, although this may have been a function of improved policing response, as arrests increased 15–20 per cent along two major lines during that year. A survey found that 36 per cent of Japanese women never use women-only cars, and only 4 per cent said they always used them (Loukaitou-Sideris *et al.*, 2008, p. 40). About half the women in a Dhaka, Bangladesh, survey called for women-only bus services, but only 2 per cent of women in Pune, India, thought this a viable option, preferring more buses in general so that there is less crowding (Peters, 2001, p. 15). There is considerable debate as to whether this response puts the burden on women to protect themselves by withdrawing from the male gaze into second-class services. As one editorial in the UK *Guardian* said in 2007: 'The onus should be on men to stop harassing women, not on women to escape them' (in Loukaitou-Sideris *et al.*, 2008, p. 41).

Phadke (2007), drawing on Wilson (1991), takes this analysis further. Women and men are always making calculations about risk in a city such as Mumbai: 'what train to catch, where to invest, what kind of insurance, to travel with a railway pass or "free", how to save one's skin during bomb blasts or on days of torrential rainfall' (2007, p. 1509). A three-year action research project undertaken by Phadke and her colleagues at Partnerships for Urban Knowledge and Research (PUKAR) in 2004–6 found that a large number of women interviewed said they would rather risk crossing railway tracks, in a city where ten people die in train-related accidents every day, than risk harassment on pedestrian footbridges. A more common strategy is avoidance of public space: in head counts at dozens of sites around the city, from downtown business streets to train stations, no more than 28 per cent of 'people in the street' were women (Phadke, 2007, p. 1511).

In focus-group discussions, there was no consensus among women or men as to the correct way to deal with the constant barrage of sexual harassment: does responding to the harasser show stern disapproval or encourage them through engaging with them? If a woman returns to the bus stop where she was harassed the next day, is she tacitly stating that she enjoys this harassment? (Phadke, 2005, p. 46). There were also differences between attitudes based on the predominant socio-economic class of the neighbourhood. In Dhavari, a slum neighbourhood, women's presence alone in streets was seen as an option rather than a necessity, by both women and men, thus leading to the implicit question, 'what were you doing there in the first place?'. In Bandra, an upmarket suburb, women working late at night were assumed to be taking on desirable middle-class working habits and reported less harassment from men, including auto-rickshaw drivers (Phadke, 2005, pp. 46–7).

Phadke thus theorizes that women's travel is governed by a 'tyranny of purpose' (Phadke, 2010, p. 5). Women are expected visibly to demonstrate their respectability, through their clothing choices and the presence of symbols of matrimony, but also through symbols of productivity. Observations in a range of public spaces in Mumbai found women alone tended to be

> carrying something, shopping, heading towards bus-stops or railway stations, but rarely, if ever, loitering around, sitting in a park or *maidan* [public square] or standing at a street corner smoking or simply watching the world go by as one is wont to see men doing.
> (Phadke, 2010, p. 5)

To return to McDowell's terms, it may have become more respectable for middle-class women to be commuters as well as childminders, but there is still a barrier to seeing women as *flâneurs*. As the quotation that began this chapter suggests, women lingering in public space still face both internalized repression (look busy!) as well as externalized oppression by men questioning their legitimacy in public space. While '"the man on the street" . . . is a synonym for the citizen, the voter, the average person . . . there is no "woman on the street" in our language; only a streetwalker, or an intruder who can be treated like one' (in Thompson, 1994, p. 313). As Katha Pollit described, in New York City in 1985:

> I found myself in midtown and decided to take a walk through Byrant Park ... [Within moments one man] invited me to take my clothes off and ... Another ... wanted to know why I wasn't smiling ... [There] were perhaps 50 men, strolling, ambling, striding along eating hot dogs, sitting on benches and reading the paper or trading illegal substances as though they had all the time in the world – and 3 women, all walking quickly and grimly, as I was now doing, as though late for an appointment with the dentist.
> (in Thompson, 1994, p. 313)

This links into a debate within feminist writing on the city. Wilson (1991) and, later, Young (1995) and Fincher and Iveson (2008) speak about the pleasures of anonymity, stepping out of routine and mundane journeys to encounter the different, surprising and erotic. But Fenster (2005), in her interviews with Jewish and Palestinian women, finds an equation of safety with belonging within a neighbourhood, and Garber (1995, pp. 25–6) speaks of the political dangers of anonymity, the threat of losing 'identity' as women to stake claims to public space. There appears to be a continual tension between anonymity and familiarity in navigation of the city, between being oneself and losing oneself. Do women have the time to get lost? Is there urban space where women can risk getting lost?

According to Phadke (2007, p. 1511), although the ultimate right to the city includes adequate infrastructure, including public transport, toilets and proximity of housing to economic and educational opportunities, in the interim, women should have a right to make informed choices about risk. She says: 'Safety does not accrue from infrastructural or institutional factors but has to be actively produced.' That is, the only way for women to achieve safety, to claim their right to the city, is by maximizing their access to public space. Rather than the right to safety, Phadke argues that women need, not 'greater surveillance or protectionism (however well meaning), but the right to engage risk' (Phadke, 2007, p. 1516). This means an absence of both internalized and externalized blame for travelling through public space without regard to time of day, manner of dress or purpose of trip.

So, women's safety might not be only – or even primarily – about protection from violence or harassment, which is omnipresent in both the public and private realms. It might be about opening dialogues and providing opportunities to negotiate risks, ranging from the real risks of travelling within public space, to the equally real risks of withdrawing from the public realm.

Policy initiatives to improve women's safety in transport

Few transport plans or policies explicitly address gender, let alone women's safety. Peters (2001, p. 4) notes that only 4 per cent of World Bank transport projects for developing countries include a gender component or actions, as compared with 15 per cent for water, 35 per cent for agriculture, 44 per cent for education and 67 per cent for population health and nutrition projects. A 2007 survey of 131 US transit authorities found that, although two-thirds feel that women have different transit security needs from men, only three agencies reported having programmes addressing these needs in place (Loukaitou-Sideris et al., 2008, p. 569).

Even when transport information is disaggregated by gender, the question of latent demand brought up by Law is difficult to address. Particularly in developing countries, household demand is gauged by interviewing heads of households, who are often men. Even in 'on-the-street' (or market, or busstop) interviews, the fact that many women are not in public space is overlooked. Only 45 per cent of women in Dhaka responded to a travel-pattern survey as part of a five-city study in the late 1990s, as opposed to 68 per cent of men, partially because many women had not travelled outside their homes in the past week. Several, however, had suggestions about public space, which might be better explored in a focus-group format (Peters, 2001, p. 18).

Women's safety audits, further discussed by Viswanath in this volume, are a tool for improving public spaces that have their origins in the Toronto Transit Commission's work with the Metro Toronto Action Committee on Public Violence Against Women and Children (METRAC), arising from the 1986 survey on women's safety on public transport discussed above. Women's safety audits, led by METRAC but including local female residents when possible, covered all of Toronto's fifty subway train stations in 1989, and were followed by similar work in relation to the suburban bus systems. This led to innovations such as transparent bus shelters, emergency intercoms in stations, elevators to subway platforms to improve accessibility, designated waiting areas at subway stations that are well lit and associated with intercoms and CCTV, and a request-stop programme that enables women to exit, at their request, between two regular scheduled stops in the evening, to reduce their walking time to their destination (Loukaitou-Sideris et al., 2008, p. 35). The latter would be a good example of providing opportunities for women to navigate risk.

The work in Toronto exemplifies a partnership model between community organizations and local authorities. In Rosario, Argentina, like Delhi a participant in the Gender Inclusive Cities Programme (see Viswanath in this volume), the Women and Habitat Network reviewed public-transport plans for women's safety concerns and made recommendations that included better signage and design of bus shelters and stations. In late November 2008, in the lead up to the International Day for the Elimination of Violence Against Women, 75,000 bus tickets were printed with the message that 'violence against women is a violation of human rights' (WICI and Jagori, 2010, p. 23).

An ambitious transit-authority partnership example comes from Transport for London, the authority responsible for the Underground (train system), buses, ferries, roads and cabs in London. As part of a commitment to gender mainstreaming in government, the national Department for Transport published a gender audit checklist with targets, in 2000. Transport for London responded with a Women's Action Plan in 2004 (Loukaitou-Sideris *et al.*, 2008, p. 37). Informed by an advisory Women's Transport Network, the first of four goals of this plan was to improve levels of real and perceived personal security. This goal was to be achieved through additional policing, better 'hub stops', with safe and well-lit waiting areas along night-bus routes, and a national accreditation system for safe stations, including lighting, CCTV, signage and customer information, staffed help points and better maintenance of vehicles and stations. Accessibility is another goal, with low-floor bus fleets (with associated bus stops and areas on the bus) that particularly meet the needs of people in wheelchairs and parents with strollers or young children. Data collection, included analysing passenger correspondence by gender, and recruitment targets for women as drivers and maintenance workers were set in accordance with the Gender Equality Act of 2007 (Loukaitou-Sideris *et al.*, 2008, pp. 36–9).

There are also a plethora of non-profit and private responses to women's transportation safety. RightRides for Women's Safety is a non-profit organization in New York City offering women, transgender and queer individuals a free, safe, night ride home from midnight to 3 a.m. in forty-five neighbourhoods. It operates with six donated cars and volunteer drivers and navigators (Loukaitou-Sideris *et al.*, 2008, p. 29). In Dhaka, Bangladesh, where 70 per cent of women work in the garment industry, usually working 12-hour days, some employers provide special transportation (Peters, 2001, p. 14). Although these stopgap measures could provide short-term solutions to afford women greater mobility in the city, it is important to see them as a small part of more transformative practices (WICI and Jagori, 2010, p. 23).

Bogota: a case study of an integrated-policy approach

Bogota has become internationally acclaimed for both its urban-safety strategy, resulting in a reduction in violent deaths, and its integrated-transport strategy, resulting in a reduction in private motorized-vehicle use (Rojas, 2002; Montezuma, 2005). Common to both these strategies is a desire to create an equitable sense of citizenship and 'right to the city' where they had not previously existed. The paradox is that the desire for encounter between classes and across gender has led to enforcement practices that have targeted the most marginalized people, including increased institutional harassment of the homeless and street hawkers (Berney, 2011).

In the early 1990s, Bogota had one of the highest homicide rates in the world and was seen by its citizens as dirty, disorganized and chaotic (Rojas, 2002, p. 5). Antanas Mockus, a philosopher who was elected Mayor in 1995, began a social transformation that was complemented by an infrastructural transformation by his successor, Enrique Penalosa, an urban planner. The aim of this social and infrastructural transformation was increased equity between rich and poor, but also a shared sense of citizenship across class, age groups and gender. The social transformation began with a comprehensive community-safety plan, part of an overall plan to *Formar Ciudad*, which means 'to form [or educate] the city' (Montezuma, 2005, p. 3). An analysis of local data on causes of violence and insecurity led to a range of measures, from making the police more accountable to the city administration and citizens, evaluating progress through monitoring all programmes and developing indicators, to developing 'civic culture' by a set of innovative public-education campaigns that sought to address everyday violence. In specific relation to safety and transport, over 350,000 'thumbs up/thumbs down' cards were distributed, so that people could communicate silently on traffic and other minor neighbourhood conflicts, rather than yelling or using their fists. The transit police, who were widely distrusted by the public, were abolished in favour of an increase in regular police patrolling public transport. Some 420 street mimes were hired to tease car drivers and pedestrians who flouted traffic laws, and 150 taxi drivers, nominated by the public as friendly, were feted by Mayor Mockus as Knights of the Zebra (Bogota's taxis are black and white) and were consulted on how to improve the safety of taxi services more generally. In terms of women's access to public space, Mockus created an annual event called Women's Night Out. At the first such event in 2002, 70,000 women received discounts at local restaurants and attended all-night parties and concerts at various venues, including the central boulevard of Bogota, which was closed off to traffic. These symbolic events were treated as no less important than the prosaic business of reducing access to guns and ammunition, reducing hours for licensed premises and creating 7,000 community–police neighbourhood partnerships (Whitzman, 2008, pp. 117–20).

Transformative cultural approaches increased property-tax revenues and created an economic climate where national and foreign-aid investment was easier to elicit. This, in turn, led to capital investments that resulted in improvements to the physical and social infrastructure in poor neighbourhoods, as well as improving access between these suburban slums and areas of employment. A master plan in 2000 led to the regularization of formerly illegal settlements, and the provision of water, electricity and paved roads to 316 mostly low-income neighbourhoods with a total of 650,000 inhabitants (Montezuma, 2005, p. 1). The *Transmilenio* bus rapid-transit system, based on programmes in Curitiba, Brazil, and Quito, Ecuador, replaced a chaotic system involving dozens of competing and under-regulated bus companies with a single-fare, integrated system that, by 2010, covered 84 km of designated public-transport lanes, with feeder buses covering most of Bogota's suburbs (Morales, 2010, p. 15). Almost 300 km of bicycle paths have been completed, and Bogota's *Ciclovia* programme, which closes off a further 120 km of roads to car traffic on Sundays and public holidays, attracts an average of 2 million participants each day to bicycling, walking and free exercise activities along the route (Power, 2010). In 2000, against fierce opposition from businessmen, Penalosa proclaimed a car-free day. Limiting car traffic has gradually become so popular (a series of public referenda have asked permission from the public for these measures) that private automobiles are now prohibited on streets two days a week (Montezuma, 2005, p. 6). The *Ciclovia* programme, in particular, is seen as a way to extend a civic culture of safety, encounter and tolerance, through reintroducing the notion of leisurely, family-based exploration of the city (Berney, 2011).

In terms of social infrastructure, a total of 917,000 m^2 of public open space have been created in Bogota. These include neighbourhood and regional parks, but also *alamedas*, or the recovery of public streets, transformed into spaces for pedestrians with the banning of car parking on streets, improvements to sidewalks, traffic signals, lighting, benches and tree planting. A network of public libraries in all neighbourhoods, located close to public-transit and bicycle routes, has been complemented by improvements to schools, with the number of youth attending school increasing by 30 per cent in 1995–2000 (Montezuma, 2005, pp. 6–7). Community economic development programmes sought to increase access to local jobs. A large-scale programme sought to improve the local environment in Usme, one of Bogota's southernmost suburbs, with very high levels of social disadvantage among its 85,000 inhabitants. Participatory practices sought to improve community leadership, while local participatory planning allowed local expertise to modify and evaluate the initial programme (Rueda-Garcia, 2003, p. 27). At a field trip held in 2004 as part of the Second International Conference on Women's Safety in Bogota, the author visited Usme, where successful, women-led employment projects included community canteens, sewing collectives and a recycling firm. All of these initiatives were intended to promote a city of shorter distances, where jobs and services would be more immediately accessible in outer suburbs.

Women's community leadership has been elicited through a bottom-up, consultative, budget-setting process based on the successful example of Porto Alegre in Brazil (Rojas, 2002). There has also been a specific women's safety programme funded as part of a Regional Safer Cities for Women programme, funded by UN Women. This programme worked within existing policies to insert a women's-safety perspective, supporting four local women's centres to involve themselves in public-space interventions, undertaking surveys, focus groups and Women's Safety Audits to diagnose particular issues and hot spots, influencing local security plans (including public-transport security) and undertaking large-scale public-education projects (Red Mujer y Habitat, 2010). To give one example, in 2008, a two-week campaign in buses and around bus stops involved hundreds of women, who held up signs communicating the message that violence against women on public transport is socially unacceptable (UN Women, 2010). This can be seen as an extension of the symbolic acts by which Mockus wished to reclaim a collective sense of urban security.

The combination of social-development and urban-design policies resulted in a 70 per cent reduction in the murder rate in Bogota between 1993 and 2005. Bogota has gone from having a higher murder rate than the rest of the country, to a murder rate that is half the national average. Traffic fatalities have also decreased by almost two-thirds over the same period (Acero, 2006), perhaps owing to a 40 per cent reduction in private-automobile use (Montezuma, 2005, p. 6).

However, these very impressive achievements do not negate the fact that the initiative has had its victims and challenges. As part of the effort to reclaim public parks, squares and streets, there have been successive crackdowns on public begging and vending. Nearly half of all street vendors in a Bogota survey in 2006 reported facing harassment from police or other officials (Berney, 2011, p. 18). Ten thousand inhabitants of the inner-city Santa Inez neighbourhood, where urban lawlessness was felt to be concentrated, were forcibly relocated so that a new park could be built (Rueda-Garcia, 2003, pp. 25–6). Signs that say 'parks are for learning how to live' also say 'vendors prohibited', which is a reversal of a culture that previously allowed informal businesses to thrive in public spaces. These new restrictions are often enforced by 'civic guides', who are themselves low-income women and men (Berney, 2011, p. 22).

Of 6 million public-transport trips per day, only one quarter use the *Transmilenio* system, and there are still economic and social barriers to the equitable use of public transport (Morales, 2010, p. 18). Poor people find the fare expensive, and the cost-recovery basis of the system means that public-transport options are limited at night and during off-peak hours. People over the age of 60 comprise 12 per cent of the population, but only 3 per cent of *Transmilenio* users. Teenagers are 21 per cent of the population, but only 6 per cent of users. Although the *Transmilenio* system is wheelchair accessible, the traditional buses are not. Women are also underrepresented on the *Transmilenio* system, partly because of the emphasis on traditional home–workplace connections and the higher fares, but also because of persistent violence and insecurity concerns (Morales, 2010, pp. 17–24).

Although the social-development bent of Mockus and the physical-planning emphasis of Penalosa can be seen in hindsight as symbiotic, the fact remains that Penalosa (who unsuccessfully ran against Mockus in 1995) eliminated most of Mockus's social-education programmes when elected in 1998 (Montezuma, 2005, p. 9). Moreover, a 12-year period of relative continuity (Mockus and Penalosa were succeeded by Luis Garzon, another progressive mayor) came to an end in 2008 with the election of Samuel Rojas, a right-wing candidate. Despite attempts to manufacture a social consensus among citizens, considerable international acclaim and demonstrable results, Bogotans appeared to tire of radical change.

This case study highlights a mainstreamed approach to women's safety in transport, where four megaplans – concerning economic development in slums, a new public-transport system, a new school system and a system to reclaim and renovate public space – came together to indirectly support women's right to safer mobility and easier access to public goods and services. All four plans were informed by both institutional and community-based initiatives that sought to promote greater gender equality. The plans addressed both increasing access to local services and improving mobility across the city, to increase both economic opportunity and sense of citizenship. Most radically, the Bogota experiment was about creating an urban culture that valued everyday access to public space via walking, cycling and taking public transport. Despite demonstrable progress in improving the most extreme aspects of violence and insecurity, it still was imperfect in promoting the right to the city, in that it targeted certain groups of 'others' (street vendors, homeless people) as sources of insecurity. Women and ethnic minorities may often equate poor men with insecure situations (DfT, 1999, p. 15), but harassment and assault are far too endemic in the public realm to be laid at the feet of a particular marginalized group.

Conclusion: women's safety, mobility and right to the city

When Lefebvre, back in 1968, wrote his famous article on 'the right to the city', he specifically contrasted the 'rhythms of daily life which are inscribed and prescribe in these "successful" spaces favourable to happiness' with his vision of suburban dystopia:

> the daily life of one who runs from his dwelling to the station . . . to the packed underground train, the office or the factory, to return the same way in the evening and come home to recuperate enough to start again the next day.
>
> (2006, pp. 151, 159)

In other words, the daily commute to Lefebvre was the opposite experience to the 'concrete' rights of the city he wanted to see: 'the rights of ages and sexes (the woman, the child and the elderly), rights of conditions (the proletarian, the peasant), rights to training and education, to work, to culture, to rest, to health, to housing ... to nature' (Lefebvre, 2006, p. 157).

The right to the city is not simply the right to access education or work. Rather, it is the right to belong everywhere, to inhabit cities through independent exploration, to influence institutions as well as attain a livelihood. It is also the right to encounter difference: not only different people, but different experiences – not only a limited 'leisure' experience, but meaningful encounters across social classes in daily life. Lefebvre (1991) further elaborates in his article on 'the production of space' that cities are created through three interrelated practices: how space is produced and used on a daily basis, how planners and other professionals represent space, and representational or symbolic space. The right to the city is not simply manifested through changes to the material realm of transport infrastructure to facilitate an effective workforce. It derives from the perceptual realms of belonging and the pursuit of happiness in public space, including the right to treat public space as a place to linger, a destination in its own right, as well as a corridor to traverse on the way to another destination.

A similar conceptual triad is found in Law's (1999) analysis of gender and power. One facet is about access to resources, or who uses which transport modes and why. A second facet is division of power: who makes decisions that affect transport and how? The last facet is related to the construction of identities, or in relation to transport, how the symbolic spaces of mobility are perceived in relation to gender. Whitzman (2007) also talks about three kinds of safety practice: making spaces safer, through lighting and other design improvements; making safe places, which in relation to transport might be the sort of supportive health, employment, social and leisure services that are easily accessible through walking and short-distance public transport; and, finally, 'discursive safe spaces', which means both making women's safety a subject of actions by institutions and activists, and using transport itself as a place for public education around urban safety. Examples of this last practice in this chapter include the anti-violence messages on Rosario's bus tickets, as well as the Women's Transport Network influencing London's public-transport design and scheduling decisions.

One final conceptual triad that is useful to understand women's safety work around transport comes from Fincher and Iveson's (2008, p. 3) three 'social logics' of planning. Planning, at its best, works on issues of *redistribution*, which is related to Law's concept of equalizing access to resources and also Whitzman's idea of access to safe places. A second social logic is *recognition* of particular concerns and needs, which is what happens when one focuses on gender (or on ethnicity, or sexuality, or disability, or age). A third social logic, and one that is a particular concern to Lefebvre's notion of the right to the city, is *encounter* with difference.

Exclusion from the right to mobility can be as obvious as a steep curb, a homophobic slur or graffiti that means navigating through a sea of penises

(Jarvis *et al.*, 2009, p. 144). But exclusion is often subtler: two women's toilets and twenty-four men's urinals at a busy Mumbai train station (Phadke, 2010, p. 10); being one of the few pedestrians interrupting the 'orderly procession of cars' (Phadke, 2007, p. 1515); or continual messages from men in authority, such as the Chief Minister of Delhi remarking in 2009 that women should not get 'so adventurous' in their use of public transport at night (Bhattacharya, 2009). Safe mobility is, thus, both an economic development and a rights issue, a matter of individual access to public space and an equitable share of collective resources. It matters because of improved life prospects through access to education and health services, but it also matters because cities can be places to create and recreate identities. Until women and men, of all ages, incomes and ethnicities, are encouraged independently to explore their urban environs, risking encounter with the uncomfortable stranger, the right to mobility will remain incompletely realized.

References

Acero, H. (2006) 'Bogota's success story', *Comunidad Secura: network of ideas and practices in citizen security*, retrieved 14 April 2007 from www.comunidadesegura.org/?q=en/node/31203.

Benard, C. and Schlaffer, E. (1984) 'The Man in the Street: why he harasses', in A. Jaggar and P. Rothenberg (eds), *Feminist Frameworks: Alternative Theoretical Accounts of the Relations between Women and Men*, New York: McGraw-Hill, pp. 395–8.

Berney, R. (2011) 'Pedagogical Urbanism: creating citizen space in Bogota, Colombia', *Planning Theory*, 10(1): pp. 16–34.

Bhattacharya, S. (2009) 'All Aboard the Ladies Special', *Infochange*, July.

Blank Noise Collective (2008) 'Step by Step Guide to Unapologetic Walking', poster, retrieved 20 May 2011 from http://1.bp.blogspot.com/_NeiopOhFSss/TBSmrKF6zsI/AAAAAAAABt8/kAWLXZh9Pmo/s1600/stepbystepguidetounapologeticwalkingposter.jpg.

Cresswell, T. (2010) 'Towards a Politics of Mobility', *Environment and Planning D: society and space*, 28(1): pp. 17–31.

Dayif, A., Abramovitch, D. and Eyal, H. (eds) (2007) *Security for Whom? Feminist Perspectives on Security*, Haifa: Pardes.

DfT [Department for Transport (United Kingdom)] (1999) *Personal Security Issues in Pedestrian Journeys*, London: Department for Transport.

Duchene, C. (2011) *Gender and Transport*, Paris: International Transport Forum of the Organization for Economic Development and Cooperation Discussion Paper 2011–11.

Fenster, T. (2005) 'The Right to the Gendered City: different formations of belonging in everyday life', *Journal of Gender Studies*, 14(3): pp. 217–31.

Fincher, R. and Iveson, K. (2008) *Planning and Diversity in the City: Redistribution, Recognition, and Encounter*, Houndsmills, UK: Palgrave.

Garber, J. (1995) 'Defining Feminist Community: place, choice, and the urban politics of difference', in J. Garber and R. Turner (eds), *Gender in Urban Research*, Thousand Oaks, CA: Sage, pp. 24–45.

Jarvis, H., Kantor, P. and Cloke, P. (2009) *Cities and Gender*, New York: Routledge.
Law, R. (1999) 'Beyond "Women and Transport": towards new geographies of gender and daily mobility', *Progress in Human Geography*, 23(4): pp. 567–88.
Lefebvre, H. (1991) *The Production of Space*, Oxford: Blackwell.
Lefebvre, H. (2006) *Writings on Cities*, Oxford: Blackwell.
Loukaitou-Sideris, A. (2004) 'Is It Safe to Walk Here? Design and Policy Responses to Women's Victimization in Public Places', Chicago: Paper presented at Research on Women's Issues in Transportation, Transportation Research Board, 18–20 November.
Loukaitou-Sideris, A., Bornstein, A., Fink, C., Samuels, L. and Gerami, S. (2008) *How to Ease Women's Fear of Transportation Environments: Case Studies and Best Practices*, Los Angeles: Mineta Transportation Institute and University of California Transportation Center.
Loukaitou-Sideris, A. and Fink, C. (2009) 'Addressing Women's Fear of Victimization in Transportatation Settings: a survey of U.S. transit agencies', *Urban Affairs Review*, 44(4): pp. 554–87.
McDowell, L. (1993) 'Space, Place and Gender Relations, Part I: Feminist empiricism and the geography of social relations', *Progress in Human Geography*, 17: pp. 157–79.
Montezuma, R. (2005) 'The Transformation of Bogota, Colombia, 1995–2000: investing in citizenship and urban mobility', *Global Urban Development*, 1(1): pp. 1–10.
Morales, E. (2010) 'Promoting the Right to the City Through a Transport System? The Case of Transmilenio, the BRT of Bogota', thesis submitted as part of the requirements for an MSc in Urban Development Planning, University College London.
Murray, C.J. and Lopez, A. (eds) (1996) *The Global Burden of Disease*, Boston: Harvard University Press on behalf of the World Health Organization and the World Bank.
Newman, P. and Kenworthy, J. (1999) *Sustainability and Cities: Overcoming Automobile Dependence*, Washington: Island Press.
Peters, D. (2001) *Gender and Transport in Less Developed Countries: A Background Paper in Preparation for CSD-9*. Background paper for Expert Workshop on Gender Perspectives for Earth Summit 2002. Berlin: Institute for City and Regional Planning, Technical University.
Phadke, S. (2005) '"You Can Be Lonely in a Crowd": the production of safety in Mumbai', *Indian Journal of Gender Studies*, 12(1): pp. 41–62.
Phadke, S. (2007) 'Dangerous Liaisons: women and men, risk and reputation in Mumbai', *Economic and Political Weekly*, 28 April: pp. 1510–18.
Phadke, S. (2010) *Gendered Usage of Public Spaces: A Case Study of Mumbai*, Delhi: Background Report for 'Addressing Gender-Based Violence in Public Spaces' Project, Centre for Equality and Inclusion, India [CEQUIN].
Power, M. (2010) 'Bogota's Ciclovia Could Teach Boris Johnson how to Run a Car-free Capital', *The Guardian*, 16 June.
Red Mujer y Habitat (2010) *Insumos para una caja de herramientas* [*Resources for a Toolkit: Programme for Cities without Violence Against Women, Safer Cities for All*], Bogota: UN Women.

Rojas, C. (2002) *Forging Civic Culture in Bogota City*, Manila: Asian Development Bank.
Rojas, E., Cuadrado-Roura, J. and Fernandez Guell, J.M. (eds) (2008) *Governing the Metropolis: Principles and Cases*, Boston: Harvard University Press.
Rueda-Garcia, N. (2003) *The Case of Bogota, Colombia, Understanding Slums: Case Studies for UN-HABITAT's Global Report on Human Settlements 2003*, London: University of London Development Planning Unit.
Silbaugh, K. (2007) *Women's Place: Urban Planning, Housing Design and Work–Family Balance*, Boston: Boston University School of Law working paper on public law and legal theory.
Thompson, D. (1994) '"The Woman in the Street": reclaiming the public space from sexual harassment', *Yale Journal of Law and Feminism*, 6: pp. 313–48.
UK Social Exclusion Unit (2002) *Making the Connections: Transport and Social Exclusion*, London: Office of the Deputy Prime Minister.
UN Women (2010) 'Develop a Communications Strategy', Virtual Knowledge Centre to End Violence Against Women and Girls. Retrieved 15 May 2011 from www.endvawnow.org/en/articles/368-develop-a-communications-strategy-.html.
Urry, J. (2004) 'The "System" of Automobility', *Theory, Culture and Society*, 21(4/5): pp. 25–39.
Wekerle, G. and Rutherford, B. (1987) 'The Mobility of Capital and the Immobility of Female Labour: transportation disadvantage in a car-centred environment', *Alternatives*, 14(3): pp. 49–54.
Whitzman, C. (2002) 'The Voice of Women in Canadian Local Government', in C. Andrew, K. Graham and S. Rankin (eds), *Urban Affairs: Back on the Policy Agenda*, Montreal: Queens University Press, pp. 93–118.
Whitzman, C. (2007) 'Stuck at the Front Door: gender, fear of crime and the challenge of creating safer space', *Environment and Planning A*, 39: pp. 2715–32.
Whitzman, C. (2008) *The Handbook of Community Safety, Gender, and Violence Prevention: Practical Planning Tools*, London: Earthscan.
WICI [Women in Cities International] (2010) *Learning From Women to Create Gender-Inclusive Cities: Baseline Findings From the Gender Inclusive Cities Programme*, Montreal: Women in Cities International.
WICI and Jagori (2010) *Conference Background Paper: Third International Conference on Women's Safety – Building Inclusive Cities*. Montreal: Women in Cities International.
Wilson, E. (1991) *The Sphinx in the City: Urban Life, the Control of Disorder, and Women*, London: Virago Press.
Young, I.M. (1995) 'City Life and Difference', in P. Kasinitz (ed.), *Metropolis: Center and Symbol of Our Times*, New York: New York University Press, pp. 250–70.
Zielinski, S. (1995) 'Access over Excess: transcending captivity and transportation disadvantage', in M. Eichler (ed.), *Change of Plans: Towards a Non-sexist Sustainable City*, Toronto: Garamond, pp. 131–56.

Chapter 4

Migrant women's safety
Framing, policies, and practices

Sara Ortiz Escalante and Elizabeth L. Sweet

> The right to the city is fulfilled when the right to difference is fulfilled too and people of different ethnicities, nationalities and gender identities can share and use the same urban spaces.
>
> (Fenster, 2005, p. 225)

> In the borderlands
> you are the battleground
> where enemies are kin to each other;
> you are at home, a stranger,
> the border disputes have been settled
> the volley of shots have shattered the truce
> you are wounded, lost in action
> dead, fighting back
>
> (Anzaldúa, 1987, p. 94)

Migrant women are continually deprived of the right to the city because of their intersecting identities: gender, race, ethnicity, migration status, etc. As already mentioned in previous chapters, women's right to the city includes the right to live free from violence and fear in more equitable, democratic, and inclusive cities (Falu, 2010, p. 16), and, in short, as Whitzman notes early in this book, 'the right to the city . . . is the right to belong everywhere' (p. 49).

This chapter analyzes the challenges and opportunities to achieve migrant women's right to the city, as well as the safety issues they still face. We provide and contextualize a literature review, examining policy approaches and presenting innovative programs that respond to violence migrant women and girls face. The chapter reviews the literature and recent data about migrant women, paying particular attention to the implications of geography and mobility for their safety, as well as to socio-economic and political issues. Next, it analyzes policies and laws as they relate to migrant women's safety, specifically to understand whether these policies incorporate migrant women and girls' needs, rights, diversity, and experiences. Finally, the chapter presents examples of programs that address the needs of migrant women. The chapter argues that planning and policy at multiple levels must respond to the issues of migrant women's safety using a two-pronged approach. While programs that attend to individual needs in a time of crisis are crucial (and require more funding and development), migrant women's safety needs to be understood and responded to as a societal responsibility, taking into consideration the multiplicity of women's circumstances and identities and how they impinge on their vulnerability to gender violence. Failing to do that limits migrant women's right to the city, their right to use urban spaces, their right to participation (Fenster, 2005), and their right to engage risk (Phadke, 2005).

Framing immigrant women's safety

Several characteristics of the current state of the limited scholarship on migrant women and girls' safety include the concentration of existing literature on domestic violence as opposed to other forms of gender-based violence (Narayan, 1995; Menjívar and Salcido, 2002; Raj and Silverman, 2002; Meth, 2003; Sokoloff, 2004; Ritchie and Eby, 2007; Anitha, 2008; Han and Resurreccion, 2008) and the dominant focus on south–north migration, preventing a more comprehensive understanding and, therefore, more effective responses to migrant women and girls' safety. Most research on migrant women and violence against women focuses on south–north migration, even though, in the last fifty years, internal migration for work in cities has greatly escalated (Parson, 2010). South–south migrants – those that migrate among countries in the South, for example, from Nicaragua to Costa Rica, or internally from one region to another within the same country – represent one-third of approximately 200 million migrants, and, in Africa and Asia, this type of migration is greater than south–north movements (Robert, 2008).

There is also mounting evidence that state structures and policies perpetuate violence against migrant women and girls. Undocumented migrant women and migrant women whose legal status depends on their husbands, family members or employers are unlikely to report violence for fear of repercussions, as well as lack of awareness and trust in law enforcement (IOM, 2009). If migrant women survive violence, they are less likely to call police if they know the police might also start deportation proceedings against them (Sweet, forthcoming). Menjívar and Salcido's (2002) important work exemplifies the focus on domestic violence and south–north immigration. They do not, however, consider the intersection of the structural violence present within the context of increased and gendered anti-immigrant policies, in the United States in particular. Parson (2010) also highlights the lack of attention given to how women's experiences are shaped by intersecting forms of intimate and structural violence, and the economic inequalities between nations that lead women from poorer countries and regions to seek employment in richer countries and cities.

Scholars have called for more research and data that would enable planners and policymakers to improve migrant women's safety (Dasgupta, 1998; Menjívar and Salcido, 2002; Raj and Silverman, 2002; Sokoloff, 2004; Sajannai and Nadeau, 2006; Sweet and Ortiz Escalante, 2010). This call reflects the need for research that provides a more nuanced and, at the same time, broader understanding of the intersection of gender violence and identities such as race, sexual orientation, and citizenship status. In other words, we must understand the interaction between these multiple identities from an intersectionality perspective, as explained in Chapter 1, and how they interact to create complicated and more oppressive circumstances.

Most of the growing body of work on gender violence and women's safety has focused on an essentialized woman (that is, a woman who essentially has one identity, that of woman), without analyzing the diversity and intersectionality of women's identities. Some exceptions are Piper (2003), Singh (2010), and Sweet and Ortiz Escalante (2010), who argue that immigrant women of color encounter more challenges when experiencing gender violence because of language and cultural barriers, immigration status, and sometimes limited social networks. It is important to understand that these multiple identities do not just add up to the sum of their parts, but they interact to create complicated and more oppressive circumstances.

In addition to understanding the impact of diversity on migrant women and girl's safety, research in different regions of the world reveals that there are insufficient state resources provided to address gender violence toward migrant women and girls (Walton-Roberts, 2008; Barton and Tactaquin, 2010). This is problematic for two reasons. First, limited resources lead service providers to turn away women in crisis or to limit the services provided. Second, only traditional social-service approaches, which frame the problem as a short-term, individual issue, are implemented. The resulting strategy is a process to fix the survivor. Strategies that address the problem as a social issue, which often need broader and more collaborative responses, are poorly funded (Walton-Roberts, 2008). Where there are programs that address migrant women and girls' safety in a more comprehensive manner, they often assume a single type of migration experience.

Policies that affect migrant women

Multiple kinds of migration and safety-related issues

Migrants can be categorized as voluntary or non-voluntary. Voluntary migrants are subjected to push and pull factors that can make women and men feel that there are no viable options other than migration. Involuntary migration includes refugees and trafficked persons. Women are 75 percent of all refugees and 52 percent of the total global population of migrants, estimated at over 220 million (Barton and Tactaquin, 2010). Women and girls who are domestic workers are an important part of this population: the International Labor Organization (ILO) estimates that there are 52.6 million domestic workers, and 83 percent of them are women (WIEGO, 2009; ILO, 2011a). Worldwide, women and girls trafficked for forced labor or sexual exploitation constitute one of the fastest growing areas of criminal activity (Cacho, 2010). According to the United Nations Office on Drugs and Crime (UNODC), sexual exploitation represents 79 percent of identified human trafficking and predominantly targets women and girls (UNODC, 2009).

Migrant women and girls' employment is typically limited to low-skilled jobs in the informal market, domestic service and sex-related industries. These kinds of economic activity are often done in private places, including homes and other unregulated spaces, i.e. the private domain, which can make women and girls more vulnerable to violence (Piper, 2003; IOM, 2009). Women and girls migrant workers are especially vulnerable to gender-based violence at all stages of their migration process: at home, when being recruited, while in transit, and at work (Waldorf, 2003; IOM, 2009). Women migrants face abuse and violence from employers, law enforcement, smugglers/traffickers, and intimate partners. Because of the growing criminalization of migrants, they are often unable to seek redress for such abuse (Barton and Tactaquin, 2010). This vulnerability is more pronounced for migrant domestic workers who live in close proximity to their employers (Waldorf, 2003). Risk of abuse is especially high for sex workers or women trafficked for sexual exploitation.

Migrant women are often characterized as suffering from double discrimination: gender and immigration status (IOM, 2010). However, women face a particular exclusion, reinforced by their immigration status. Double discrimination assumes a norm or citizen model that places women and migrants outside of this norm:

> The problem of migrant women's exclusion cannot be solved by introducing women in a pre-established analysis frame, 'adding and removing'. What do we add? Do we add gender (women) to immigrant or immigrant to gender? Immigrant women do not suffer from double exclusion (gender and migration status), but a particular type of reinforced exclusion.
>
> (Mestre, 2010, pp. 79–80)

Thus, the double-discrimination perspective should be problematized, because it associates men as the norm, and also ignores multiple intersectionalities between gender, immigration status, ethnicity, and race (Mestre, 2010).

Trafficking often takes place in spaces of conflict and transition,[1] where women become more vulnerable in highly chaotic and dangerous situations and where law enforcement is limited – they may lose income-generating opportunities, social networks, adequate shelter, and healthcare (Martin and Callaway, 2009). In 2008, 63 percent of the 155 countries and territories that provide information on human trafficking to the UODC had passed anti-trafficking laws addressing the major forms of trafficking, and 16 percent had passed laws that only cover certain types of trafficking. Therefore, only one-fifth of the 155 countries have yet to develop laws specific to human trafficking (UNODC, 2009). Despite legislative efforts to increase women's and girls' safety, law enforcement is limited, in part owing to issues of sovereignty that prevent effective international implementation and prosecution of responsible parties not complying with these laws (Martin and Callaway, 2009, p. 59). The lack of enforcement is evident by the existence of trafficking of women and girls in 175 countries (Cacho, 2010, p. 15). It is estimated that, 'every year 1.39 million people in the world are trafficked and submitted to sexual slavery and a great majority are women and girls' (Cacho, 2010 p. 15).

Geography, mobility, and policy

Policies that regulate space and mobility must be contemplated when analyzing migrant women's safety. Space refers to household forms, workplaces, and communal areas where social spatial relationships are developed, normalized, and contested. Western/US–Eurocentric research on gender violence has accentuated the private–public divide of where violence happens, and, when applied in non-Western contexts, it has limited use. In particular, domestic violence and intimate-partner violence are associated with the private sphere or the home. However, in places where 'home' does not exist, the private–public bifurcation is inadequate for understanding violence against women. Meth (2003), for example, documents a case in South Africa with women living in informal settlements. She questions how safety can be measured when 'home' does not exist because a person lives in a shack:

> Clearly women in these situations have less security to utilize as a defense against domestic violence. They cannot slam the door, lock someone out or secure the windows. These women live in public space, which has very few means of protection and has variable, complex boundaries.
> (Meth, 2003, p. 324)

However, it cannot be assumed that living in formal housing increases women's safety, because, although for some women homes can be liberating, for others, they can be frightening and dangerous (Whitzman, 2007). Therefore, the analysis of gender violence should focus on violence in the public and private sphere, in addition to women's social relations and experiences of violence in different spaces and contexts (Meth, 2003).

Mobility includes different aspects of movement and transportation to, from, and within residential, work, and public spaces, as well as the process of migration. Both farm workers and domestic workers, for instance, in high-income countries, face mobility challenges that increase susceptability to violence. In the U.S. state of California, an estimated 1 million farm workers have precarious working conditions: taking sick leave and missed work can lead to loss of employment (Villarejo *et al.*, 2000). Approximately 28 percent of farm laborers are women, and 80 percent experienced sexual harassment (Villarejo *et al.*, 2000). The spatiality of farm work, in remote areas and with often-limited transportation, makes women particularly vulnerable to sexual harassment and violence. In research conducted with 150 Mexican and Mexican-descent farm-working women, Morales Waugh (2010) illustrates how they remain in poverty owing to low pay and seasonal employment. They also frequently rely on family or friends, which may imply that their jobs depend on their abusers, so that it is difficult to leave or end the abuse. Additionally, undocumented women fear deportation (Morales Waugh, 2010). The high rate of sexual harassment experienced by women in the Morales Waugh study suggest that agricultural companies are not enforcing harassment policies, if these policies exist at all.

Migrant women engaged in domestic work are also highly vulnerable to gender violence, in part owing to restricted mobility. Demand for domestic workers is strong in North America, Hong Kong, Japan, Malaysia, Singapore, and South Korea, and in many Arab states. The ILO's Bureau of Statistics Database shows that domestic work is an important source of employment for women. Women migrants from Mexico and other parts of Latin America make up most of the domestic workforce in the United States. In Latin America and the Caribbean, domestic workers are 10–18 percent of employed women and represent 60 percent of internal and cross-border migrants, who move from countries such as Bolivia and Peru to Argentina and Chile. Domestic workers also represent over 40 percent of employed women in Arab countries, especially in Qatar, Saudi Arabia, the UAE, 11 percent in the Philippines, 11 percent in Botswana, and 16 percent in South Africa (WIEGO, 2009; ILO, 2011a).

Worldwide, domestic workers are the single largest group of unprotected workers, largely excluded from labor legislation and often denied fundamental rights, such as freedom of association and social protection (ILO, 2008). 'Regardless of the manner in which domestic work is regulated by national laws, standards on domestic work fall below labour standards set for other categories of workers' (Ramírez Machado, 2003). Arab countries such as the UAE, Saudi Arabia, Lebannon, Bahrain, or Qatar, do not regulate the private sphere, and migrant domestic workers are classified as foreigners rather than workers (ILO, 2008). The exclusion of domestic workers from the application of labor standards and policies is discriminatory, because it is a sector dominated by women and girls, and it is disproportionately unprotected. Additionally, its origin and intention are rooted in sexual stereotypes associated with this form of work (Waldorf, 2003). Understanding this bias, in March 2008, the ILO Governing Body, with some supportive governments among its members, agreed to start the standard setting procedure for a Convention on Domestic Work (WIEGO, 2009). Successfully, in June 2011, the ILO's 100th Conference adopted the Convention on Decent Work for Domestic Workers, which requires governments to protect the human and labor rights of domestic workers and defines minimum standards for decent working conditions (ILO, 2011b). This is a positive step forward, although it will be necessary to monitor its application and implementation.

Responses to gender violence: the intersection of migrants, programs, policies, and laws

There have been three different policy approaches to gender violence among immigrant women. They include mainstream national policies and strategies, criminal justice responses, and community-based responses. *Mainstream national policies and strategies* often use the same tools for native-born women and migrant women, without accounting for the different circumstances migrant women face. At the local level, migrants can sometimes access services used by native-born women, but they might find barriers such as language, cultural misunderstandings, and difference of perceptions (Menjívar and Salcido, 2002). Only rarely are social services designed specifically for migrant women. *Criminal justice responses* to gender violence emphasize reporting abuse to authorities and do not contemplate the implied risks for migrant women who report abuse within the legal system. *Community-based responses* often work from a traditional social-service approach, which relies on crisis intervention and 'treats' survivors of violence as if they had a 'medical' condition. The survivor is treated for her condition through counseling and removal from the space where the violence has occurred. In some cases, community-based responses offer women alternative approaches to violence linked to the specificities of their experiences, closer to their communities, and involve community collaboration, which aims to build trust, raise consciousness, and challenge societal norms that perpetuate violence against women and girls. The effectiveness of this alternative approach is reflected in research conducted with women survivors in Canada, which advocates for using feminist participatory planning in order to include women at risk of violence in the planning process. Using this process enabled women survivors of gender violence to help build local communities of women who are no longer victims of abuse (Rahder, 1999). This is an important step in the process to orient the practice of service providers, planners, and policymakers to recognize and respond to diversity issues and increase migrant women's right to the city.

The mainstream policies and strategies to address gender violence and the criminalization of immigrants in the United States, Canada, and other Western countries have increased the vulnerability of migrant women to violence, in addition to resulting in other negative impacts. The sudden removal of partners, for example, upon whom they rely for immigration status, can create devastating financial and communication problems (Singh, 2010). In many Western societies, police are symbols of protection, but, for survivors of violence who lack legal status, the police offer few assurances of safety, given the likelihood of deportation (Singh, 2010):

> immigrant victims are disproportionately harmed, rather than helped, by 'aggressive' policing and prosecution ... in many immigrant communities keeping quiet rather than publicly acknowledging gender violence is often preferred, largely in response to the pressures associated with managing widely racist and xenophobic perceptions that women abuse is an immigration and minority problem ... immigrant victims often have to make difficult decisions about disclosing violence; while they undoubtedly want the abuse to stop, the potential of jeopardizing the integrity of their communities or inciting stereotypes imposes several barriers to coming forward and seeking assistance.
> (Singh, 2010, pp. 32–3)

In addition, the criminal justice approach to violence against women does not recognize or remedy the cause of violence against women; rather, it merely shifts the focus of violence against women from a social issue to one pertaining to individuals (Singh, 2010). Responding to gender violence as an individual issue rather than a structural and social problem results in women's revictimization, instead of addressing the root cause of violence and recognizing women's agency: 'women generally feel revictimized, rather than helped by the law' (Singh, 2010, p. 55).

Violence against women is present across all countries, but the impact of gender violence can vary by community (Anitha, 2008). Singh (2010, p. 34) suggests, 'Strategies to counter women's abuse must acknowledge how race, class, citizenship and other structural locations intersect with gender, and complicate a women's experience of violence as well as their interactions with the criminal justice system.' Walton-Roberts' (2008) research on Sikh women in British Columbia, Canada, also argues that institutional incompetence in situations of domestic violence actually facilitate ethnic silence with regard to systemic social problems.

Immigration laws are part of the large group of policies that often create circumstances where violence against women becomes part of the employment itself, as in trafficking and sex work, but also enacted by a state-sanctioned, or socially constructed, context that allows, and probably even furthers, the violence against migrant women (Piper, 2003). Gender violence among immigrant women is usually not situated as a human-rights issue but understood as an immigration legal concern, regulated through immigration laws. There have been different responses to gender violence among migrants, both at the government and at the local level in receiving communities. Governments have enacted and amended immigration laws that are making it easier for migrant women to find protection. 'U' visas in the United States, for example, provide undocumented survivors of violence temporary legal status and work permits. Also, in Spain, immigration laws incorporate strategies to protect migrant women who are survivors of violence. Spain is an example of where new gender-equality legislation has increased Spanish women's rights, while decreasing migrant women's rights, because equality is measured through the access of women to the public sphere of production (Mestre, 2010). However, production in private spaces such as domestic work is not recognized or measured. The parameter of gender equality continues to be measured on a scale dominated by men. Migrant women, who have become the largest group on which national women rely to do domestic work and care for dependents, often in the informal economy, are not treated as equals to national women.

Thus, policies that protect immigrant women are not the same as those that protect 'national' women, and therefore a different approach is required to address all women equally. The problem of gender violence faced by women and girls with insecure migration status is 'a human-rights issue, not one of immigration and needs to be tackled as such' (Anitha, 2008, p. 199). Therefore, using the immigrant-rights approach, as opposed to a human-rights approach, is problematic, because women without citizenship are relegated to a lesser status without redress or protection by the state, as they do not 'belong' in their state of residence:

> The export of labor is not approached purely as an issue of migration policies but is increasingly emerging as part of holistic development policies covering the political and social spheres. The issue of trafficking or export sex workers needs to be treated as part and parcel of such development policies.
>
> (Piper, 2003, pp. 741–2)

Menjívar and Salcido (2002, pp. 915–16) note that:

> Laws, definitions and channels of information need to be adjusted to recognize the increasing presence of immigrant women ... [so that] immigrant women will be informed, in their own language, of community services, that will educate them about their rights, empower them, and enable them to improve their immigrant-specific situation so that they can live dignified lives.

Although mainstream policies, the criminal justice approach, and traditional social services addressing individual problems are important, they do not address the global structural issues. These issues, which include high demand for sexual workers and the capitalist system that demands higher profits, often at the expense of workers' salaries, permit and might even perpetuate violence against women.

We regard alternative, community-based approaches as the most appropriate for migrant women and girls in the current global context, and we will discuss some examples in more detail below, in the section on best practices. Ideally, this kind of community-based approach has to be in coordination with government responses that include a gender perspective and a 'women's right to the city' approach, as well as legal and policy mechanisms to address migrant women's safety issues. Few countries or cities have broadly embraced a 'right to the city' approach in their policies, strategies, or legislations that seek to narrow the urban divide. Some examples are Ecuador, which in 2008 recognized in its new constitution the right to the city; Australia's Victoria Charter of Human Rights and Responsibilities (2006), which recognizes that everyone is equally entitled to participate in, and contribute to, society and (the) community; and Dakar, Senegal, where municipal leaders and local authorities in 2003 endorsed a 'Civic and Citizens' Pact' that acknowledges the diversity of cultures and beliefs among all residents, and where community-based organizations have agreed to act in a socially responsible way (UN-HABITAT, 2010). However, we are not aware of any that specifically address migrant women's rights to an inclusive and safe city.

Responses to violence and migrant women and girls

This section presents responses that address the needs of migrant women and ensure their right to the city, spaces, safety, economic security, and mobility. These practices challenge the mainstream approaches to gender violence and exemplify alternative, community-based responses to migrant women's safety. Community-based organizations can be the most promising mechanism to ensure migrant women and girls' safety (Rahder, 1999; Whitzman, 2008; Singh, 2010; Sweet and Ortiz Escalante, 2010) and 'a key medium for addressing emotional geographies of safety and fear' (Panelli *et al.*, 2004, p. 450). However, their work must be supplemented and supported by government policies, funding, programs, and legislation. The Canadian province of Manitoba's Labour and Immigration Department, for example, has created a Division on the Status of Women, with specific programs and resources for migrant women.

Three cases are presented in this section, from different areas of the world, representing different responses to gender violence and migrant women and girls. Although this is not an exhaustive list of the innovative and alternative approaches to gender violence facing migrant women and girls, each responds to some of the concerns laid out previously: migration process, diversity of experiences and identities, geographies of migration, mobility issues and types of violence and their intersection, and legal frameworks.

Casa Segura: a community response in Chicago, United States

In response to the stabbing death of an immigrant woman from Mexico by her husband only two blocks from a police station, immigrant women, mostly from Mexico, formed the group Casa Segura (Safe House). They developed an alternative response to gender violence in their community. They collectively understood violence as the product of economic disempowerment, which facilitated violence against women. Additionally, they understood that the cultural and social norms in Latino communities prevented many women from recognizing their situations as violent, which prevented them from seeking help or developing exit strategies.

The women developed a multilayered approach to serve their *'hermanas del mismo dolor'* (sisters who experience the same pain). First, they decided to organize themselves outside the not-for-profit system. They were not willing to submit themselves to the rules and constraints of 501-c3[2] status within the United States.[3] They wanted autonomy. Most of the women had negative encounters with not-for-profit organizations that use a traditional social-services response of 'fixing' the survivor. The women wanted an alternative model, which included the following strategies: support groups, safe houses, individual assistance, development initiatives (cooperatives), street theater, and an annual march/protest to remember Lilia Ortiz, the woman murdered by her partner.

Casa Segura formed three groups of eight to twenty women, which also included their daughters who would revolve in and out of groups. The groups used Paulo Freire's popular education model for raising consciousness to challenge myths about women's duties and responsibilities to families and husbands. They distributed flyers asking: 'Are you having problems in your relationship?', 'Are you fighting or arguing a lot with your husband?', 'Do you want to learn how to live a happier life?'. They did not use the language of 'domestic violence' but instead used more culturally accepted ways of questioning issues of abuse that might not always involve physical but rather psychological, economic, and/or sexual violence against women.

During group meetings, participants would engage in activities such as learning to knit and cook while sharing experiences. These activities were therapeutic, because the gentle, repetitive movement of knitting was soothing. They also built skills, as products from knitting could be sold to generate income or goods for family consumption. Women from the groups became group leaders, and their leadership and meeting-facilitation skills improved. Also, through street theater, they engaged community members in performances that presented familiar situations in the home and at work, where women and men are often victims of systemic structural violence and racism.

Participants displayed signs in their windows that said '*casa segura*,'[4] which communicated that this home is a safe space to talk, take refuge, or have a meal. Twenty-sixth-street, a major Mexican business and residential area of Chicago, had many of these signs displayed, giving women a safe place to stay where there were no rules that needed to be obeyed and no restrictions. Each person was willing to let someone stay with them for a week and could refer women to other '*casas seguras*' if needed. The network of Casa Segura demonstrated a community response to gender violence that was developed, managed, and implemented by migrant women.

The activism associated with this community group contributes to building a safer and more inclusive community and it does so by analyzing structural elements of violence from a women's-safety perspective. At the same time, Casa Segura promotes women's right to the city: right to participation, right to use the space, right to engage risk in the community, and right to belong, making Latina women's safety issues a community concern and increasing their visibility.

Figure 4.1 Casa Segura's (Safe Home) street theater performance to raise awareness about the intersection of gender-based violence, patriarchy, and class struggle (Chicago, Illinois, 2006)

Author/Performer: Ana Romero

Red Nacional de Trabajadoras del Hogar: a community response to south–south migration in Mexico

In 2006, the Red Nacional de Trabajadoras del Hogar en México (National Network of Home Workers in Mexico) was formed by uniting several civil and other associations that worked with domestic workers. Using a gender perspective, their goal is to support the labor, human, cultural, and collective rights of women domestic workers who have diverse ethnic identities. In Mexico, there are over 2 million domestic workers, of whom 90.8 percent are *campesinas*, or indigenous workers who have migrated from rural areas to cities for work (Red Nacional de Trabajadoras del Hogar, 2010).

Their three main activities include leadership training, communication and dissemination of information, and collaboration with other groups. Training activities include workshops to become *promotoras* to support the organization of domestic workers, and to promote the defense of labor, human, cultural, and collective rights of domestic workers. Their communication activities revolve around educating the general public about the value and rights of domestic workers. They also work with other groups internationally to promote the rights of domestic workers, feminist agendas, and other union movements (Red Nacional de Trabajadoras del Hogar, 2010).

This group is important because it both addresses domestic workers' issues and understands the dynamics of south–south and intra-country migration. They also use a human-rights framework for their activities, as well as approaching the issues that domestic workers face as a social collective problem needing collaborative responses. The risk of gender violence is one of the issues they face. By providing information and leadership skills to women who, for the most part, can be isolated in their places of employment, they provide tools for participating in the development of more inclusive and safer cities.

Women's League of Burma: refugee women organizing against structural violence against women

The Women's League of Burma (WLB) was established in 1999, at the second Forum of Women's Organizations of Burma, to find a common platform to work together and promote the role and participation of women in the struggle for democracy and human rights, at the national and international levels. Currently, there are thirteen member organizations that represent women from all nationalities in Burma. The WLB believes firmly that the participation of women in the national reconciliation and peace-building process is essential.

Burmese women are increasingly vulnerable to violence, including rape and various forms of sexual violence, owing to the increased militarization and anti-insurgency measures in ethnic states implemented by the Burmese regime. This has driven many women to leave their homes and migrate to neighboring countries, where they remain vulnerable to acts of violence, because of their migration status as refugees.

In June 2002, the Shan Women's Action Network (SWAN), a founding member of WLB, jointly produced a report, 'Licence to Rape,' with the Shan Human Rights Foundation (SHRF) documenting 173 rape incidents involving 625 women and girls in Central Shan State from 1996 to 2001. The report attracted considerable international media attention, and friends and networks both locally and internationally have supported the resulting campaign 'Stop Licence to Rape in Burma.'

In August 2003, WLB launched a 'Stop State Violence against Women' campaign, and, in November 2003, WLB organized the first human-rights-documentation training for Beijing Plus 10. Fifteen women from nine organizations based in Thailand attended the training workshop. The workshop and its discussions generated much interest and inspired more women to do human-rights documentation and compile data to produce reports.

WLB's Third Congress decided specifically to address the issue of violence against women as a WLB program, which was named Women Against Violence (WAV). The objectives include: empowering women's organizations, both members and non-members, to work together at the community level to address the issue of violence against women, and to advocate on these issues both locally and internationally.

After several meetings among network partners with extensive experience in violence-against-women issues in the region, WAV formulated and conceptualized its program. The program aims to enable each women's organization to carry out action-oriented activities with a feminist perspective, together with other groups in their areas, and with WLB as a whole. From July to December 2005, WAV organized consultation meetings in eight areas: four in Thailand, two in India, one on the China–Burma border, and one in Bangladesh. Based on the findings of the consultations, in 2006, working groups of six to ten members from different organizations were formed in six different areas to address issues of violence against women at the community level.

Activities of the regional working teams include documenting women's stories or data on violence-against-women cases and providing practical assistance to women who have suffered from violence, including counseling, temporary shelter, medical support, and also linking with other NGOs for legal redress. These teams also organize activities on commemoration days such as International Women's Day, Aung San Suu Kyi's birthday and Stop VAW Day (16 Days of Activism).

One of the challenges faced by the three programs is how to measure outcomes and evaluate their impact. As Margaret Shaw exposes in Chapter 11, the evaluation of women's safety is 'one of four "hard to measure" areas along with poverty, empowerment and conflict' (Shaw, p. 192). Not only is it hard to measure, but, where quantitative data do exist, they are often inaccurate and not comparable because of ineffective data collection, under-reporting of incidents, and the use of different definitions of violence and safety by criminal justice, social-service, and health-care agencies (Hiselman, 1999). The programs presented faced a big challenge – their lack of resources limits their capacity for action. Only WLB is already gathering quantitative and qualitative data. For the most part, limited resources are focused on implementing programs and offering services to survivors, and, after that, few or none of the resources are left for monitoring and evaluation. In addition, most evaluation processes focus on quantitative indicators and outcomes, which, if reliable, frequently miss the nuanced and deep descriptions of effectiveness and outcomes. The challenge is to increase qualitative indicators in these processes. As women's safety is a difficult issue to measure, we need to develop multi-method approaches that use a gender perspective, respond to local conditions, and are designed to capture longitudinal data, enabling a portrayal of the dynamics and opportunities of women's safety.

Even with limited evaluations, the programs highlighted have been able to address some of the concerns initially presented in this chapter. Casa Segura exemplifies how a community can respond with alternative approaches to the mainstream and criminal approaches used in the United States and Europe, using a popular education model and providing services adapted to the experiences of Latino women in Chicago. The example from Mexico

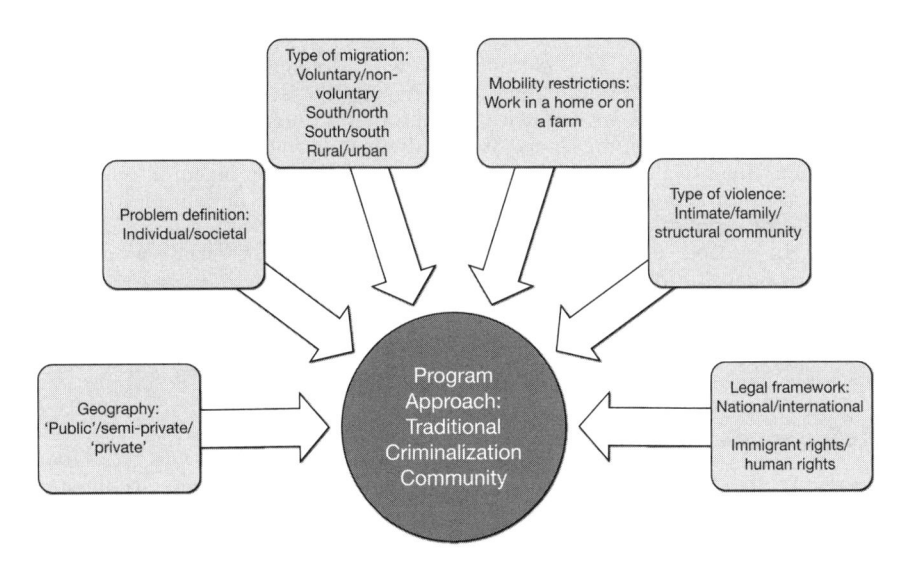

Figure 4.2 Multiple factors that should be considered when developing approaches to safe cities for migrant women and girls

reflects the need to expand the analysis beyond north–south migration and document south–south migration between countries, but also within the same country, from rural to urban areas and from small cities to the capital, to increase the visibility and awareness of certain types of work, such as domestic work. The case of the WLB reflects forced south–south migration and how refugee women challenge structural violence while in exile. Although no one program can respond to all the variables and situations of violence that migrant women and girls face, the chart in Figure 4.2 might serve as a way to conceptualize the complicated nature of violence in the life of migrant women and girls.

Conclusions

This chapter has reviewed the literature on migrant women's safety and gender violence, analyzed policies and approaches to violence against women, and presented three different responses to improve migrant women's safety. In the literature, we found that there is a need to document and research how violence affects migrant women and girls differently, in all its forms and spaces, and consider the intersections of gender with ethnicity, origin, mobility, sexual orientation, class, age, etc. Thus, future research has to go beyond the private and public division and analyze violence as a social and structural problem, and not as an individual issue, as well as understand how mobility challenges women's safety.

Notes

1. Conflict and transition might include: war, economic transition, political transition, social upheaval, natural disasters, or terrorist attacks.
2. 501-c3 is the formal government registration of an organization as a not-for-profit organization in the United States. Although having 501-c3 status permits organizations to apply for funds from foundations and other organizations, there are also restrictions, including the inability to participate in political lobbying and other political activities.
3. For an in-depth understanding of these constraints, see INCITE! Women of Color Against Violence (2007).
4. Several of the women who formed Casa Segura were also part of a group that developed Women for Economic Justice (WEJ). For a detailed description of this group, see Sweet and Ortiz Escalante (2010).

References

Anitha, S. (2008) 'Neither safety nor justice: the UK government response to domestic violence against immigrant women,' *Journal of Social Welfare and Family Law*, vol. 30, no. 3, pp. 189–202.

Anzaldúa, G. (1987) *Borderlands/La Frontera: The New Mestiza*, San Francisco: Aunt Lute Books.

Barton, C. and Tactaquin, C. (2010) 'Advancing rights for migrant women,' available at: www.awid.org/Library/Advancing-Rights-for-Migrant-Women, accessed March 29, 2011.

Cacho, L. (2010) *Esclavas del Poder: Un Viaje al Corozón De La Trata Sexual de Mujeres y Niñas en el Mundo*, Mexico DF: Grijalbo.

Charter of Human Rights and Responsabilities Act (2006), Victoria, Australia, available at: www.google.com/url?sa=t&rct=j&q=&esrc=s&source=web&cd=2&ved=0CC4QFjAB&url=http%3A%2F%2Fwww.opi.vic.gov.au%2Ffile.php%3F251&ei=oR0dT8quDcrL8QPd7KmyCw&usg=AFQjCNFT9DpgFBznUhqnTG-RExdObguAHQ, accessed September 2011.

Dasgupta, S.A. (1998) 'Women's realities: defining violence against women by immigration, race and class,' in R. Kennedy Bergen (ed.), *Issues in Intimate Violence*, Sage: Thousand Oaks, pp. 209–19.

Falu, A. (2010) 'Violence and discrimination in cities,' in A. Falu (ed.), *Women in the City: On Violence and Rights*, pp. 15–37.

Fenster, T. (2005) 'The right to the gendered city: different formations of belonging in everyday life,' *Journal of Gender Studies*, vol. 14, no. 3, pp. 213–31.

Han, C.K. and Resurreccion, B.P. (2008) 'Struggling alone: gender, migration and domestic violence among Thai women in Bangkok,' *Asian Journal of Women's Studies*, vol. 14, iss. 1, pp. 34–73.

Hiselman, J. (1999) 'Intimate partner violence in Illinois,' *Illinois Criminal Justice Information Authority: Trends and Issues Update*, [Online], vol. 1, no. 8.

ILO (2008) 'Promoting the rights of women migrant domestic workers in Arab States: the case of Lebanon,' Issue Brief 1, Beirut, Lebanon: International Labour Organization, Regional Office for Arab States.

ILO (2011a) 'Global and regional estimates on domestic workers,' Domestic Work Policy Brief 4, International Labour Organization.

ILO (2011b) 'PR No. 15A – text of the Convention Concerning Decent Work for Domestic Workers,' International Labour Organization, available at: www.ilo.org/ilc/ILCSessions/100thSession/reports/provisional-records/WCMS_157836/lang–en/index.htm, accessed August 12, 2011.

INCITE! Women of Color Against Violence (2007) *The Revolution Will Not Be Funded: Beyond the Non-Profit Industrial Complex*, Cambridge, MA: South End Press.

IOM (2010) 'Factsheet: taking action against violence and discrimination affecting migrant women and girls,' International Organization for Migration, available at www.iom.int/jahia/webdav/site/myjahiasite/shared/shared/mainsite/published_docs/brochures_and_info_sheets/violence_against_migrant_women_factsheet.pdf, accessed April 26, 2012.

Martin, S. and Callaway, A. (2009) 'Women, conflict and trafficking: towards a stronger normative framework for protection,' in S.F. Martin and J. Tirman (eds), *Women, Migration, and, Conflict: Breaking a Deadly Cycle*, Dordrecht: Springer, pp. 41–61.

Menjívar, C. and Salcido, O. (2002) 'Immigrant woman on domestic violence: common experiences in different countries,' *Gender and Society*, vol. 16, no. 6, pp. 898–920.

Mestre, R. (2010) 'Mujeres, nueva ciudadanía y trabajp: ¿de qué mujeres hablamos?,' in M. Freixenet Mateu (ed.), *Dones migrades treballadores: anàlisi i experiències locals contra la desigualtat*, Barcelona: Institut de Ciències Polítiques i Socials, pp. 75–106.

Meth, P. (2003) 'Rethinking the "domus" in domestic violence: homelessness, space and domestic violence in South Africa,' *Geoforum*, vol. 34, pp. 317–27.

Morales Waugh, I. (2010) 'Examining the sexual harassment experiences of Mexican immigrant farmworking women,' *Violence Against Women*, vol. 16, no. 3, pp. 237–61.

Narayan, U. (1995) '"Male-order" brides: immigrant women, domestic violence and immigration law,' *Hypatia*, vol. 10, no. 1.

Panelli, R., Little, J. and Kraack, A. (2004) 'A community issue? Rural women's feelings of safety and fear in New Zealand,' *Gender, Place and Culture*, vol. 11, no. 3.

Parson, N. (2010) '"I am not [just] a rabbit who has a bunch of children!": agency in the midst of suffering at the intersections of global inequalities, gendered violence and migration,' *Violence Against Women*, vol. 16, no. 8, pp. 881–901.

Phadke, S. (2005) '"You can be lonely in a crowd": the production of safety in Mumbai,' *Indian Journal of Gender Studies*, vol. 12, no. 1, pp. 41–62.

Piper, N. (2003) 'Feminization of labor migration as violence against women,' *Violence Against Women*, vol. 9, no. 6, pp. 723–45.

Rahder, B.L. (1999) 'Victims no longer: participatory planning with a diversity of women at risk of abuse,' *Journal of Planning Education and Research*, vol. 18, pp.221–32.

Raj, A. and Silverman, J. (2002) 'Violence against immigrant women: the role of culture, context, and legal immigrant status on intimate partner violence,' *Violence Against Women*, vol. 8, no. 3, pp. 367–98.

Ramírez-Machado, J.M. (2003) 'Domestic work, conditions of work and employment: a legal perspective,' *Conditions of Work and Employment*, Series No. 7 (Ginebra, OIT), p. 93.

Red Nacional de Trabajadoras del Hogar (2010) '¿Quiénes somos en la red?' available at: http://redtrabajadorasdelhogar.blogspot.com/search/label/Informaci%C3%B3n%20general%20de%20la%20red, accessed on April 7, 2011.

Ritchie, D.J. and Eby, K.E. (2007) 'Transcending boundaries: an international, interdisciplinary community partnership to address domestic violence,' *Interdisciplinary Community Development*, vol. 15, no. 1.

Robert, E. (2008) 'Mujeres, migración, remesas y relaciones de género. Evidencias a partir de tres casos: Colombia, República Dominicana y Guatemala,' UN-INSTRAW, available at: www.google.com/url?sa=t&rct=j&q=&esrc=s&source=web&cd=1&ved=0CCcQFjAA&url=http%3A%2F%2Fwww.un-instraw.org%2Fdownload-document%2F662-mujeres-migracion-remesas-y-relaciones-de-genero-tres-casos-al-y-c.html&ei=2H-UT42qDKby6QH9uZC3BA&usg=AFQjCNEikUzCUB5Pot_VLysuTjf0Nr9Wbg&sig2=KYkZBUMrTdO1nN_XRaHaCQ, accessed April 26, 2012.

Sajannai, N. and Nadeau, D. (2006) 'Creating safer spaces for immigrant women of colour: performing the politics of possibility,' *Canadian Woman Studies*, vol. 25, no. 1/2, pp. 45–52.

Singh, R. (2010) 'In between the system and the margins: community organizations, mandatory charging and immigrant victims of abuse,' *Canadian Journal of Sociology*, vol. 35, no. 1, pp. 31–62.

Sokoloff, N.J. (2004) 'Domestic violence at the crossroads: violence against poor women and women of color,' *Women's Studies Quarterly*, vol. 32, no. 3/4.

Sweet, E.L. (forthcoming) 'New configurations of racism after 9/11: gender and race in the context of the anti-immigrant city,' in J. Betancur and C. Harring (eds), *Reinventing Race, Reinventing Racism: The 40th Anniversary of the Kerner Commission*, The Netherlands: Brill Publishers.

Sweet, E.L. and Ortiz Escalante, S. (2010) 'Planning responds to gender violence: evidence from Spain, Mexico and the United States,' *Journal of Urban Studies*, vol. 47, no. 10, pp. 2129–47.

UN-HABITAT (2010) 'State of the world's cities 2010–2011. Bridging the urban divide: the right to the city,' UN-HABITAT.

UNODC (2009) 'Global report on trafficking in persons,' United Nations Office of Drugs and Crime, available at: www.unodc.org/unodc/en/human-trafficking/global-report-on-trafficking-in-persons.html, accessed August 16, 2011.

Villarejo, D., Lighthall, D., Williams III, D., Souter, A. and Mines, R. (2000) 'Suffering in silence: a report on the health of California's agricultural workers,' Woodland Hills, CA: The California Endowment.

Waldorf, L. (2003) 'Human rights protections applicable to women migrant workers,' New York: UNIFEM-CEDAW Panel on Addressing Women Migrant Workers' Concerns.

Walton-Roberts, M. (2008) 'Weak ties, immigrant women and neoliberal states: moving beyond the public/private binary,' *Geoforum*, vol. 39, pp. 499–510.

Whitzman, C. (2007) 'Stuck at the front door: gender, fear of crime and the challenge of creating safer space,' *Environment and Planning A*, vol. 39, pp. 2715–32.

Whitzman, C. (2008) *The Handbook of Community Safety, Gender and Violence Prevention*, London: Earthscan.

WIEGO (2009) 'Women in informal employment: globalizing and organizing,' available at: http://wiego.org/informal-economy/occupational-groups/domestic-workers, accessed April 26, 2012.

Part II

Interventions

Chapter 5

Gender Inclusive Cities Programme

Implementing change for women's safety

Kalpana Viswanath[1]

Introduction

Women's experience of the city is an area of research that has gained credibility with the growing numbers of people living in cities and increasing awareness about gender discrimination and violence. In recent years, there has been significant research and action around women's access and safety in urban spaces (Wilson, 1991; Massey, 1994; Andrews, 2000; Low, 2005; Whitzman, 2008; Falu, 2009). Although the work on creating safer cities for women had its early beginnings in the late 1980s in Canada, the United Kingdom and Australia, it soon spread around the world, and today there is work being done in over forty countries across six continents (Women in Cities International, 2008). The increase in safer-cities initiatives around the world has led to a broadening of the contours of the agenda. From a focus on safety and crime prevention, it has broadened to inclusion of the recognition that gender intersects with other identities and marginalization to produce exclusion in complex ways.[2]

The spread of work has resulted in greater awareness of the issue and it has provided an opportunity to reflect on some of the more successful strategies, as well as those that have had less impact. This is critical to assess how best to bring about change. The Gender Inclusive Cities Programme (hereafter referred to as GICP) is a significant advance of the existing work that has been done in the area. All knowledge builds upon earlier knowledge, and the GICP brings together learning from over two decades of work on creating safer cities for women. More specifically, it builds upon the knowledge of several ongoing programmes in other countries. In Canada, after the pioneering work that resulted in structures within city governments to address women's safety, Women in Cities International (WICI) carried out several studies, including one across four cities in Canada. The study aim was to explore the adaptation of the Women's Safety Audit (WSA) methodology with marginalized groups of women, including women with disabilities, immigrant women and indigenous women (Women in Cities International, 2010). The project used a participatory approach that focused on building partnerships between community-based organizations, municipal governments and other stakeholders.

The GICP also builds upon the learning and activities of the UN Women Regional Programme on Safer Cities, being implemented in Latin America across several cities with the Red Mujer y Habitat network. In general terms, the Regional Programme seeks to build knowledge and broaden public debate on violence against women and safety in order to contribute to reducing violence and building safer cities for all. It addresses the right of women to lead a life free from violence in private and public spaces (though with a focus on public spaces) and the right to experience and enjoy cities.

In this chapter, I engage with some of the key concerns and debates around creating safer and more inclusive cities, using the findings and lessons from the GICP, which is being implemented in four cities across the world. The GICP experience provides an opportunity to analyse strategies and changes in different contexts and cultural settings.

The Gender Inclusive Cities Programme: an overview

The GICP is a three-year programme (2009–11) that has been implemented by WICI and supported by the UN Trust Fund to End Violence against Women. It is a four-country study that seeks to add to the knowledge base on women's safety and inclusion in cities, their nature, causes and effects and to explore effective strategies to bring about change. Although the entry point remains women's safety, the broader notion of gender inclusion has been used, not only to address violence and fear, but also to engage institutions (both government and civil society) to deal with inclusion as a principle.

The main aim of the programme has been to improve gender inclusion in participating cities by increasing the safety and accessibility of women in public spaces. Along with this, the goal is also to increase knowledge and provide evidence about the dimensions of the problem, its consequences and effective responses, so as to generate debate and interest among key stakeholders. As it is being implemented across several continents, it has also provided an opportunity to understand commonalities and differences across contexts and cultures.

GICP is a challenging and complex initiative that brings together partners from across the globe.[3] There are four participating cities spread across four continents, with implementation in each driven by a local NGO (Figure 5.1).[4] The process of knowledge generation and exchange has been central to its functioning.

The four participating cities are Rosario (Argentina), New Delhi (India), Dar es Salaam (Tanzania) and Petrozavodsk (Russia). Rosario has more than 1 million inhabitants and shares with other Latin American cities situations of urban violence and insecurity that have become one of the citizens' main causes of concern.[5] Delhi, the capital of India, is a fast growing megacity. Among the large cities within India, Delhi records among the highest levels

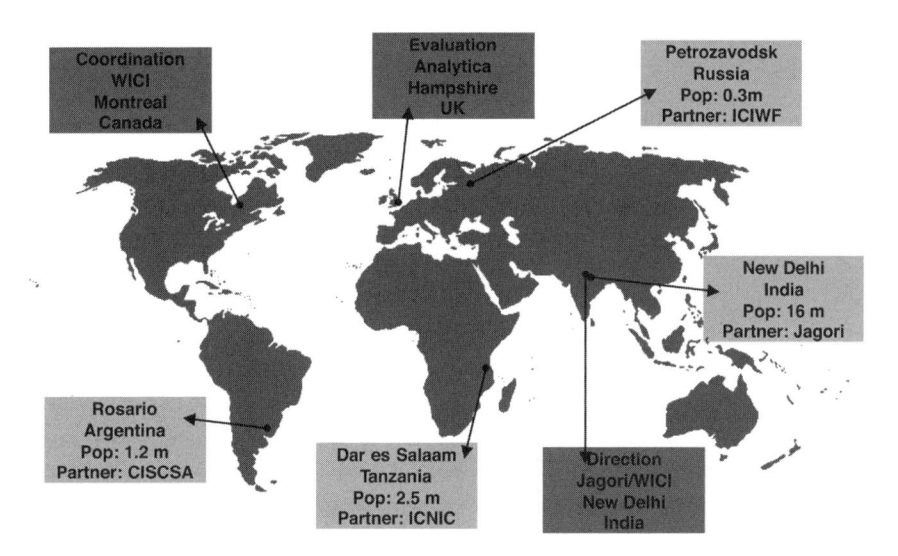

Figure 5.1 Participating cities, populations and partners

of reported crimes against women. Like many other cities in developing countries, the pace and model of urban development are increasingly excluding the poor and marginalized populations. Dar es Salaam, like many fast-growing cities in Sub-Saharan Africa, is facing rapid urbanization amid weak institutional capacities and frameworks to support efficient service delivery, including urban safety and security.[6] Petrozavodsk, the capital of the Karelia Republic in north west Russia, with a population of approximately 300,000 citizens, has been facing problems associated with a lack of safety in the streets, poor infrastructure, alcoholism and drug abuse among the youth.[7]

In each of the cities, a partner organization has led the initiative to collect data, create partnerships and plan interventions. CISCSA (Exchange and Services Centre, Southern Cone, Argentina), an organization working on women and urban planning, is based in Cordoba, approximately 250 miles from Rosario. Rosario is one of the cities in Argentina that have a participatory budget and strong citizen involvement in governance. The GICP has extended the work to the south and north-west districts after the initial phase in the west district with the Regional Programme. CISCSA, set up in 1985, works with a strong women's-rights framework and is a member of the Latin American Women and Habitat Network. Similarly, in New Delhi, Jagori, a women's resource centre, has been working on violence against women and women's rights since 1984. The GICP in Delhi builds upon the existing work on safety in the city, which started in 2005, and upon more general VAW programmes. In Dar es Salaam, the International Centre for Network and Information on Crime – Tanzania (ICNIC-T) is a relatively new NGO that works on urban crime and violence. The aim of this group is to progress work by UN-HABITAT and the government under the Safer Cities Programme established in 1997. Although the work focused on creating safer communities, there was less focus on gender as a key determinant of safety. The GICP study is the first project of the group, although several of the members had previous experience of working on the issue of community safety. The International Centre of the Independent Women's Forum (ICIWF), set up in 1994, is a Moscow-based organization that has been working in Petrozavodsk in partnership with local organizations on women's safety. Safety audits were conducted in selected communities, and partnerships with local government are being explored.

The kind of organization that was selected influenced the course of the programme. In some cities, the entry point was crime prevention, whereas in others it was women's safety. This played an important role in determining the nature of the intervention. This is an important point to consider while choosing partners for a cross-regional study. Although there are numerable factors that will influence the programme, it is key to identify factors that influence particular outcomes. Thus, in the GICP, one of the partner organizations had a strong crime-prevention entry point that clearly was reflected in the implementation. This will be discussed in greater detail below.

It has been an ambitious programme, spanning four continents for the purpose of learning how women can play a key role in creating safer communities and cities. It has not been formulated as a comparative study, but rather one that aims to learn and examine how tools, methodologies and practices can be used across contexts and cultures. The GICP provides an opportunity for innovative programming and cross-cultural learning.

A key facet of the programme has been the development of tools for diagnosing and understanding the complex nature of women's safety and gender inclusion. As existing data are often insufficient, it is critical to be able to establish the problem in its entirety. The GICP partners each spent almost a year establishing the nature of the problem, using a variety of data-collection tools.

The programme is underpinned by the belief that enhancing women's inclusion and their right to the city requires a multistrategic approach. WSAs are a tried and tested methodology to engage women and communities in identifying safety risks. This methodology lends itself to stakeholders being clearly defined and engages them strategically. Through the process, several stakeholders were identified, including the transport authorities (Delhi and Petrozavodsk), local government (all cities), police (Dar es Salaam and Delhi), community groups (Rosario) and others. The programme has also reinforced the belief that, in order to bring about long-term changes and sustained measures of safety, a fundamental rethink is required in the way that cities are conceived, planned and managed, along with changes in attitude and ideological beliefs about women and their rights.

Adaptability of research tools

A defining feature of the GICP has been the range of research tools and methodologies that were used to derive a complete picture of the nature of fear and violence that women face in each city. Data were also collected on the existing infrastructure, mechanisms and stakeholders that play a part in addressing the issue. As the participating cities are very diverse in terms of size, level of socio-economic development and culture, it was important to have a deeper understanding of the nature of concerns and the level of political commitment to address these concerns.

Both primary and secondary data were collected using quantitative and qualitative methodologies. In order to understand the policy environment, an extensive listing of all local and national policies and initiatives around women's rights, women's empowerment and violence against women was done in each city. City plans, budget outlays, legal provisions and service delivery were researched. This provided a template of existing government commitment to making cities safer and more inclusive for women.

Primary data were collected through a street survey and focus-group discussions. The street survey was designed in collaboration with all the partners and was pilot-tested in each site. The GICP is one of the first to use a street survey on such a large scale to understand women's experiences and perceptions of their own safety in the city. The rationale behind a street-based survey, in contrast to a home-based survey, was to design a survey that interviewed women who were in the process of negotiating different public spaces in the city.[8] It was an experiment that turned out to be very successful in three cities, but less so in one. The survey could only be successful if women were willing to answer personal questions about their experience of fear and violence.

In Delhi and Rosario, almost 100 per cent of the respondents expressed willingness to respond to questions on personal experiences of sexual harassment, which provided rich data over a large spread of women in terms of age, class, residence and income. In Dar es Salaam, this figure was 84 per cent, which also provided a significant sample. In contrast to this, in Petrozavodsk, 77 per cent of the women respondents were not willing to answer personal questions. This led to inadequate data in one city and a lack of comparability across cities. The success of the tool in three cities provided invaluable data in a short period of time. However, the reluctance in Petrozavodsk led to an important reflection about the social and cultural contexts. These contexts need to be factored in when doing a cross-cultural study.[9]

To complement the quantitative data, focus-group discussions were carried out in each city to allow for a rich tapestry of women's voices and to focus specifically on some groups that might not have been heard during the street survey. Feminist theorists have reiterated that all women cannot be seen as a single category, and it is thus essential to understand differences in identity among more marginalized or vulnerable groups of women. Thus, in Delhi, focus-group discussions were conducted with homeless women, transgender people, women call-centre workers (who have to move around the city at night) and women with disabilities, among others. In Rosario, a similarly diverse group of women was addressed, including elderly women, young women and transgender people. In Petrozavodsk, young mothers were included, as were women bus drivers, as a group that has to negotiate public spaces at all times of the day. In Dar es Salaam, young men were also included as part of the discussion.

Ensuring consistency across cities posed a challenge to the process of data collection. Although the GICP provided extremely detailed guidelines for carrying out these activities, it is important to recognize that local priorities also play a competing role in determining how the tools are actually implemented. For example, in Dar es Salaam, the focus-group discussions were not carried out with vulnerable groups, but rather with key stakeholders, in order to understand and have a discussion about the role to be played by them. It was essential to maintain a level of flexibility to allow for these local variations.

In addition to these methods, WSAs were carried out in the sites chosen for intervention. WSAs are a tool both for data collection and for women's empowerment. Thus, they play a significant role in any programme on women's safety. The WSAs provided detailed, site-specific information on the provision of infrastructure, services and usage of public spaces. Further, key stakeholders were indentified through the process, and interventions were deliberated. Michaud (2004) states that a fundamental condition for successful initiatives is to address these issues and to create the space for dialogue to occur between municipalities and women.

The GICP, in its choice of cities and methodologies, was able to address a variety of concerns. Early work on creating safer cities was largely focused on developed nations (the United Kingdom, Canada, Australia), and the emphasis tended to be on physical design and urban planning (Whitzman, 2007, p. 17). The GICP recognizes that the growth of cities, especially in the developing world, is a story of marginalization of the poor and vulnerable (Klodawsky, this volume). Thus, the range of issues that came to the forefront included poverty, drugs, lack of faith in the police and deep-seated patriarchal attitudes as playing a role in creating unsafe and exclusive cities.

The anatomy of gendered fear and violence in the city

The findings from the different methods of data collection demonstrate the extent of the problem and commonality across different countries in the world. The lack of safety for women was evident in all cities to varying degrees. It is now increasingly recognized that it is not only violence but also fear that plays an important role in controlling women's behaviour and their ability to access urban spaces (Viswanath and Mehrotra, 2007; Falu, 2009). Approximately 40 per cent of women in Rosario, Delhi and Dar es Salaam were fearful of sexual harassment while using public spaces, whereas, in Petrozavodsk, almost 30 per cent of women reported the same. Across the cities, women reported that they felt vulnerable by virtue of their gender. It was commonly reported that, whereas women are comfortable in some parts of the city during the daytime, they felt less safe at night. Nevertheless, women also reported facing incidents of harassment in the day. The highest number was in Delhi, where almost 80 per cent reported facing harassment in daytime, with approximately 50 per cent in Petrozavodsk, 40 per cent in Dar es Salaam and 35 per cent in Rosario.[10]

The data indicate that all women do not share the same experience in accessing the city. Their experience is shaped by factors such as age, economic status, ethnicity, migrant status and other factors. Thus, young women face specific vulnerabilities, as do new migrants or women with disabilities. Through the focus-group discussions, an attempt was made to hear the voices of the more vulnerable users of public spaces. In two cities, focus-group discussions with transgender people were conducted to understand the specific vulnerabilities that they face. Their extreme marginalization was evident, and they often reported feeling unsafe in both familiar and unfamiliar spaces.

Whereas sexual and violent assaults are seen as criminal offences, the seemingly milder forms of harassment such as verbal comments, touching and staring are often not taken very seriously. In reality though, these forms of harassment are an everyday experience for women negotiating spaces in cities, and these experiences affect their ability to work, study and move around freely. The data from the four cities show that verbal forms of harassment were the most common, followed by visual harassment, including staring (see Table 5.1). Studies carried out in Latin America also found

Table 5.1 Types of harassment faced by survey respondents in the past year (%)

Type of harassment	Dar es Salaam	Delhi	Petrozavodsk	Rosario
Verbal	51	44	38	36
Physical	14	13	12	8
Visual	36	16	18	24
Flashing	28	2	12	3
Stalking	15	15	4	22
Violent physical attack	13	1	1	7
Others	2	0	1	0
None	25	45	48	42
Total respondents	503	998	113	718

82 K. Viswanath

similar patterns, where different forms of violence and violation are an intrinsic part of women's experience of the city (Rainero, 2009).

Several types of public place were reported as insecure for women. The roadside was where most women felt vulnerable to sexual harassment. Other spaces where many women experienced incidents were on public transport or while waiting for public transport. In Delhi and Dar es Salaam, around 20 per cent of women also reported sexual harassment at marketplaces, while the corresponding figure for the other two cities was less than 10 per cent. In each city, poor, or lack of, infrastructure had a significant impact on safety and women's ability to negotiate public spaces with confidence, with poor lighting cited as a major problem (Figure 5.2).

Figure 5.2 also demonstrates that the absence of effective policing was seen as an important factor contributing to women's insecurity, with over 80 per cent in Rosario reporting this, and approximately 50 per cent in the other cities. Women in all the cities also reported fearing spaces where men were using or dealing drugs and alcohol. Men moving in groups also evoked fear and concern in women. This was mentioned specifically in and around sports fields and other such areas where men tend to dominate. This finding points to the importance of unpacking perceptions of 'others' and including men, especially young men, in the discussions around making communities safer.

It is interesting to note that lack of respect for women was also cited as an important factor, with almost 40 per cent identifying this issue in Rosario and Dar es Salaam. This option was included in the survey to assess whether women identified the role played by ideological and cultural attitudes in their

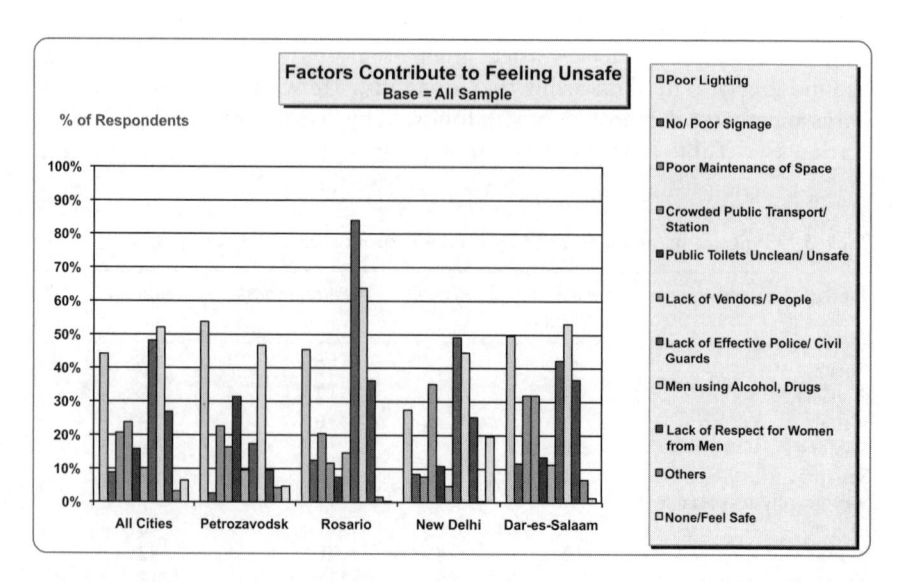

Figure 5.2 Factors causing women to feel unsafe

Table 5.2 Women's responses to sexual harassment (%)

Nature of response	Dar es Salaam	Delhi	Petrozavodsk	Rosario
Nothing	71	41	47	52
Confronted the perpetrator	11	43	8	16
Reported it to the police	7	2	5	12
Reported to municipal guard or agency	1	0	1	1
Asked bystanders for help	7	5	12	7
Reported it on a helpline/ to another service	1	0	0	1
Told/asked for help from family	7	16	8	15
Told/asked for help from a friend	4	22	22	15
Others	1	0	0	0

everyday functioning. This finding, along with the one of vulnerability due to gender, clearly indicates that the problem of women's lack of safety and fear has deep-rooted sources and motivations and will have to be dealt with through solutions that address attitudes of the population in general, in addition to more concrete interventions, such as urban design and improved public transport or policing.

Although fear and actual experiences of violence seem to define women's experiences of urban spaces, the reality is that women and girls continue to use these spaces, as they offer opportunities for work, leisure, education and mobility. It is therefore important to understand how women deal with violence, fear and exclusion.

Across the four cities, almost 50 per cent of women reported that they did not do anything when faced with sexual harassment. Less than 10 per cent reported the incident to the police, and very few asked for help from bystanders (Table 5.2). These findings point to the fact that women still carry the burden of responding to sexual harassment themselves and do not ask for help from either the police and authorities or from bystanders and community members. In a similar vein, Rainero (2009) argues that, although violence against women in cities is widely prevalent, the weak nature of responses leads to rationalization and its being seen as part of everyday life.

In the absence of large-scale public or police support, girls and women have developed multiple strategies to deal with violence and fear (Viswanath, 2010). A large percentage of women restrict their own movements, especially after dark (72 per cent in Dar es Salaam, 42 per cent in Delhi, 82 per cent in Rosario and 53 per cent in Petrozavodsk), by avoiding going out or not going out alone. Many also carry items, such as a pin or chilli spray, to use in self-defence. These findings indicate how women are not able to access certain parts of the city, at certain times of the day. This has an impact on their ability to affirm their 'right to the city', which is an assertion of the right of all individuals living in cities to liberty, freedom and the benefits of city life (Shaw et al., this volume).[11] The right to safety and inclusion must be subsumed under the right to the city, which has been defined as the right to 'change ourselves by changing the city' (Harvey, 2008, p. 23).[12] This notion presupposes the right of individuals to have a role in defining what they want and expect from a city, thereby making it a collective project that people have a right to be part of.

Building partnerships and synergies

It is possible to pick out two key learning points that have emerged from the implementation of interventions – the centrality of partnerships in the process and the importance of creating synergies across programmes to build momentum for an issue. Together, these two form the core of any sustainable work around this issue.

A key element of the programme has been building partnerships with a range of stakeholders. The programme encouraged each city and partner organization to decide its own priorities, based on the local context, findings from the research and the existing priorities and strengths of each organization. This has, of course, meant that comparison between sites has been neither possible nor envisaged as part of the programme. The four cities have very different profiles, and it would have been unrealistic to expect any useful or reliable data for comparison in a short period of three years. The aim was rather to look at each city as a case study for documenting different initiatives and partnerships and to derive good practices from this process.

The GICP and earlier work have clearly established the role of a range of possible stakeholders, including the police, municipal governments, service providers, community groups, youth groups, educational institutions and others. Partnerships are central, not only for a broad-based intervention, but also to build in sustainability at institutional levels (Whitzman, 2008).

The unfolding of project activities in each city led to the privileging of select partnerships. The role of the police as a stakeholder has varied greatly among the cities. In Rosario, CISCSA decided not to engage with the police, as women were hesitant to approach them owing to the expected response and the fact that the community-based women's groups did not feel they were strong enough to work with them at this stage. Instead, they focused on working with the community and with local-government stakeholders. Their earlier work with the UN Women Regional Programme had already provided them with the capacity and tools to work with local government, and this turned out to be a strategic move. Their aim of working with communities was to mobilize women to create opportunities for the public spaces to be utilized by more people through cultural and recreational activities, with the aim of revitalizing the spaces. The endeavour was to create a sense of ownership through street art, public competitions and cultural events, while simultaneously giving people an opportunity to use and occupy public spaces in a way that promotes community spirit. Theorists have argued that urbanization in many Latin American countries has created extreme divisions in society – with gated enclaves on one side and impoverished communities, with precarious access to services and transportation, on the other (Caldeira, 2005; Moser and McIlwaine, 2006). In such a context, restoring the accessibility of urban spaces has an important symbolic role as well.

CISCSA's continuous engagement with officials from the local government and, in some cases, the participatory budget gave them confidence to engage with local government. The creation of partnerships at the data-collection stage promotes greater participation by a range of actors, as they have a deeper sense of ownership of the process (Whitzman, 2008). In Rosario, the engagement with local government and community-based mobilization led to innovative strategies. The programme implementation took place during a year when an election was held, and the women from the communities prepared a broad-based agenda of the kinds of change they envisaged, which they presented to the candidates. The agenda included concrete demands to address women's lack of safety and access to the city. Community-based-awareness actions and advocacy on the women's agenda provided a counterpoint to engage the community and local government on issues of women's safety in a holistic and sustainable manner. This focus on a local, community-women-led intervention based on prevention is the result of partnerships that emanate from below (Andrew and Legacy, this volume).

In Dar es Salaam, the police were among the key stakeholders who were engaged in the process of working to create safer communities. Although lack of faith in the police and lack of resources for improved policing were cited as problems during data collection, better policing and renewed community policing were recommended. It is pertinent to recognize that key partnerships are also determined largely by the kind of group leading the initiative. Whereas, in Rosario, it was led by women groups and community groups, in Dar es Salaam, it was led by an NGO with a strong crime-prevention perspective, which had links with both local government and police and was thus able to obtain police support. Community policing was developed in both of the selected sites, and the volunteers were trained and provided with some basic equipment. The groups therefore obtained legitimacy and a mandate to function within the community. Further, this was not a new initiative, as the idea of neighbourhood-watch groups had already been tried (although not in these neighbourhoods). Residents are willing to contribute, and there has been support from the local police and other municipal structures at the ward level, such as the Safety and Security Committees.

In such a case, it is very easy for the watch group to be seen as a body that is separate from the community. Effort must therefore be made to ensure constant dialogue and interaction with community members, so as to ensure that the initiative remains a partnership where the community has a voice. The moment it is no longer perceived as such, it will become one more mechanism of power and not of empowerment. Creating partnerships and working with communities requires a subtle understanding of power and how it can get reproduced.

In Petrozavodsk, the local group was able to bring a range of actors around the table, including local government and police, to sign a memorandum to work together on women's safety. Unfortunately, the process of translating this into concrete action or commitment at the local level has not followed easily. With changes in government personnel and changed priorities, it is not always possible to engage with partners. This reinforces the point that the work of creating partnerships takes time and is often punctuated by two steps backward for every step forward, owing to political exigencies, changes in priorities and lack of commitment and resources. In every city, this was the case to some extent, but in Petrozavodsk, where the local engagement was very low to begin with, the task was more complex. As mentioned earlier, the first challenge was not only to get women's safety on the agenda, but also to get visibility for the issue. A lot of the effort was spent on dialoguing with the local authorities and police. However, there was not a critical mass of women and communities who were engaged with the issue to keep pressure on local authorities to respond.

It is a continuing challenge to keep partnerships meaningful to all concerned. Who takes leadership in the partnership and the relative importance of the role of government and non-government actors must be determined (Whitzman, 2007). With local-government commitment, the initiative stands a good chance of sustainability, but, without the involvement of community groups and women's groups, it could remain a top-down programme that does not take root in communities. On the other hand, without the involvement of local government, the initiative runs the risk of remaining very small and often unsustainable. A successful safe-city initiative needs to have commitment from a range of stakeholders located at different levels and with different functions, along with a diversity of users of city spaces. Partnership building implies reciprocity between partners, and, in building community safety, the focus shifts from merely addressing violence to finding root causes and prevention (Andrew and Legacy, this volume).

In Delhi, the group was able to build upon earlier engagements to create a strong partnership with the Delhi Transport Corporation (DTC). Whereas work in an earlier phase had focused on public messaging and gender sensitization of drivers and conductors, this phase was designed to take it to the next level of institutionalizing the partnership through influencing the curriculum of driver and conductor training and creating trainers within the organization. As in Rosario, this partnership is also a result of concerted work across programmes. Jagori launched their Safe Delhi campaign in 2005 and, in the first phase, conducted a series of safety audits across the city and had a visible public campaign using different media and communication methods.[13] Alongside the GICP, Jagori was also involved in a safer-cities programme with the South Asian UN Women office, which offered the opportunity to build synergies across the two programmes to have a much wider impact. This led to a formal partnership with the Delhi government, through which a baseline survey was carried out across the city and received wide media attention. Further, a strategic-framework document was prepared in consultation with a wide range of stakeholders that provided a roadmap of the steps to be taken for a comprehensive intervention. The work with the DTC needs to be seen within this larger framework of partnership and public interest in the issue that was generated.

The growing safer-cities-for-women movement has expanded the agenda of safer cities to include a clearer political overtone, beyond the realm of urban planning and management. Women's right to safety in the city incorporates the inclusion of women's concerns and a gendered analysis of all processes in the city (Shaw and Andrew, this volume). In Rosario, the placing of the women's agenda clearly demonstrates this broadened agenda and the concern to influence the political agenda with the understanding that this level of change is required for a deeper political commitment and sustainability beyond programmes or projects. Similarly, in Delhi, the linkages made with a range of city actors, including the department of women, urban planning authorities, the police and transport authorities, have led to a broad-based approach to safety which has led to the formulation of a strategic framework that identifies seven areas of intervention to create a sustained effect.[14] The GICP has contributed to this process of expanding the discourse and linking safer cities for women to wider notions of the right to the city and urban governance.

Notes

1 Many people have contributed to the thoughts developed in this chapter, which is the product of rich discussions over the past few years: first and foremost, the four partner organizations, and specifically Paola Blanes, Anna Mtani, Liza Bozhkova and Anupriya Ghosh; my colleagues Melanie Lambrick, Marisa Canuto and Sohail Husain; and advisors to GICP, specifically Carolyn Whitzman, Caroline Andrew and Margaret Shaw.
2 The recently held Third International Conference on Women and Cities in New Delhi, in November 2010, had the subtitle 'Building Inclusive Cities' and had participation from people across forty-five countries and included women's groups, NGOs, local government, urban planners, police and other stakeholders. The conference released the Delhi Declaration at the concluding session, and this encapsulates all the concerns. For more information, please see www.womenincities.org/pdf-general/delhi_declaration_call_to_action_web.pdf

3 It is funded by the UN Trust Fund to End VAW and managed by Women in Cities International (WICI), an NGO based in Montreal.
4 The International Centre for Network and Information on Crime – Tanzania (ICNIC-T) – Dar es Salaam; Jagori – New Delhi (http://jagori.org); Red Mujer y Habitat, Rosario (www.redmujer.org.ar); The Information Center of the Independent Women's Forum (ICIWF) – Petrozavodsk (www.owl.ru/eng/women/org001).
5 The government of Rosario has implemented socially inclusive and participatory policies as a response to this situation, without using repressive policies. Also, the government has developed gender-equity policies through the Women's Machinery and, in particular, a Programme for Addressing and Preventing Gender-based Violence, implemented in partnership with community women's networks.
6 In recognition of increasing rates of crime, violence and fear of victimization, especially against vulnerable groups such as women, children and youth, the Dar es Salaam City Council, in collaboration with UN-HABITAT, initiated the Safer Cities Programme to enhance safety and security through crime prevention and reduction. The programme responds to the government's call for a systematically and well co-ordinated partnership between the local authorities, central government, institutions and citizens.
7 The ICIWF and other women's organizations of Petrozavodsk City have been working together for more than ten years. An ongoing initiative involving ICIWF in collaboration with the community is the support and development of the 'neighborhood communities' in Petrozavodsk City. The goal of this initiative is to help members of the Petrozavodsk community improve their quality of life and have a beneficial effect on the policy-making process in the city. The neighbourhood groups have been able to organize themselves to make real changes in their local communities, as well as within their local-government decision-making processes.
8 It is pertinent to mention that the team was aware of the possible pitfalls and gaps that would arise from using this methodology, and it was discussed in detail during the planning meeting with members of the advisory committee.
9 This could come up as a stumbling block in other cities also, and it is essential to know how to deal with it. For example, a household survey may elicit better responses, or questions of a more personal nature should be kept out of a street survey in areas where there may be resistance. The reluctance to answer can also be a sign that the issue is still not visible, and an awareness campaign might be necessary. It could also mean that women are not used to speaking about such private concerns, and thus a different format needs to be used for data collection.
10 We must be careful in interpreting this finding. As many women do not use public spaces on their own after dark, the number of incidents may be less than during the day, when a large number of women are in public spaces on a regular basis.
11 *World Charter on the Right to the City* (2004–5) (www.env-health.org).
12 This concept was first proposed by Henri Lefevbre in 1968. It has been further developed by David Harvey (2008), to broaden the concept from an individual right:

> The question of what kind of city we want cannot be divorced from that of what kind of social ties, relationship to nature, lifestyles, technologies and aesthetic values we desire. The right to the city is far more than the individual liberty to access urban resources: it is a right to change ourselves by changing the city. It is, moreover, a common rather than an individual right since this transformation inevitably depends upon the exercise of a collective power to

reshape the processes of urbanization. The freedom to make and remake our cities and ourselves is, I want to argue, one of the most precious yet most neglected of our human rights.

13 See http://safedelhi.jagori.org/ for more information on the campaign.
14 In 2010, Jagori prepared a strategic framework document, along with the Delhi government, UN Women and UN-HABITAT. This document can be found at http://jagori.org/wp-content/uploads/2006/01/Strategic_Framework.pdf

References

Andrews, C. (2000) 'Resisting Boundaries: Using Safety Audits for Women', in K.B. Miranna and A.H. Young (eds), *Gendering the City: Women, Boundaries and Visions of Urban Life*, Rowman and Littlefield, Lanham, pp. 157–68.

Caldeira, T. (2005) 'Fortified Enclaves: The New Urban Segregation', in S.M. Low (ed.), *Theorizing the City*, Rutgers University Press, New Brunswick, pp. 83–107.

Falu, A. (2009) 'Violence and Discrimination in Cities', in A. Falu (ed.), *Women in the City: On Rights and Violence*, Women and Habitat Network of Latin America, Chile, pp. 15–38.

Harvey, D. (2008) 'The Right to the City', *New Left Review*, vol. 53, September–October.

Low, S. (ed.) (2005) *Theorizing the City*, Rutgers University Press, New Brunswick.

Massey, D. (1994) *Space, Place and Gender*, University of Minnesota Press, Minneapolis.

Michaud, A. (2004) *A City Tailored to Women: The Role of Municipal Governments in Achieving Gender Equality*, Federation of Canadian Municipalities, Montreal.

Moser, C. and McIlwaine, C. (2006) 'Latin American Urban Violence as a Development Concern: Towards a Framework for Violence Reduction', *World Development*, vol. 34, no. 1, pp. 89–112.

Rainero, L. (2009) 'A Contribution to the Debate on the City, Public Space and Safety from a Feminist Perspective', in A. Falu (ed.), *Women in the City: On Rights and Violence*, Women and Habitat Network of Latin America, Chile, pp. 165–77.

Viswanath, K. (2010) 'Women Imagining the City', in B. Chaturvedi (ed.), *Finding Delhi: Loss and Renewal in the Megacity*, Penguin, Delhi, pp. 55–67.

Viswanath, K. and Mehrotra, S. (2007) 'Shall We Go Out?: Women's Safety in Public Spaces in Delhi, in Review of Women's Studies', *Economic & Political Weekly*, vol. 42, no. 17, pp. 1542–8.

Whitzman, C. (2007) 'Stuck at the Front Door: Gender, Fear of Crime and the Challenge of Creating Safer Space', *Environment and Planning A*, vol. 39.

Whitzman, C. (2008) *The Handbook of Community Safety, Gender and Violence Prevention: Practical Planning Tools*, Earthscan, London.

Wilson, E. (1991) *The Sphinx in the City: Urban Life, the Control of Disorder and Women*, University of California Press, Berkeley.

Women in Cities International (2008) *Women's Safety Audits: What Works and Where?*, UN Habitat, Nairobi.

Women in Cities International (2010) *Together for Women's Safety: Creating Safer Communities for Marginalised Women and Everyone*, Women in Cities International, Montreal.

Chapter 6

The role of partnerships in creating inclusive cities

Caroline Andrew and Crystal Legacy

Introduction

In 2008, the UN-HABITAT Safer Cities Programme released *The Global Assessment on Women's Safety* report. The then Executive Director of UN-HABITAT, Anna Tibaijuka, articulated in the Foreword of this report:

> We need full and meaningful participation of women and girls to make cities safer for them. Governments at all levels have a vital role and responsibility in engaging women and girls and men and boys as equals in decision-making, policy and strategy development addressing violence against women and girls. Ending violence against women requires collective action and we need to recognise that safer cities for women and girls are better cities for everyone.
>
> (UN-HABITAT, 2008, p. 3)

This chapter is about the *collective action* referred to above: at least, to one of the principal forms of collective action that has emerged in recent years – the formation of partnerships. Even more specifically, this chapter is looking at the establishment of partnerships between community-based feminist or women-centred groups and local governments, as well as other relevant partners. The central focus of the chapter is on telling the stories of such partnerships, of their efforts to build successful collaborations with local governments, of their successes and failures (or limits to success). However, before doing this, it is important to outline the debates that exist around the possibility for such partnerships to advance the interests of women. There are very different positions articulated as to whether links between women's organizations and state agencies are necessarily co-optation in the interests of the state, either to pursue other state objectives or to reduce overall state funding by the delivery of services through non-state organizations. Some authors clearly see all these links as co-optation; however, other authors present positions suggesting that there can be a potential to advance women's interests through closer collaboration with state agencies. We will briefly describe these debates, before going on to present ways of understanding and analysing partnerships in order to evaluate their potential for advancing the interests of women and girls.

Partnerships as co-optation?

Links between the state and community-based groups have been analysed as one of the forms of co-optation that the state has used in the period of neo-liberal restructuring (Lamoureux, 2005). These kinds of links have been a specific example of the more general argument illustrating 'how the gendered subject of the post-war welfare state has been progressively erased through the complementary processes of invisibilization and individualization' (Brodie, 2008, p. 166). Using community-based groups to deliver services has been part of this new governance regime: 'It emphasized partnerships and shared responsibility across the state and community sectors of the welfare diamond, with the public sector financing services and the community sector delivering them' (Jenson, 2008, p. 194). An integral part of this co-optation was that overall funding was reduced and replaced, at least in part, by the voluntary labour of the community sector. Gender was invisibilized, either through recasting social-policy objectives in terms of the child, the family or social investment (McKeen, 2004; Abu-Laban, 2008), or through the application of managerialist approaches that have 'marginalized the intersubjective, consciousness-raising practices which are central to feminism' (Robson and Spence, 2011, p. 288).

In other cases, the argument has been that the state is focusing on gender, but really to achieve other objectives. One such illustration of this is the analysis of the Women-Friendly City projects in South Korea (Ahn, 2011). In Ahn's (2011) analysis, the argument posits that the real objective of the government-funded programme was to try to increase the low birth rate in South Korea by improving public facilities for middle-class mothers. It was at best a mother-friendly or family-friendly city policy, but not a women-friendly policy, as it hid gender inequalities instead of highlighting them.

On the other hand, other authors have maintained that the post-neo-liberal political environment is more varied and more diverse, and perhaps also both more ambiguous and more contradictory. This was the position taken by Sandra Grey and Marian Sawer, in their analysis of women's movements across the world:

> The trajectory of most women's movements has been towards more institutionalised, unobtrusive, cultural and discursive collective action repertoires. The articles show that these changes have been the result of internal movement processes, the transnational diffusion of feminism through civil society networks, and the shifting political, economic,

cultural, and institutional environments that activists have confronted and targeted for change.

(Grey and Sawer, 2008, pp. xv–xvi)

This is also the position presented by Rachel Laforest (2011, p. 129) in her analysis of the emerging relations between voluntary-sector organizations and the state. She talks of the new governance model that emphasizes 'horizontality and partnership', which began to emerge in the 1990s, with voluntary organizations that provided services gaining influence as compared with those engaged in advocacy. Laforest is not making a normative argument, but simply recognizing the growing importance of the language of collaboration and partnership.

These references nicely set up our specific argument in this chapter: that the outcome of partnerships cannot be determined in advance, and that it is necessary to examine examples of real partnerships between community-based women's groups and local governments in order to evaluate whether or not these partnerships have led, or can lead, to improvements in the lives of women. Once having examined this question, we must also ask additional questions about the nature of these partnerships in order to unpack the general category of women and determine which women were advantaged and which were not. We need, therefore, to set up a framework for examining partnerships.

The theory and practice of partnerships

The literature on partnerships is expanding and includes reflections on the reasons supporting their use, their development and the challenges associated with forming and executing a successful partnership, as well as the unique advantages partnership-based decision-making brings. In part, the increasing interest in partnerships as a contemporary procedural approach to problem-solving, particularly when the solution requires co-ordination and co-operation across a range of organizations, reflects a shift from government to governance in modern societies.

The significance of this shift is variously defended on the premise that no one actor is capable of single-handedly solving a problem, and, furthermore, the multiple scales of political action between tiers of government are required to negotiate the complexity involved in many of society's most difficult to solve social issues. A definition of governance that captures some of these changes comes from Gilles Paquet (2011, p. 30), who states that governance is the effective mechanism of co-ordination in situations where power, resources and information are widely distributed. In the context of this definition, partnerships need to be examined so that we can understand the concrete arrangements that affect and may influence the distribution of power, resources and information; how partnerships change over time; and, crucial to the analysis in this chapter, what has been the experience of women and women's organizations in these partnerships.

To begin to unravel what makes partnerships effective in some contexts but not in others, Chris Huxham, in her article 'Theorizing collaborative practice' (2003), evaluates a number of themes on the topic of collaboration that have been written about in the theoretical literature and looks at these themes in terms of the real experience of collaboration that occurs within partnerships. Huxham's analysis is theoretically sensitive while rooted in practice and focuses on partnerships as a way of establishing common aims, addressing power differences and building trust, as well as achieving a membership structure that broadens the partnership's access to resources and creates leadership within the communities affected. For a number of these themes, Huxham's position is that, although the theory of partnerships suggests that these factors need to be there from the beginning, in practice they can and should develop over time. For example, common aims are far more likely to develop through the partnership-building process, which permits concrete activities to generate and develop these common aims. The same process relates to trust as well. It is crucial for trust between partners to exist in order for the partnership to be successful, but it is important to note that some partnerships are required between groups who possess deep-seated distrust issues. Thus, it is often the case that the partnership-building process is slow, to allow time for trust to evolve. Rather than use trust as the starting point to establish a partnership, partnerships should focus on the processes of trust building, which is a more inclusive means of engaging all necessary parties who, at the beginning of the collaboration, may not share a trustful relationship.

Power is also treated in the concrete context of practice, and the lesson to be learned, according to Huxham, is that power is often exercised in numerous ways. The differing access to resources among groups remains one of the elements of power, but it is not the only one. The others can be seen in examining the ways partners negotiate decisions, and these typically change throughout the stages of the partnership. One of the examples that Huxham gives is that, in the initial stages of a partnership, a crucial lever could be the ability to write proposals and find funding to support the activities of the partnership. But, once funding has been successfully obtained, this usually means that staff are hired, and, once this is achieved, the staff can exercise their power through a variety of channels, and not simply through the control of finances.

Huxham's analysis of membership structures is particularly interesting, as it draws out the complexity surrounding membership. This includes people changing positions and remaining in the partnership, although no longer representing the same organization; people remaining in the same organization and in the partnership, but speaking for themselves and not representing their organization; members who belong to a number of organizations, but may not be representing any one of them in the partnership; and changes in the structure and/or mandate of partnership members, which may result in changed roles in the partnership, but without any explicit discussion of the change in the organization. These examples all illustrate situations that can cause tensions in partnerships on a very concrete level. For Huxham, the structural complexities of partnership membership reinforce the importance of continuously nurturing and re-engaging the partners on the aim of the partnership.

Finally, leadership: Huxham argues that leadership must be understood in a very practical way. Leadership is what drives change, and, from this definition, Huxham argues that there need to be two kinds of leadership or two kinds of action by leaders: collaborative leadership and strong action. These two different types are not always in collaboration. Our description of the case studies below will try to use the framework elaborated by Huxham as a way of evaluating the processes followed by the partnerships.

At the same time, there are also some other theoretical insights that can build our capacity to evaluate the effectiveness of the partnership in terms of the improvement of women's lives, but also in terms of the ways in which the processes increased the empowerment and sense of agency of women. For example, Carolyn Whitzman's work in examining community-safety planning also conceives of this in terms of important stages in a process. Whitzman's (2008) analysis identifies six stages in the community-safety planning process, which are: (1) developing partnerships; (2) diagnosing a problem; (3) developing a work plan; (4) implementation; (5) monitoring and evaluation; and (6) modification, maintenance and mainstreaming. Quite a lot of importance is given to stage 1, as partnerships can support a more inclusionary approach to problem-solving which, in turn, differentiates this process from one that is expert-driven. Other authors also emphasize the importance of collaborative, inclusive and indeed partnership-focused processes leading to more inclusive outcomes.

Focusing briefly on the collaborative aspect of partnerships, which Ansell and Gash (2008) have termed 'collaborative governance', this is defined by them as a situation where 'one or more public agencies directly engage non-state stakeholders in a collective decision-making process that is formal, consensus-oriented and deliberative and that aims to make or implement public policy or manage public programs or assets' (Ansell and Gash, 2008, p. 544). Vangen and Huxham (2005, p. 4) posits that collaborative governance delivers a policy, a programme or an idea that could not be realized without having engaged a broader range of stakeholders. By adopting an inclusive process, it is possible for different forms of knowledge to interact with one another (Healey, 1997, p. 219).

The broader social and cultural context, which both defines the problem and surrounds the problem, is relational in nature and is known only by regarding the tacit knowledge possessed by the users of the space (Gertler,

2003, p. 78; Amin and Cohendet, 2004, p. 89). As mentioned above, one notable advantage to a partnership approach is the ability to draw upon different kinds of knowledge that exist within the partnership. Consistent with the work on intersectionality, as seen in a later chapter in this volume, the tacit ways of knowing a problem, when supported through an inclusive method of partnership building, enables people's experiences to be shared in a way that allows the nuances of experience influenced by age, gender, class etc. to be known. These nuances evolve through the sharing of knowledge emanating from people's experiences (tacit knowledge), as well as their technical and expert-based knowledge, which might stem from formal training.

Focusing on tacit knowledge in the first instance, Lindblom and Cohen (1979) describe this knowledge as knowledge obtained through social learning, which is the product of listening to the actual experience of the individual. Indeed, social learning is common to collaborative processes (Healey, 2006, p. 540) where the action of listening to others results in a more nuanced account of challenges that need to be addressed (Lindblom and Cohen, 1979, p. 19). The kind of social learning described here is subsequently shared through networks, face-to-face contact, trust and 'cultural proximity' (Gertler, 2003, p. 86; Amin and Cohendet, 2004, p. 89), which typically evolves through partnerships. The learning that is experienced by individuals engaged in the partnership may result in the transformation of relationships and roles within the social network because of the opportunity for different ideas and knowledge to be exchanged (Forester, 1999, p. 115).

Following the stages of the community-safety planning process outlined by Whitzman (2008), the next phase of diagnosing the problem also requires the inclusion and interaction of different types of expertise and knowledge. When diagnosis is undertaken through a partnership approach, the combination of expert and tacit forms of knowledge delivers a shared understanding of the problems (Lindblom and Cohen, 1979; Nonaka, 1994, p. 20). The challenge becomes the transmission of this tacit knowledge, so that the problem is understood and the solutions are articulated between groups that might not share the same language (Gertler, 2003, p. 84).

By embracing an inclusive process of finding solutions that will enable women to feel safe in public space, the tacit knowledge of those that use the space (or have felt excluded from that space) is considered a legitimate source of knowledge (Caspary, 2000). Focusing on building social intelligence, which is achieved when expert and tacit knowledge interface, helps to open up the range of problem-solving possibilities and understandings about how to move forward (Caspary, 2000). The literature on tacit knowledge (Polanyi, 1958, 1966; Lindblom, 1973; Lindblom and Cohen, 1979) and the 'experience' of the individual (Nonaka, 1994, p. 19; Reed, 1996) has contributed to the argument that people's everyday experience shares a necessary place within the partnership-development process and in the creation of solutions. An inclusive partnership that celebrates the different forms of knowledge the partners possess is essential to (1) generating a nuanced and considered understanding of what the problem is and (2) generating a collective response founded on creative and innovative solutions. The mixture of different types of knowledge is therefore also important in understanding the processes of partnerships.

Along with providing a forum for knowledge exchange, inclusively designed partnerships can also be avenues for enabling vulnerable populations to have a voice. If inclusive, membership of a partnership can offer more opportunities to marginalized groups, partly because of the visibility this gives these groups; partnerships also provide a space to vulnerable groups to own solutions, and this ownership can be a shared ownership with policymakers and other stakeholder groups in the city who are engaged through the partnership. Vulnerable communities can be empowered through partnerships, and partnerships can also bring about the benefit of access to a broader range of resources and knowledge upon which to draw. When determining policies in planning, where the beneficiaries are those who are most vulnerable, the motivation on the part of the political authorities to adopt a partnership approach is also to come up with solutions that are owned by all the partners.

In examining our case study below, we will look first of all in terms of Huxham's five themes and then add to this by seeing how they have incorporated the different forms of knowledge and whether this has led to a greater capacity to give space to the voice of marginalized women.

Together for women's safety: creating safer communities for marginalized women and everyone

Having outlined both the reasons behind the setting up of partnerships and the ways these partnerships are set up, we have opted in this chapter to give a detailed and very concrete description of one partnership aimed at creating safe and inclusive cites for the full diversity of women and girls. We have already described the way in which we will look at this partnership, first through Huxham's five themes and then followed by the diversity of forms of knowledge and the potential of enabling marginalized women to have a voice in establishing inclusive and safe cities. This evaluation of process is the central focus of the chapter, but we will also ask the question of outcomes, to allow us to examine these partnerships in two ways: the degree to which they are egalitarian partnerships, and the results of the partnerships in improving the lives of the full diversity of women and girls.

The case study is a Canadian-based partnership project that ran from 2007 to 2010. Established by WICI, this project brought together four communities in the establishment of a partnership that saw community-based women's groups and their local governments working collaboratively. This partnership was built around the adaptation of safety audits to suit a diverse group of women and, following on this, building partnerships between community-based organizations, municipal governments and other key local stakeholders. Four community organizations participated. These were Women of the Dawn, an Aboriginal counselling organization in Regina, Saskatchewan; Le Centre des ainés, an organization bringing together seniors (and, in this case, women members recruited from the organization's walking club) in Gatineau, Quebec; Catholic Crosscultural Services in Peel, Ontario, who work with immigrant and visible minority women; and Action des femmes handicappées de Montréal, Quebec, an organization that works with women with disabilities.

WICI had done a lot of work, both in Canada and internationally, on the use and adaptation of safety audits. It is a tool that was first developed in Toronto and was adapted through its use in Montreal. Subsequently, safety audits have also been picked up and used across the world. From the work already done, WICI knew the importance of adapting the tool to take account of the particular circumstances in which it was being used. In particular, it was clear that an intersectional approach was necessary in order to successfully take account of the socio-economic and cultural dimensions of the particular use of safety audits. The idea behind the proposal was to build very consciously on this intersectional analysis by choosing to work with a number of groups, across Canada, whose focus was on a particular group of women. Thus, the overall project would focus on the ways in which collaboration between community-based women's groups and their municipal government would vary according to the nature of the intersectional dimension focused on by the various groups. The proposal identified the four groups, two of which (Regina and Peel) had already worked with WICI on an earlier project. Indeed, the entire project was the result of a phone call from the co-ordinator of Women of the Dawn asking WICI to help the group conduct safety audits in Regina, as she had seen reference to the tool and felt it would be a powerful tool for improving the condition of Aboriginal women in Regina. The other two groups came from suggestions made by the project officer at Status of Women Canada, based on her extensive knowledge of women's groups across the country. As we will see throughout the description of this partnership, the guidelines for funding projects used by Status of Women Canada play a very important role in the organization of the project. For example, the project could only fund limited opportunities for the groups to meet together, and yet, as we will show, this was one of the most useful elements of the project. The proposal included three safety audits for each of the groups, and the project started with WICI providing training and support on the safety-audit process. The project used the principles of design from a women's point of view that had been developed by the City of Montreal (Women in Cities International, 2010, p. 7), and the training allowed the participants from each of the groups to discuss how these general principles could relate to their circumstances.

When the four women's groups were brought together, there was considerable sharing and learning about how to form partnerships with local governments. WICI continued to provide support, both for the safety audits themselves and to help the groups with their connections to their local governments. In this case, the power to implement fell on the municipal governments, and, certainly, one of the lessons of creating partnerships between local governments and community-based women's groups is that this is a long-term process and not something that is achieved in a short period of time. The financial resources came from Status of Women Canada, but, on a daily basis, the financial resources were held by WICI and distributed to the four community groups according to the project proposal and within the funding regulations of Status of Women Canada. The human resources were those of the four groups and of WICI, but, for the project to be successful, the deployment of human resources was also necessary on the part of the municipal governments. Their willingness to allocate human resources gave them considerable influence over the project's outcomes. The municipalities' willingness was much related to the current priorities of the individual municipal governments. In Gatineau, as we will describe later on, the municipality already had a budget for renovating the park being audited by the women, and so their recommendations after their audit came at the perfect moment for implementation.

The partnerships of interest to this chapter are the four specific partnerships established between the groups and their municipal governments, as well as the overall partnership between WICI and the four groups, for facilitating the establishment of processes that enhanced the lives of marginalized groups of women. In the examination of the partnership between WICI and the groups, it is clear that, in terms of Paquet's definition of governance with regard to the sharing of power, resources and information, there was sharing, but overall the partnership was not fully egalitarian, as WICI had control over the financial resources on a daily basis. However, information was shared, in that each of the groups knew far more about its particular reality than did WICI, and WICI depended on the groups for conveying this tacit knowledge to WICI and to the other groups. In addition, from interviews carried out with the participants from the four communities, the participants 'felt that the project brought them a sense of empowerment. It validated their experiences and strengthened their capacities – including their leadership skills' (Women in Cities International, 2010, p. 41).

Drawing on Huxham's themes, the question of common aims is particularly interesting. Indeed, the four groups had some quite different reasons for wanting to participate in the project: the Regina organization was interested in connecting to the cross-Canada campaign, which focused on the missing Aboriginal women, whereas the Peel organization was interested in adding a new type of activity to its anti-violence work with immigrant women. In working together, the four groups gained a shared understanding that the project involved the inclusion of multiple forms of diversity, going beyond each of their original perspectives. The partnership-building process supported face-to-face interaction between the four groups, which delivered agreement on what constituted the common aims, while also fostering trust among the partners. It was in Gatineau that the most concrete partnership emerged between the municipal government and the group involved in the safety audits. Here, Huxham's analysis of power is interesting. Gatineau had some money in the budget to do improvements to a local park, and, just at the right moment, the safety-audit recommendations for the park were presented to the municipality by the Centre des ainés. This group is not particularly powerful in the broad context of Gatineau politics, but, by producing practical information at the right moment, it increased its power to influence the municipality. In light of Huxham's interest in membership structures, one insight was that WICI was a member of each process, yet as a non-local participant and, sometimes, as a member that could play a significant role in terms of perceived expertise it often carried more weight than a local-community representative.

The leadership on the project was exercised by WICI, and the double tracks of leadership, as discussed by Huxham, fit accurately the project experience of a combination of inclusive, supportive leadership and more directive leadership when conditions required it. In addition, at the community level, participants described their involvement as having enhanced their leadership skills, through the fact that they had learned to speak in public, organize activists and bring together women to act collectively. Some of the participants also reported that they had been able to transfer their new leadership skills to their work environments. At the same time, the very short time frame of the project (three years) did not really allow for full development of leadership skills. So, without detailing each of the factors described by Huxham for each of the specific partnerships at the four sites, this case study has demonstrated the usefulness of these themes in evaluating the process of partnership building.

In addition, the different kinds of knowledge being brought to bear in the project are also examined here. This project clearly meets the criterion of involving different forms of knowledge, in that the four groups certainly brought tacit knowledge of safety in their communities. Not only did they bring this tacit knowledge, the process validated their sense that their tacit knowledge was important. The municipal knowledge was perhaps less present in all of the communities than had been originally hoped for. The example of Gatineau does show the useful combinations of different sorts of knowledge. After the safety audit of the underground parking lot of City Hall, the photographs taken by the community women, supported by their verbal descriptions of their feelings of insecurity, made a clear impact on the City staff that the verbal description alone might not have achieved.

Overall, the project did allow for the voices of marginalized women to be heard. As we have indicated earlier, the interviews undertaken with project participants clearly demonstrated their sense of empowerment at being heard and having spoken. There were positive results, and there was the building of confidence, but certainly one of the lessons is the very slow process of partnership building with municipalities and the need for time. Similarly, and this was an important benefit, all the participants gained an increased understanding and appreciation of intersectionality. They had the opportunity to compare experiences, to be able to understand other realities and to understand how these realities were similar yet different from their own. This allowed each of the groups to feel listened to and heard, but also to feel that they had listened to and heard other experiences that enriched their own.

Outcomes

It is not easy to generalize about the outcomes of partnerships, as each partnership has specific outcomes that relate to its specific local context. However, looking at the examples described here, one can say that partnerships rarely have an equal distribution of power, resources and information, but that there is *some* distribution, and that, in many cases, the contributions of community-based women's groups are around information and knowledge exchange. The earlier discussion about the importance of tacit knowledge and the voices of lived experiences certainly underlies much of the contribution of the community-based women's groups. The challenge is, then, for this information to be given credibility, and this requires skillful strategies, both to retain the authenticity of the voices, and yet to convey the information in such a way that it can be heard by the other partners. Our example of the WICI-led partnership project with women's community groups in four communities in Canada does indicate that it did lead to improvements in women's lives.

This chapter concludes that the movement to form, and use, partnerships has been beneficial to the women's movement. Partnerships create secure and inclusive cities, as they establish a basis for including groups at the table, or in the partnership, while recognizing differences between the groups and acknowledging different levels of power, resources and information. Being part of a partnership gives greater opportunities for influence and activity. This is not to say that the movement towards partnerships necessarily builds a more socially egalitarian society, but it does at least give tools to equity-seeking groups. For the focus of interest in this book, the creation of safe and inclusive cities for the full diversity of women and girls, these tools are particularly important, as this volume underlines. Longer versions of the stories would illustrate even more clearly the use of concrete tools, and, indeed, this will be achieved in the other chapters of this book.

References

Abu-Laban, Y. (ed.) (2008) *Gendering the Nation-State*. Vancouver: UBC Press.
Ahn, S. (2011) *Gender and Space: A Critical Approach to Women-Friendly City Projects in South Korea*. Conference Presentation, Frankfurt.
Amin, A. and Cohendet, P. (2004) *Architectures of Knowledge: Forms, Capabilities and Communities*. Oxford, UK: Oxford University Press.
Ansell, C. and Gash, A. (2008) 'Collaborative governance in theory and practice', *Journal of Public Administration Research and Theory*, 18(4): 543–71.
Brodie, J. (2008) 'Putting gender back in: women and social policy reform in Canada', in Y. Abu-Laban (ed.), *Gendering the Nation-State*. Vancouver: UBC Press.
Caspary, W.R. (2000) *Dewey on Democracy*. London, UK: Cornell University Press.
Forester, J. (1999) *The Deliberative Practitioner: Encouraging Participatory Planning Processes*. London, UK: The MIT Press.
Gertler, M.S. (2003) 'Tacit knowledge and the economic geography of context or the undefineable tacitness of being (there)', *Journal of Economic Geography*, 3: 75–99.
Grey, S. and Sawer, M. (2008) *Women's Movements: Flourishing or in Abeyance?* London: Routledge.
Healey, P. (1997) *Collaborative Planning: Shaping Places in Fragmented Societies*. London, UK: Macmillan.
Healey, P. (2006) 'Relational complexity and the imaginative power of strategic spatial planning', *European Planning Studies*, 14(4): 525–46.
Huxham, C. (2003) 'Theorizing collaborative practice', *Public Management Review*, 5–3: 401–23.
Jenson, J. (2008) 'Citizenship in the era of "new social risks": what happened to gender inequalities?', in Y. Abu-Laban (ed.), *Gendering the Nation-State*. Vancouver: UBC Press.
Laforest, R. (2011) *Voluntary Sector Organizations and the State: Building New Relations*. Vancouver: UBC Press.
Lamoureux, D. (2005) 'Les tentatives d'instrumentalisation de la société civile par l'État', in F. Saillant and E. Gagnon (eds), *Communautés et socialistes*. Montréal: Liber.
Lindblom, C. (1973) 'The science of "muddling through"', in A. Faludi (ed.), *A Reader in Planning Theory*. Oxford, UK: Pergamon Press, pp. 151–69.
Lindblom, C. and Cohen, D. (1979) *Usable Knowledge: Social Science and Social Problem Solving*. London, UK: Yale University Press.
McKeen, W. (2004) *Money in Their Own Name: The Feminist Voice of Poverty 1970–1995*. Toronto: University of Toronto Press.
Nonaka, I. (1994) 'A dynamic theory of organizational knowledge creation', *Organization Science*, 5(1): 14–37.
Paquet, G. (2011) *Gouvernance collaborative*. Montreal: Liber.

Polanyi, M. (1958) *Personal Knowledge: Towards a Post-Critical Philosophy*. London, UK: Routledge and Kegan Paul Ltd.
Polanyi, M. (1966) *The Tacit Dimension*. New York, US: Doubleday & Company.
Reed, E.S. (1996) *The Necessity of Experience*. London, UK: Yale University Press.
Robson, S. and Spence, J. (2011) 'The erosion of feminist self and identity in community development theory and practice', *Community Development Journal*, 46(3): 288–301.
UN-HABITAT, Safer Cities Program (2008) *The Global Assessment on Women's Safety*. Nairobi: UN-HABITAT.
Vangen, S. and Huxham, C. (2005) 'Aiming for collaborative advantage: challenging the concept of shared vision', Advance Institute of Management Research Working Paper Series, London.
Whitzman, C. (2008) *The Handbook of Community Safety, Gender and Violence Prevention: Practical Planning Tools*. London: Earthscan.
Women in Cities International (2010) *Together for Women's Safety: Creating Safer Communities for Marginalized Women and Everyone*. Montreal: Women in Cities International.

Chapter 7

What it looks like when it's fixed

Collaboration towards a shared vision of city safety

Barbara Holtmann

Introduction

This chapter examines a methodology for facilitating safety strategies for communities, through the lens of how this might make women safer. The methodology is a social-transformation model that follows a process and delivers a systems model (Capra, 1982) and action plans for a safe community in which opportunity abounds. The methodology specifically makes use of the ideas of *safety*, and its opposite, *unsafety*, as a conscious and calculated turn away from the idea of *security*, which carries with it a perceived threat or danger – and a mode of operation and thought that concerns crime, violence and criminal justice. The term unsafety is intended to convey a state in which many communities exist, where they neither feel nor are safe, most of the time. The focus on safety (and turn away from security) suggests the inclusion of a range of sources and sectors in the discussion, which and who may not be included in a conversation about security, but can contribute in meaningful ways to a discussion about safety.

The methodology has previously been used to facilitate local discussions in and around specific geographic sites or communities. It is particularly useful in a closed system, that is to say, where there is a concern or objective that is shared by many stakeholders and focused on one site. This may be a neighbourhood, a public space, a school or an institution, but could also be a village, town or city. At the Third International Conference on Women's Safety (Delhi, November 2010), the methodology was applied not to a local site but to a global question of safety of women in cities, by 200 women from sixty-five cities in forty-five different countries in the developing and developed worlds. For the first time, the methodology, which is designed to confront and interpret complex social problems and create a vision of 'what it looks like when its fixed', was applied to a problem of safety of women in a virtual site, a city that is safe for women. The outcome of the visioning exercise and the application of the methodology by the women at the conference indicated that women across the world share a vision of the safety they strive for, and also of the elements that must come together to constitute a safe community of opportunity for women. The methodology was applied to determine what the city looks like when it is fixed, from the perspective of women.

Women suffer particular forms of unsafety in cities, associated with massive discursive problems linked with patriarchy and with small, pragmatic problems associated with design and space, and much in between. The methodology allowed the participants at the conference to contribute in their capacities as stakeholders from a range of cities, and to identify who can be called on to take part in moving towards the vision of what the city looks like when it is fixed, such that women experience safety.

Evolution of the methodology

The methodology evolved over more than a decade of work motivated by various stakeholders to facilitate local crime-prevention strategies. As understanding emerged that framed crime and violence more as by-products of other social insecurities and cracks in social safety nets, the model was broadened to facilitate local safety strategies that looked very different to the original crime-prevention strategies. The methodology can be, and is now, applied in sets of circumstances where crime and violence are not necessarily the primary target of the strategies, but are often symptoms of a different kind of problem. In this case, the concern is women's safety in the context of poverty reduction and social inclusion.

The first piece of work that contributed to the methodology as it stands today was a study undertaken in the Central Karoo (CSIR, 2006), a rural semi-desert area in the middle of South Africa. The work was undertaken at the request of the South African Police Service (SAPS) and funded by the European Union. The aim of the project was to learn about crime and violence and how to mitigate crime and violence in rural areas. The methodology was a mix of data collection, consultative workshops, an international literature review and expert interviews. The characteristics of the area quickly demonstrated that, ten years after the end of South Africa's infamous apartheid system, little had changed for most poor people in these small towns and surrounding areas. The social engineering of the past had created geographical barriers between the rich and the poor, the so-called coloured[1] people having been forced to live as far away as possible from the 'white' town centre and suburbs. This meant that they lived a significant distance away from services, shops, job opportunities, sports and leisure facilities and good education. Women were always at the bottom of the hierarchical pile: apartheid laws discriminated against them for both their race and their gender, oppressing them in a way that was different from the way men were oppressed, with different impacts. Black women could not own property and they could only access very limited education and legal rights. Often, the only way for a poor coloured (or African) woman to put food on the table for her babies was to leave them behind in the rural township and to walk some distance to the 'white' town to seek work, which usually took the form of cleaning houses or taking care of the babies of well-off women. In these rural towns, white women rarely worked themselves. Instead, they would almost certainly have at least one 'maid', probably two, to clean house and look after the children. Similarly, coloured women could work on farms in a domestic role or as menial labour. Many were paid 'in kind', with food and shelter being seen as sufficient remuneration. On wine farms in the Western Cape, the 'dop' system, whereby workers were paid in part with wine, contributed to a hard-to-break habit of heavy drinking on Fridays, which still perpetuates in many communities today. Wages, where they were paid, were low (Parry et al., 2008). As a result of the men leaving for the cities to seek better-paid work, apartheid policies effectively undermined the stability of poor families, separating them from one another, and very often children were left vulnerable to childhood diseases, unsupported by loving parenting, adequate health care and nutrition (Wilson and Ramphele, 1989).

Although these characteristics are specific to a particular time and circumstance in South Africa, they highlight ways in which oppression and exclusion from rights and services impact the unsafety of women and compound ubiquitous patriarchal and paternalistic attitudes and behaviours in many developing environments (Wilson and Ramphele, 1989).

Any work aiming for an inclusive understanding of local challenges and obstacles to safety had to include targeted strategies for hearing women's voices and for creating space for women's issues to be unpacked and affirmed. It would be easy to develop a strategy that ignored both the issues and opportunities pertinent to women's engagement. As the lead agency, the SAPS, was in itself a deeply patriarchal and discriminatory institution, it was unlikely that such an oversight would be challenged. At that time, police units that dealt with sexual offences, child abuse and domestic violence were known in the SAPS as 'the nappy brigade', and any issue identified as being a priority for women was downgraded accordingly (Holtmann, 2001). There was a move to have only women police deal with crimes against women; this, fortunately, was resisted and was never implemented, as it would have reduced the status of both the crimes and the women police officers in a way that would have been hard to mitigate.

Other hierarchies complicated the consultation and evidence-gathering process. Although, when the methodology was designed, it was envisaged to gather rich information from widely inclusive consultative workshops, these proved difficult to manage. Magistrates, prosecutors, police-station commanders and head teachers led the conversation – and, as a result, only issues they regarded as important were typically captured. Local business people (likely to be white) didn't come to the sessions at all, demonstrating that they didn't see themselves as part of either the problem or the solution.

After many one-on-one discussions with different members of the community and repetitive invitations, each time reframed in response to a growing understanding of the dynamics, workshop attendance picked up and became more inclusive. In an attempt to create egalitarian discussion and debate, the methodology was adapted to invite participants to draw their inputs as images rather than to articulate them with words. In the event, this generated very different and much richer learning than discussion, under these circumstances, could have delivered (CSIR, 2006).

As this methodology has now been used for over a decade, it is possible to identify a number of ways it benefits a gendered perspective on matters of both unsafety and safety. First, women, who were often reluctant to speak out in mixed groups, also proved more comfortable with drawing as a way to express themselves, whereas men, especially senior officials, often struggle to let themselves go at the beginning of such an exercise (although they rarely hold out for long: once they see the images emerging on paper, their need to contribute inevitably overwhelms their fear of not being able to draw well). Women also draw things that they may not be comfortable talking about in mixed company. This allows for issues such as sanitation and the impact of menstruation on girls and women to be presented in an agnostic, unembarrassing way (Abrahams *et al.*, 2006). Distances between home and services and home and potential work are easily visible. Overcrowding, lack of privacy, the impact of alcohol abuse on domestic violence and neglect, the proximity of illegal taverns and of health hazards such as waste-dump sites and the lack of facilities for community activity also emerged. Women take the drawings into the dimension of the night: they draw women walking to and from work under the moon and streetlights; they draw toilets and transport hubs that have proper lighting.

Prior to using the drawing methodology, discussions had often deteriorated into long complaints and blaming sessions. Many came to the workshops because they wanted to vent their frustrations. It was clear that many participants held little hope; often, this reflected their inability to contemplate an optimistic future. In the years of using this methodology, it has been apparent time and again that dreaming of, and planning, a better life is not encouraged among poor people, particularly not poor women and children. It is apparent that, as in practical matters, there is a hierarchy in dreaming, and poor women, at the most vulnerable end of many societies, are excluded from creative processes, and they are often unable to articulate their dreams without encouragement. This severely hampers their ability to contribute ideas to strategies for addressing the social problems they identified, as a vision of that better life is necessary to be able to identify strategies that can take a community towards it. As it was the intention to develop inclusive strategies, it was essential to shift the collective mindset from one of complaint and hopelessness to one of ideation and some optimism.

This approach was not to disrespect or ignore very real challenges and obstacles to safety, but to encourage the articulation of a vision worth achieving. In the early days of this work in the Central Karoo, it was shocking how difficult this was. Asked to draw their environment in an ideal way, participants could not, for instance, see beyond the deeply entrenched oppression of alcohol abuse on their communities; they did not draw out the proliferation of illegal outlets for alcohol,[2] but instead drew images of crèches to look after the children while their mothers were drinking, a row of taxis to take the drunk people home and a clinic to treat the people who hurt themselves while drunk. Women often included childcare and crèches as enablers for extending their education and for seeking work. This reflected their disconnection with even the limited opportunities available to their male counterparts for mobility and access (CSIR, 2006).

An outcome of the work in the Central Karoo was a better understanding of 'the cycle of crime and violence'. This provided a systemic snapshot of the inherent unsafety of local communities. There were generic features that characterized a context more likely to entrench vulnerability and victimization than to provide a safety net that would contain crime and violence and provide opportunities to break the cycle.

These features were broadly articulated as follows:

- The relationship between crime and poverty (Liu *et al.*, 2004), with particular focus on the way in which poverty increases vulnerability to crime: for instance, a woman who leaves her children with inadequate protection while seeking work; and the increased impact of crime experienced by poor people: for instance, a poor woman will not easily recover from the theft of a mobile phone used as a business tool in a micro-enterprise (Holling, 2001). Another example came from a school where the chain flushing mechanisms for the toilets were stolen, and the school replaced them with string that was difficult for the children to reach. Children often fell into the toilets while trying to flush them.[3]
- The instability that comes from high levels of migrant activity in communities, where there is a constant flow of people coming in to seek opportunities that are already scarce, causing conflict and competition, and minimizing natural oversight and protective relationships among neighbours, friends and relatives and through long-term relationships, networks and associations (Young, 2002). Many people also believe that, for their children to lead a better life, they should go to a school in the next community rather than in their own neighbourhood, the assumption being that anything will be better than what is locally available. This results in daily migrant patterns that put children at risk while they travel to and from school (Burton, 2006). It wastes precious resources on travel costs and disconnects parents, especially mothers, from having a relationship with their children's schools.

- Many years of violence and victimization have contributed to a pervading sense of being overwhelmed and inadequate (Weingarten, 2003); this is described as uselessness, where people do not believe they have a function or a purpose, and where those around them make no demands on them, nor challenge them, nor are they ever affirmed for doing something useful (Jewkes *et al.*, 2001). This results in low self-esteem that is sometimes interpreted as a lack of willingness to work or contribute, but is rather an imposed and self-perpetuating state of inertia.
- There is a high, easy availability of weapons. Guns are typically used in the domestic context to intimidate and control women and children, often in conjunction with alcohol abuse. Many women described this intimidation as being a ritual part of their lives, beyond their control and largely unreported to the police or any other authority (Vetten, 2006). Guns are also used to enable property crimes against strangers, and, in many cases, crimes are committed with the sole purpose of acquiring a gun to be able to commit more rewarding crimes.
- Alcohol abuse and other drug abuse are central to vulnerability, abuse and victimization in these communities (Parry *et al.*, 2008). Alcohol is experienced as a gateway drug: in many instances, other drugs are introduced into school communities through sites where there is underage or illegal drinking. Girls are vulnerable to sexual abuse when drunk or high; mothers who abuse substances give birth to children with Foetal Alcohol Syndrome and are often abusive or neglectful of their children; children who drink or take other drugs are more prone to being disruptive of the learning environment, more likely to drop out of school, more likely to join gangs and more likely to parent unplanned children (Tomlinson and Landman, 2007).

These factors, when compounded with fragmented families, leave children vulnerable to abuse, neglect and the normalization of violence as the default way to respond to frustration, anger and conflict (Engle *et al.*, 2007). Mothers are most often ill-equipped for parenting, and they lack support from fathers or extended family. It is hard or impossible for them to meet the basic needs of their children, who are often, as a result, hungry, disruptive and inattentive at school or truant from school, and they lack corrective behaviour or support (Frank, 2005). Children are tempted to commit crimes, not because they make a conscious choice, but because nobody is guiding them to make choices at all (George and Finberg, 2001).

Older women, as primary caregivers in the community, were often in the front line of response to neglected children. They provided feeding schemes, afterschool and even foster-care programmes, funded from their own very limited resources. Discussions on these interventions offered interesting windows into the complexity of local relationships. For instance, a group of women described how, notwithstanding their ongoing efforts, they felt angry. Parents were not taking proper care of their children; the government was not fulfilling its promises of a better life for all; and even the children themselves were often abusive and dishonest. The discussions with the women drew out these tensions and alerted them to the possibility that they were resentful in their interactions with the children, and that this was affecting their care. The women were horrified to realize that they might be acting to the detriment of the children, rather than providing loving, supportive care (CSIR, 2006).

At the end of this study, the learning was captured in a very simplified and simplistic way (see Figure 7.1, 'Breaking the cycle of violence' below) (CSIR, 2006), as a tool for testing and exploring the conclusions drawn (Hobdell, 1996). It took a long time and many consultations and expert engagements of one kind or another to move from what was essentially a systemic analysis of the problem space to begin to brave the solution space. The cycle of violence model (CSIR, 2006) didn't create new knowledge, but it brought many pieces of sector-specific knowledge together in a way that was innovative and useful, because it presented what the author came to term 'unsafety' as a failing, fragile system, drawing its inspiration from systems theory (Brown, 2008). This is different from traditional approaches that draw from terminology such as crime and violence and are dependent on criminological or victimological theories. Although it took a long time,

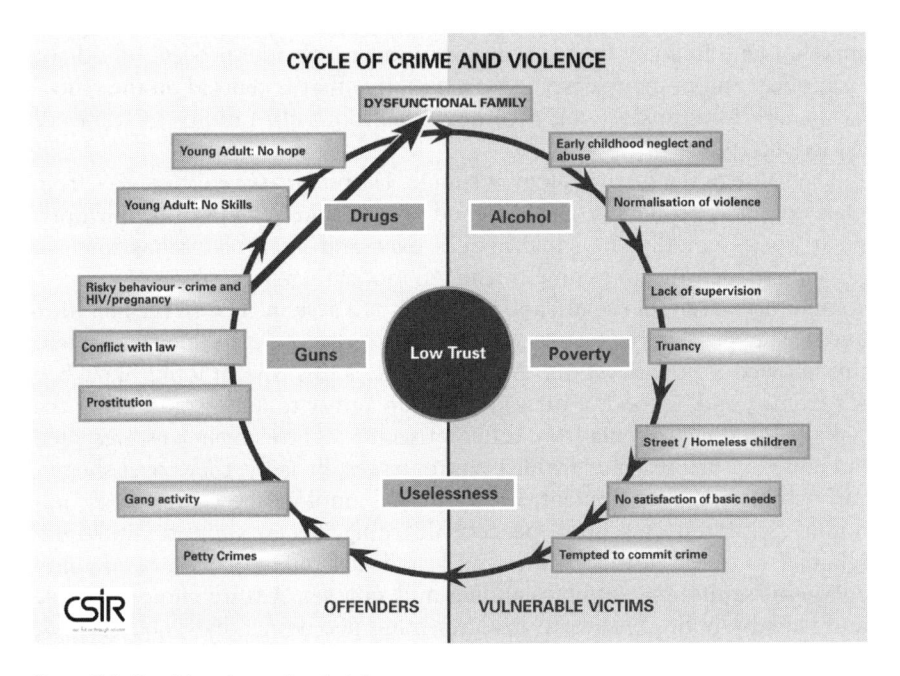

Figure 7.1 Breaking the cycle of violence

the model and methodology that emerged to assist in the creation of planning strategies for safety also drew from business studies, including systems theory and design thinking (Brown, 2008).

The systemic nature of the approach brings both a requirement for inclusivity and opportunities for vulnerable and marginalized groups. Underpinning a systems view of community or society is the principle that no one part can succeed as long as any one part is failing (Allen, 2001). When women are not safe, this limits opportunities for all. Thus, the safety of women, for instance, is not seen solely as a benefit for women, but rather as a benefit for all. The motivation for improving the circumstances and experiences of women is an inclusive vision of a safe community in which all are safe. This opportunity must be carefully managed: when framed in a collective context, women's safety strategies are often articulated simply as protectionist, and yet the real need is for strategies that enable women to move from being a vulnerable group, which often entrenches their victim status. The real investment must be in making cities safe for all, and in this there are benefits also for youth, migrant groups and the elderly, as there is overlap among their needs (Viswanath and Mehrotra, 2007).

What it looks like when it's fixed

Asking the question 'what does it look like when it's fixed?' is the starting point for developing strategies and action plans motivated by a range of stakeholders. In some cases, local government leads the process; in others, the police, and in many cases it is an initiative that is centred on the school as the site for transforming a community from vulnerability to resilience (Hobdell, 1996).

The value in the methodology is simple. Despite massive differences from place to place, problem to problem and time to time, groups of people draw what are essentially the same images over and again. This has made it possible to identify common elements, to model them as a vision of a 'fixed' community or school or park and test them, as a system, against the literature and with experts in the sectors whose work is about specific elements. First, this allowed for the question: 'Are they right, is this what it looks like when it's fixed?', and, second, it offered the opportunity to understand better the linkages among elements from different sectors. The elements, as presented in Figure 7.2 below, span a wide range of issues. Broadly, they cover shelter, early-childhood development, happy play, school as the centre of a community, children at school, peaceful learning, social support, nutrition, reliable transport, infrastructure, well-managed public places, community cohesion, sanitation, family planning and safe sex, leisure choices, visible and friendly police, access to justice, young people making good choices, well-managed and limited access to alcohol, and opportunities for skills building and livelihoods. Both the literature and experts confirmed that these were elements that underpin a safe community (Holtmann, 2011). Using a systems approach, it was also clear that the elements themselves were less important than their relationship with, and impact on, one another. Hungry children could not contribute to peaceful learning; children who were doing nothing were more likely to do something wrong; truancy from school, combined with inadequate leisure opportunities, was more likely to result in alcohol abuse, which was likely to lead to teenage pregnancy (Burton, 2006). The cycle of neglect, abuse and violence was perpetuated in environments where many of these things were absent, rather than just one (The Parent Centre, 2009). A community where children are fed and school is the centre of community is more likely to provide peaceful learning, and thus more opportunities for pro-social activity. Better social support will contribute to young people making better choices, and the cycle will be broken. Any one or two of these interventions may not be enough, which may require the system itself to be shifted.

Unsafety in communities has a very negative impact on the ability of schools to deliver their mandates (Burton, 2006). Children bring their domestic problems to school, educators reflect the best and worst of local conditions, and the school is often a contested space. In Korogocho, a slum in Nairobi, Kenya, Ngunyumu School struggles to provide an education in an environment where the air is heavy with the toxicity of the nearby city garbage dump,

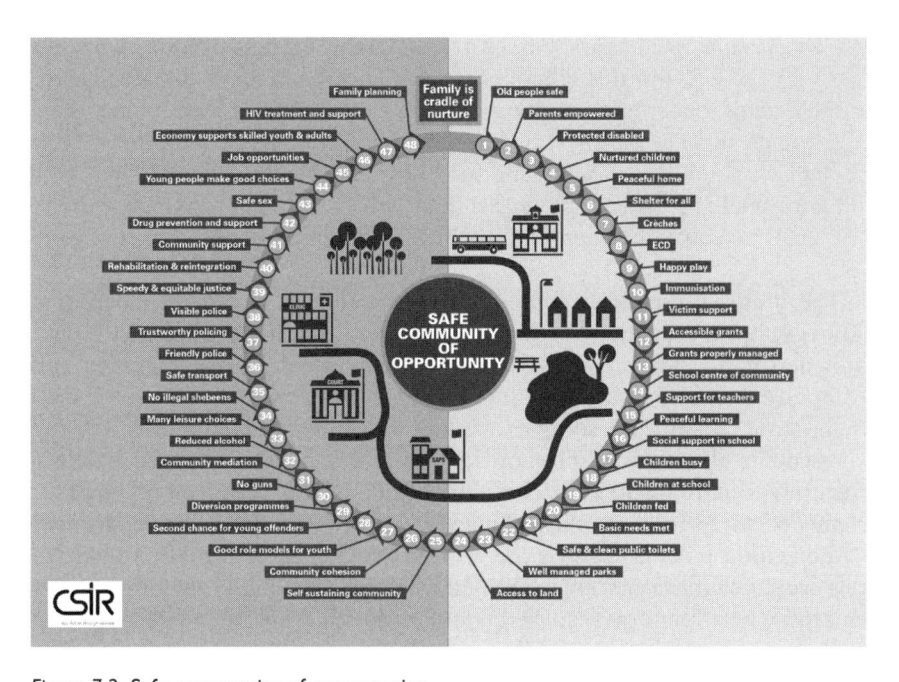

Figure 7.2 Safe community of opportunity

while Marabou storks circle above. In 2008, post-election violence wracked Korogocho, the school was vandalized, hard-won facilities such as water tanks and toilets with basins were broken, and the taps were stolen. Liquor outlets surround the school and against the fence men laze drunkenly in the heat between bouts of drinking. Attempts at food gardening have been thwarted, as goats roam among the children in the dusty playground.

A working group of approximately forty community members was established by UN-HABITAT Safer Cities Nairobi, for the purpose of upgrading the school. This group was widely diverse, including the Nairobi Council Education Department and various community and school governing structures. In the course of a five-day workshop, the methodology elicited a vision for the school, which articulated 'the best life for each child'. Sanitation and nutrition emerged as central themes, with sanitation for girls paramount. Without running water, the toilets are dank and foul. Girls use pieces of litter from near the school fence when they go to the toilet, and, when they begin to menstruate, many skip school for several days each month. These are not easy conversations to have in a mixed group in Kenya. Religion is ever present, and neither Muslim nor Christian clerics are comfortable in such discussions. Despite difficulties and a major focus on infrastructure, the women in the workshops prevailed and ensured that sanitation was one of three issues to be addressed as a priority for the school.

In South Africa, a teacher[4] at one school said,

> I've been here 21 years. Fifteen years ago the mothers of today's fifteen-year-old girls left this school pregnant. This year a lot of them will leave pregnant too – there's nothing for them to do outside of school, nowhere safe for them to go; anyway they don't have dreams and ambitions. They get drunk on Friday night and sometime they'll get pregnant. They were a problem to their mothers and their babies will be a problem to them. I can't change anything by myself. The whole thing needs to change.

The model presents the school or community as a system; it is not a strategy, but a snapshot of what it looks like when it's fixed. It is a vision and destination. Because it has many elements, everyone involved can recognize their vision in it and find a role for themselves in moving towards it, because, despite its complexity, it is finite, it is manageable. Having verified the elements of the model, every participant is required to place themselves at the centre of the model and link to specific outcomes or elements. An example of this is Figure 7.3 below, in which the Department of Education has highlighted the elements for which it has a mandate. In this way, collaborators are identified as those who share outcomes. Gaps emerge where there are no stakeholders to take on the achievement of outcomes. Identifying and finding stakeholders to fill these gaps becomes a part of action planning to take the process forward.

Figure 2.1 Warwick Junction: internationally recognized gender-sensitive land-use planning
© Gerald Botha: 'Working in Warwick: including street traders in urban plans'

Figure 4.1 Casa Segura's (Safe Home) street theater performance to raise awareness about the intersection of gender-based violence, patriarchy, and class struggle (Chicago, Illinois, 2006)
Author/Performer: Ana Romero

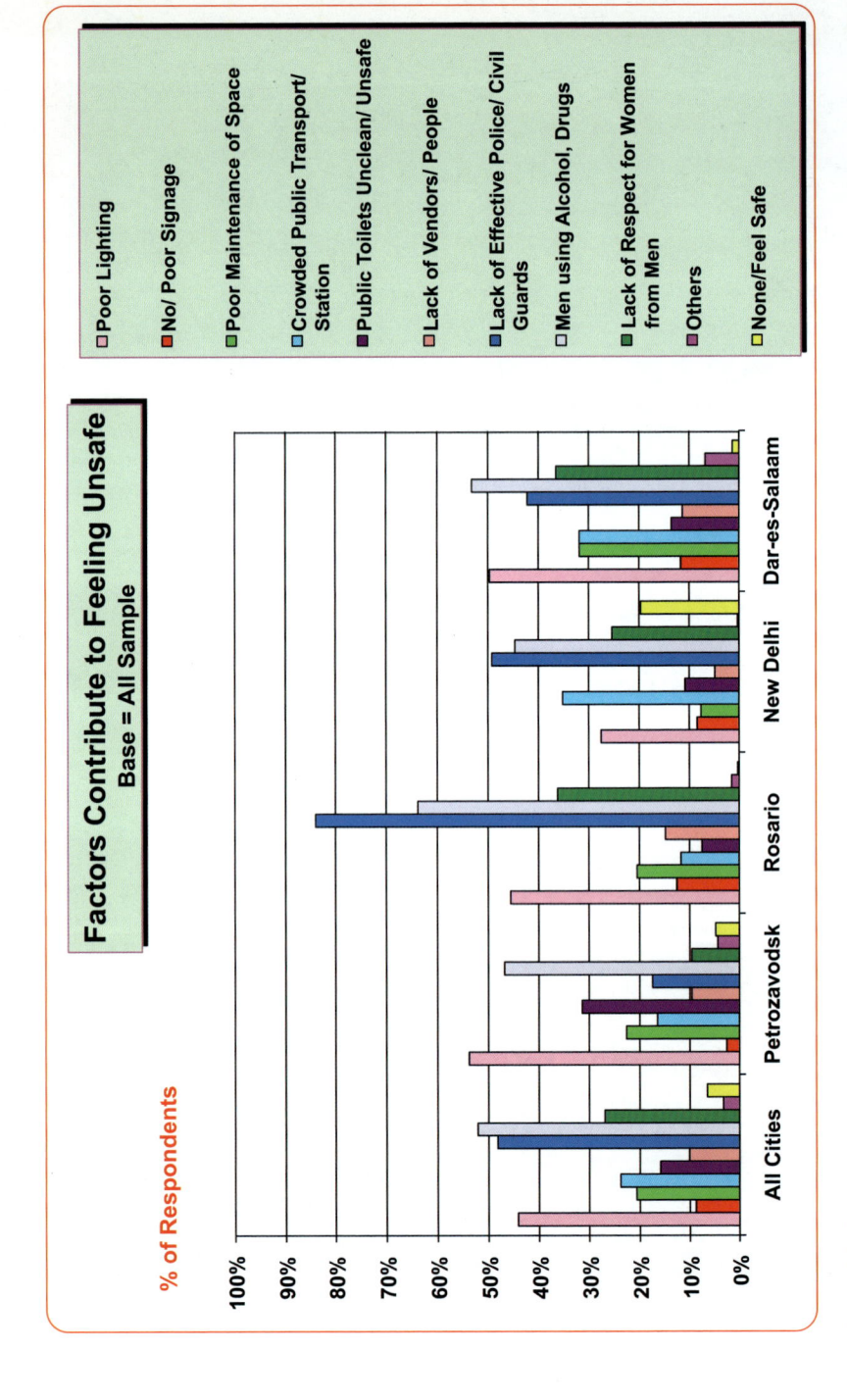

Figure 5.2 Factors causing women to feel unsafe

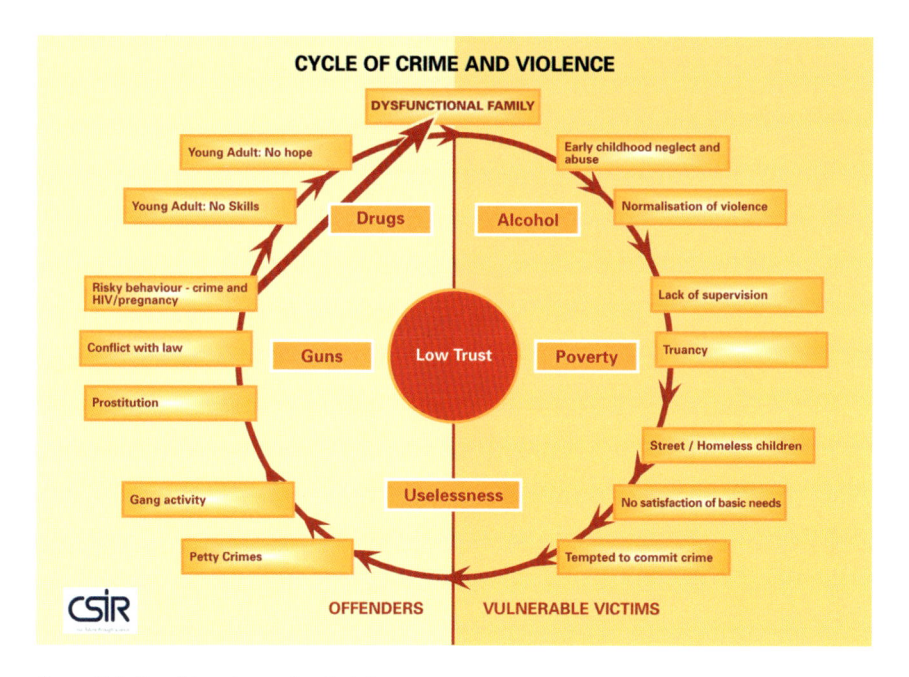

Figure 7.1 Breaking the cycle of violence

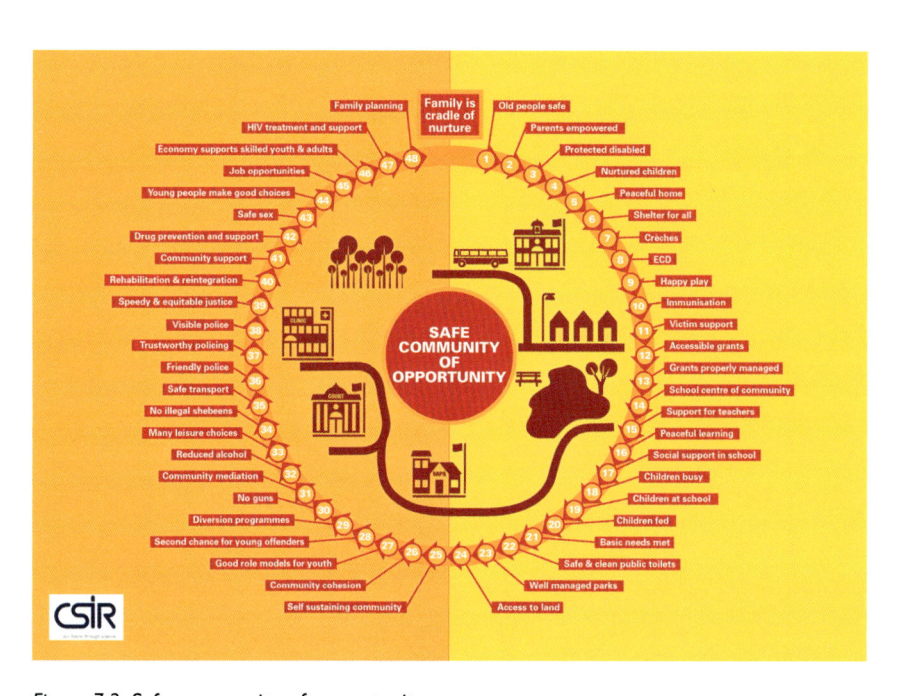

Figure 7.2 Safe community of opportunity

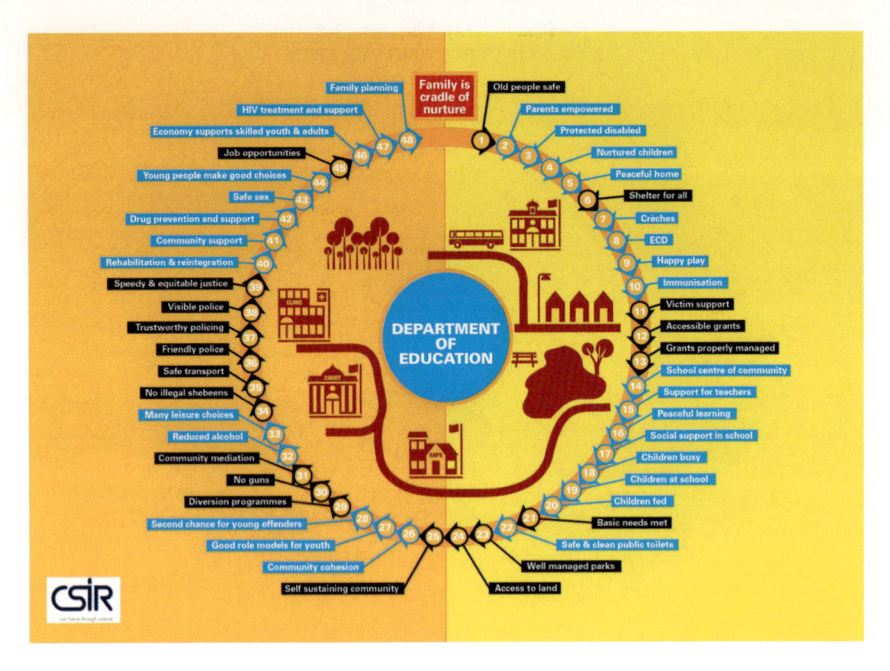

Figure 7.3 Department of Education

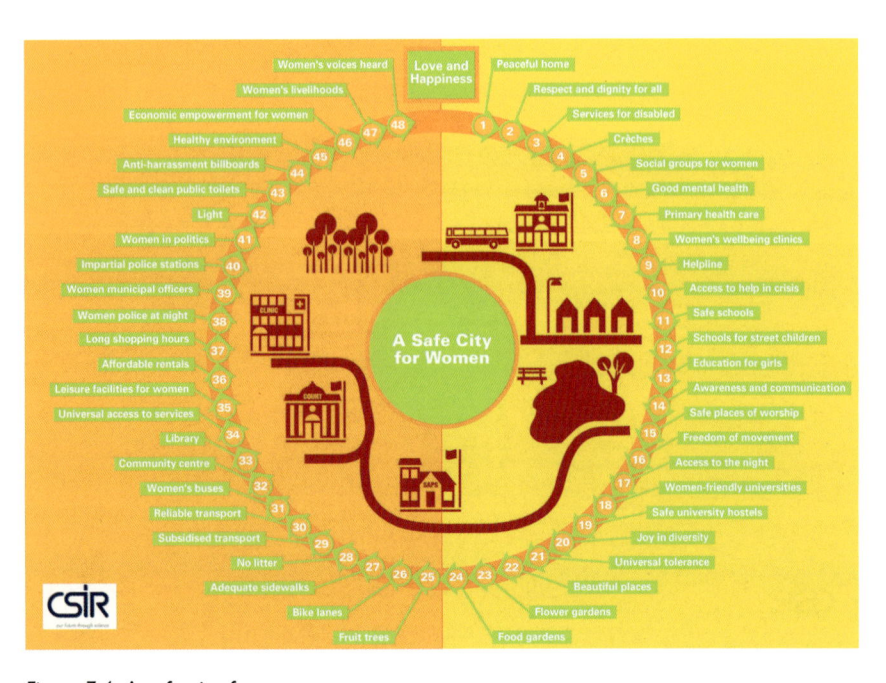

Figure 7.4 A safe city for women

Figure 8.3 Woman in a community toilet complex
Source: Jagori

Figure 8.4 Muddy streets in all seasons
Source: Jagori

Figure 8.5 Girls fetching water from a water tanker in Bhalswa
Source: Women's Feature Service

Figure 8.6 Man cleaning the drain outside his home, Bhalswa
Source: Jagori

Figure 8.7 Woman cooking outside her home on her 'veranda' over the drain, Bawana
Source: Jagori

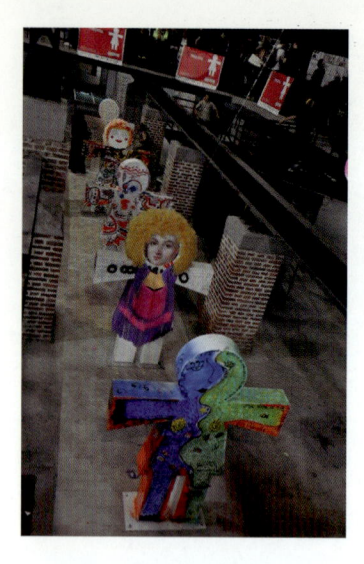

Figure 10.2 Several recovered women figures in Rosario, Argentina

Source: 'Mujeres por la cuidad' Campaign, Latin American Women and Habitat Network

Figure 10.3 Y R U LOOKING AT ME, *Blank Noise* action heroes

Source: © Jasmeen Patheja

Figure 10.4 'Mohini. Age 19. A stranger rubbed himself against me', *Blank Noise* action heroes

Source: © Jasmeen Patheja

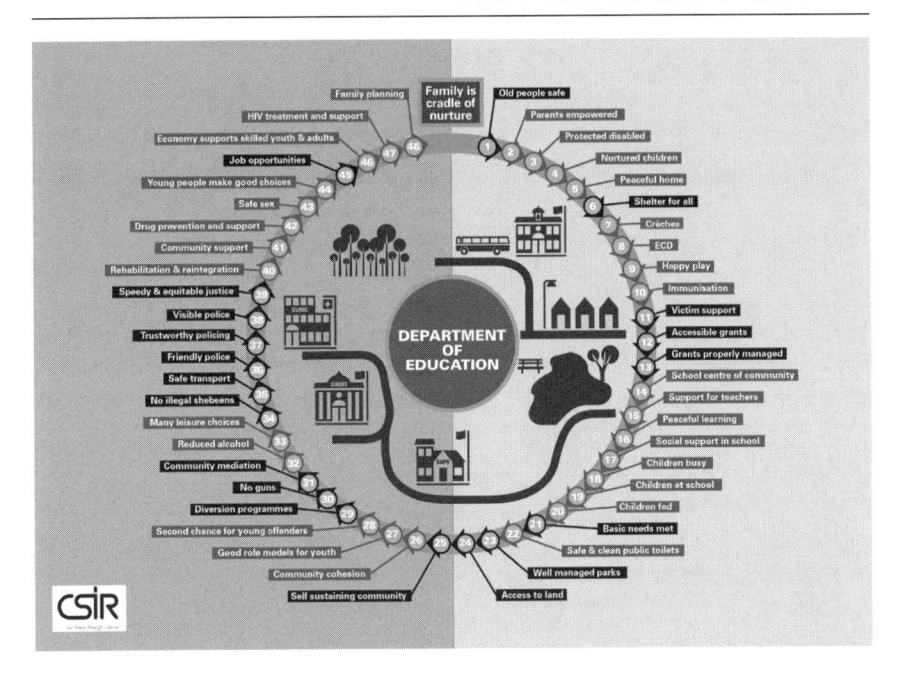

Figure 7.3 Department of Education

The Delhi conference

Using an opportunity presented by a gathering of 200 women, from sixty-five cities in forty-five countries, at the Third International Conference on the Safety of Women in Cities in November 2010, a facilitated visioning process offered some new elements to the model (see Figure 7.4 below). Although many of the elements that emerged from the visioning exercise in Delhi reflected elements common to the safe community of opportunity model in previous exercises, this exercise contributed new elements reflecting the views and dreams of women. These elements have since been incorporated into the methodology and have delivered insights that are useful to all, not just to women. The methodology has thus been strengthened, using the lens of women, to provide a more nuanced approach in other settings.

New elements that emerged in Delhi were focused on both the private and the public spheres. There was a focus on women's health and well-being with the inclusion of women's well-being clinics, social groups for women and a helpline. Access to education was emphasized, with specific reference to education for girls, women-friendly universities and safe university hostels. The women focused on the delivery of public services, in particular: women municipal offices, women police at night, women's buses and women in politics. This focus is sometimes contentious, as it may perpetuate rather than

114 B. Holtmann

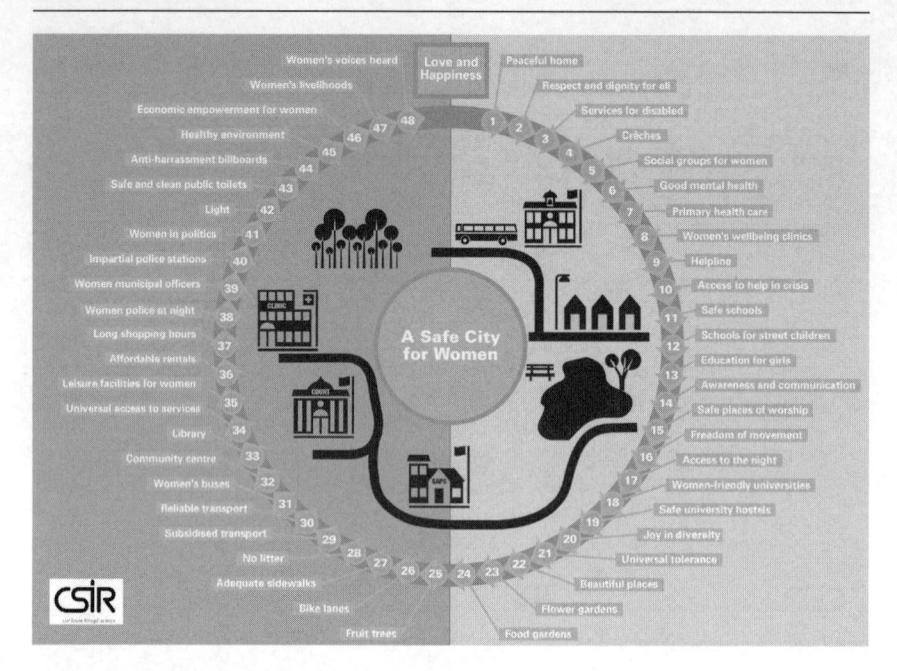

Figure 7.4 A safe city for women

ameliorate the risk of the isolation of women and the risk of being exposed to men. It is perhaps significant that, when women dream of safety, they are hesitant to imagine themselves fully integrated into the existing world and would rather wish for protection against a perceived threat. The women also brought a perspective of beauty, love and joy: love and happiness, joy in diversity, beautiful places and flower gardens. The participants reinforced dreams of economic empowerment, livelihoods, light and mobility and added the element of women's voices being heard, providing a poignant reminder that women are often excluded from strategic processes and discussions. These elements would never be proposed without women in the design process, and yet can often not be achieved other than in a process where only women are consulted.

Conclusion

The Delhi conference contributed depth and insight to the model that would never have been achieved without women in the design process, looking specifically through the eyes of women. Often, however, processes aimed to benefit women consult only women, and this is sometimes to the detriment of the outcome. Just as important as the lens of women are the lenses of men, the elderly, children, youth and all marginalized groups and stakeholders. An advantage of the methodology is that it provides an optimistic platform within which all these views can be captured and used to articulate a shared vision of a safe place for all. Without a conscious focus on women's issues, the need for women-friendly transport, services, social and education facilities is not necessarily incorporated into planning processes (Whitzman, 2008).

The model and methodology are inclusive and create a platform for all participants to bring their personal perspectives, as well as their institutional perspectives, to both the visioning and the planning processes (Dator, 1998). Although the process offers participants an opportunity to benchmark and measure progress towards transformed social impact, this chapter has dealt with its value solely in terms of the way in which it facilitates the articulation of a shared understanding of vulnerable social systems, delivering a collective vision itemized in achievable, interlinked elements across sectors and interests. The model promotes the identification of practical collaborative partnerships, rather than sector-specific safety strategies, reminding us that, when women dream, they don't dream of protection but of a place in which they can achieve their full potential and live their best lives (Viswanath and Mehrotra, 2007), without needing protection.

Notes

1 In South Africa, and in particular in the western part of the country, 'coloured' people are those who are neither black nor white and have a combination of indigenous and European ancestry.
2 In one small town, Laingsburg, the population of 7,000 mostly poor people was served by sixty-seven illegal liquor outlets, whereas there were no sports facilities in easy walking distance, and the secondary school was a long walk across town.
3 This was told at a workshop that took place in a school in Newcastle, South Africa, on 18 August 2011.
4 This comment was made during a personal interview with the author at a school in Wellington, South Africa, 27 July 2011.

References

Abrahams, N., Mathews, S. and Ramela, P. (2006) 'Intersections of sanitation, sexual coercion and girls safety in schools', *Topical Medicine and International Health*, vol. 11, no. 7, pp. 751–6.
Allen, P.M. (2001) 'The dynamics of knowledge and ignorance; learning the new systems science', in Matthies, H.M.W. and Kriz, J. (eds), *Integrative Systems Approaches to Natural and Social Dynamics*, Heidelberg, Berlin.
Brown, T. (2008) 'Design thinking', *Harvard Business Review*, June 2008.
Burton, P. (2006) 'Easy prey. Results of the National Youth Victimisation Study', *SA Crime Quarterly*, vol. 16, available at: www.issafrica.org/uploads/CQ16 BURTON.PDF, accessed 23 January 2012.
Capra, F. (1982) *The Turning Point, Science, Society and the Rising Culture*, Simon & Schuster, New York.

CSIR (2006) 'Central Karoo Study', unpublished, Pretoria.

Dator, J. (1998) 'The future lies behind! Thirty years of teaching futures studies', *American Behavioral Scientist*, vol. 42, pp. 298–319.

Engle, P.L., Benley, M. and Pelto, G. (2007) 'Strategies to avoid the loss of developmental potential in more than 200 million children in the developing world', *Lancet*, vol. 369, pp. 229–42, available at: www.who.int/maternal_child_adolescent/documents/pdfs/lancet_child_dev_series_paper3.pdf, accessed 23 January 2012.

Frank, C. (2005) 'How social service delivery can prevent crime', *Crime Quarterly*, vol. 13, Institute for Security Studies, available at: www.iss.co.za/pubs/CrimeQ/No.13/Frank.pdf, accessed 23 January 2012.

George, E. and Finberg, A. (2001) *Scared at School: Sexual Violence Against Girls in South African Schools*, Human Rights Watch, New York.

Hobdell, K. (1996) 'Working with victims of violent crime', in Stanko, E. (ed.) *Perspectives on Violence*, vol. 1, The Howard League Books, London.

Holling, C. (2001) 'Understanding the complexity of economic, ecological and social systems', *Ecosystems*, vol. 4, pp. 390–405.

Holtmann, B. (2001) 'Gender bias in service delivery to victims of crime', Masters dissertation, University of the Witwatersrand, Johannesburg.

Holtmann, B. (2011) *What It Looks Like When It's Fixed*, Self-published, sponsored by PWC, Johannesburg.

Jewkes, R., Vundule, C., Maforah, J. and Jordaan, E. (2001) 'Relationship dynamics and teenage pregnancies in South Africa', *Social Science and Medicine*, vol. 25, pp. 733–44.

Liu, J., Raine, A., Venables, P.H. and Mednick, S.A. (2004) 'Malnutrition at age 3 years and externalising behavior problems at ages 8, 11 and 17 years', *American Journal of Psychiatry*, vol. 161, pp. 2005–13.

Parry, C., Morojele, N. and Jernigan, D. (2008) 'A sober South Africa', in *Action for a Safe SA*, South Africa the Good News, Sandton.

The Parent Centre (2009) *Annual Report. 2009*, available at: www.kwikwap.co.za/parent/docs/Annual%20Report%202009.pdf, accessed 23 January 2012.

Tomlinson, M. and Landman, M. (2007) '"It's not just about food": mother–infant interaction and the wider context of nutrition', *Maternal and Child Nutrition*, vol. 3, pp. 292–303.

Vetten, L. (2006) *Mapping the Use of Guns in Violence Against Women; Findings From Five Case Studies*, Paper presented at the Firearms Injury Prevention Conference, April 2006, Durban.

Viswanath, K. and Mehrotra, S. (2007) '"Shall we go out?" Women's safety in public spaces in Delhi', *Economic and Political Weekly*, vol. 42, no. 17, pp. 1542–8.

Weingarten, K. (2003) *Common Shock: Witnessing Violence Every Day; How We Are Harmed, How We Can Heal*, Dutton, New York.

Whitzman, C. (2008) *The Handbook of Community Safety, Gender and Violence Prevention: Practical Planning Tools*, Earthscan, London.

Wilson, F. and Ramphele, M. (1989) *Uprooting Poverty, The South African Challenge*, David Philip, Cape Town.

Young, J. (2002) 'Crime and social exclusion', in Maguire, M., Morgan, R. and Reiner, R. (eds), *The Oxford Handbook of Criminology* (3rd Edition), Oxford University Press, Oxford.

Chapter 8

Safe access to basic infrastructure
More than pipes and taps[1]

Prabha Khosla and Suneeta Dhar

Introduction

This chapter uses the results of a two-and-a-half-year action research project entitled, Action Research Project on Women's Rights and Access to Water and Sanitation in Asian Cities, to examine women's rights to the city in the context of their daily activities. Its focus is on poor women in *Jhuggi Jhopri* (JJ), relocation colonies in Delhi. The research was undertaken from 2009 to 2011, with programmatic interventions in 2010 and 2011. The action research was a collaborative effort between Jagori in Delhi, India, and WICI in Montreal, Canada. Financial support for the project was provided by the International Development Research Centre (IDRC), Canada.

The key objective of the action research was to test and adapt the WSA in the context of essential services – water, sanitation, drainage, solid waste and electricity – and for its use in low-income urban communities.

The overarching context informing the action research was to identify the gender gap in services; to identify the impact of inadequate and inappropriate infrastructure, facilities and services on women's and other marginalized groups' access to water and sanitation, including drainage, solid-waste management and electricity; and to link this to the gender gap in women's safety and security and the gender gap in governance of municipal infrastructure, facilities and services.

The right to the city

We explore the findings of the research from the perspective of the right to the city and the everyday experiences of low-income women and men, young and old, in settlements of evicted slum-dwellers. The findings also strongly validate the urban feminist theoretical framework of the infrastructure of everyday life. Before discussing the research outcomes, we briefly elaborate these theoretical frameworks.

The 'Right to the city' is still a nascent concept. Although Lefebvre (1968, 1996) has often been cited as exploring this concept initially, in the 1990s, the initiatives of the Council of European Municipalities and Regions (CEMR) led to further exploration of the practical meaning of the rights of urban residents. In 2006, one of these inquiries led to the publication of the European Charter for Equality of Women and Men in Local Life.[2] The Charter identifies six fundamental principles that need to inform the practice of local and regional governments in implementing equality between women and men in cities. Local and regional governments are invited to join and implement the Charter and its commitments through the development and implementation of equality action plans in a number of identified areas and within two years of signing the Charter.

Harvey (2008) is also recognized as advancing the concept of the right to the city. However, the meetings of activists, workers and professionals at the World Social Forums from 2002 to 2005 have given the right to the city a tangible definition based on an analysis of the implications of neo-liberalism for urbanization. Globally, urbanization under neo-liberalism has created divided cities, in geographical terms as well as socially, politically, culturally and economically, with greater inequalities between richer and poorer residents. Cities have become polarized, with wealthy neighbourhoods of exclusive and gated communities, shopping malls and entertainment complexes on the one hand, and, on the other, the exclusion by eviction and displacement of poorer residents and their communities to the periphery of the city. Under these conditions, ideals of urban identity, citizenship and belonging become much harder to sustain (Harvey, 2008, p. 32).

The World Charter for the Right to the City[3] is the product of deliberations from the World Social Forums. It recognizes that the right to the city interconnects and is interdependent with all recognized international human-rights conventions. It was conceived as an integrated right. Thus, it is inclusive of the right to land, ways of subsistence, work, health, education, culture, housing, social protection, security, healthy environment, sanitation, public transportation, leisure, the right to information, water and access and supply of domestic and urban public services, justice, the right to association and free speech, and planning and management of cities.

Fortunately, there is also a new initiative from United Cities and Local Governments (UCLG), the international organization of local governments, to also define the mandate of local governments within a human-rights framework. At its last conference, held in Mexico City in November 2010, the UCLG adopted the Global Charter-Agenda for Human Rights to the City. It too invites local governments to sign on and develop an action plan for implementation in consultation with their residents.[4] It remains to be seen how the implementation of the rights framework by local governments can bridge the divided city, especially in terms of the rights of the urban poor to a healthy living environment.

It is also important to underline that, for millions of women and girls around the world, any possibility of exercising the right to the city is curtailed by their restricted access to public spaces. Women and girls in all cultures live with varying degrees of fear of violence in public spaces, as well as in the home. In public spaces, including at work, there is always the threat and reality of verbal and non-verbal sexual harassment and assault. Additionally, millions of women and girls around the world are brutalized daily by violence from their partners and family members in their own homes. Women's and girls' safety in the home and in public is an area that needs immediate and effective action to enable women and girls to exercise their right to the city in all other ways.

As our interest is in the daily lives of evicted poor women in Delhi, we are particularly concerned about how the rights frameworks will actually incorporate and implement equality and equity for low-income women and men in slums and informal settlements. Recognizing that so many international conventions and declarations on women's rights have been adopted by countries around the world, including India, positive changes in low-income urban women's daily lives are often difficult to discern. At this point, it is worth stressing that all societies are informed by strong patriarchal traditions and structures, and, as Kapur (2010, p. 3) says, 'Is it possible to anchor substantive equality as a practical means to breathe life into everyday decision-making which is informed by social context realities, i.e. lived lives of women – the holistic goal of a human rights-based approach?'.

Globally, urban social movements that successfully confront the daunting forces of neo-liberalism in city development are also nascent, and the challenge to create equitable and sustainable cities remains.

The infrastructure of everyday life

The proposition that urban planning and management should be informed by an understanding of everyday life was first explored in Sweden in 1979. Swedish women proposed a better everyday life in which a more humane infrastructure would play a central role. This evolved into a decade-long project called *New Everyday Life* (Forskargruppen, 1987). The latter not only comprised a critique of the present conditions but also a vision of a harmonious, creative and just society. The central motives for action were children's and women's needs, as well as the social reproduction of all people and nature (Horelli, 2002, p. 2). It proposed the creation of an intermediate system of infrastructure and services for the shared provisioning of daily living, such as collective cooking, cleaning, shopping and child minding.

Gilroy and Booth (1999, p. 309), among others, also attribute the expansion of this approach to the work of others (such as Healey *et al.*, 1997) who built on Giddens' (1984, 1990) concept of everyday life as a web of social relations through which we accomplish human existence in daily, weekly, yearly, life-span and intergenerational time. Healey elaborates that this can be encapsulated in how people accomplish daily life; their strategies for survival and coping; the tasks of acquiring the material means of existence, the social supports such as social care, emotional support and moral developments; and the enrichment of life through enjoyment.

The work of EuroFEM, a network of European women scholars, in the 1990s, provided substantive new critiques and pilot projects to explore the practical application of a gender-sensitive approach to the built environment (Gilroy and Booth, 1999, p. 311). For a contemporary discussion of the concept of the infrastructures of daily life, see Jarvis with Kantor and Cloke (2009, pp. 127–56).

With this background, Gilroy and Booth (1999, p. 310) developed a model to illustrate the conceptual modes of everyday life (see Figure 8.1).

This model is very apropos to many cities planned in a conventional urban-planning frame. The slums and relocation colonies of the research in Delhi do not fall under the purview of any existing planning paradigm, not the least, a master plan's definition of land-use planning and urban neighbourhoods. However, the research findings clearly validate the need for the application of a gendered mode of urban planning to the upgrading and/or redevelopment of slums and the establishment of any new relocation colonies.

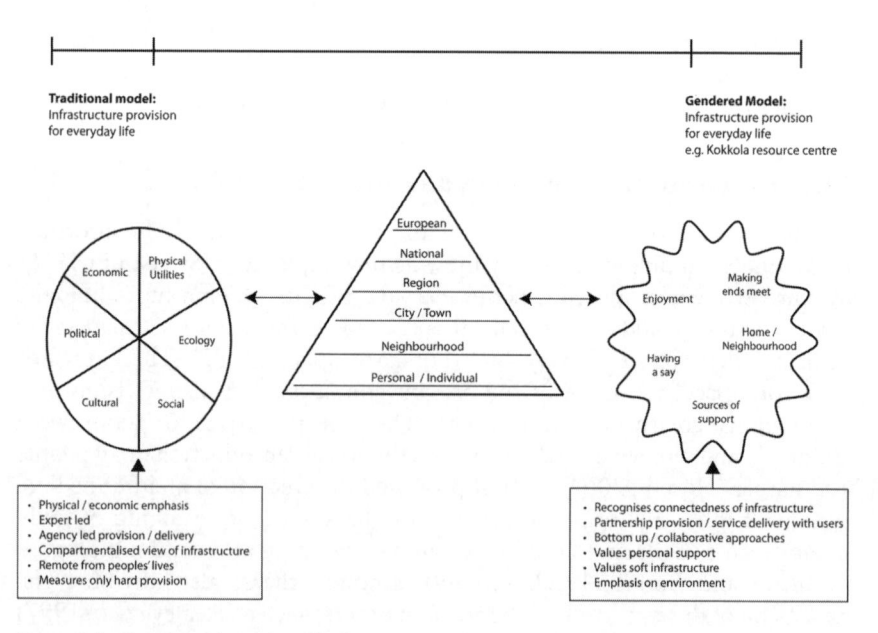

Figure 8.1 Conceptual modes of infrastructure for everyday life
Source: Gilroy and Booth, 1999, p. 310

Low-income women and their families and communities have the right to live in the city with dignity and self-respect. They have the right to gender-sensitive infrastructure and services that will make daily living easier and better than what they live with today. And they have a right to plan and design cities. Gender-sensitive resettlement areas for evicted slum-dwellers will give local residents a better standard of living and greater opportunities to what cities offer.

A brief note on Delhi's urbanization and the growing exclusion of the poor

In 2010, the urban population passed a critical point, with more than 50.6 percent of the world's population (3.49 billion) living in urban areas (UN-HABITAT, 2010, p. 55). Estimates indicate that, by 2030, all developing regions, including Asia and Africa, will have more people living in urban than rural areas (UN-HABITAT, 2010, p. 10).

In India, the pace of urbanization is slower than in the rest of the world, and projections indicate that, by 2030, 575 million people (41 percent of the population) will be in urban areas (Hashim, 2009, p. 5). According to the latest National Sample Survey Organization (NSSO) reports, there are over 80 million poor people living in the cities and towns of India. The slum population is also increasing, and the Town and Country Planning Office (TCPO) estimates from 2001 indicate that over 61.80 million people were living in slums (Ministry of Housing and Urban Poverty Alleviation, Government of India and United Nations Development Programme, 2009).

Among the findings of the 2011 Indian Census, it has been noted that, for the first time since 1921, urban India has added more numbers to its population in a decade than rural India. The urban population is 91 million higher than it was a decade ago (Sainath, 2011).

From the early 1900s, Delhi has evolved as a divided city. It has witnessed continual displacements of the poor, urban working classes, who have sustained the city while being deprived access to basic needs and rights (Roy, 2010). It is reported that the number of people below the poverty line in Delhi has nearly doubled – from over 1.1 million in 1999–2000 to over 2.2 million in 2004–5 (Economic Survey of Delhi, 2007–8). Approximately 33 per cent of the population of Delhi lives in so-called slum dwellings, and another 18 per cent live in JJ resettlement colonies or unauthorized colonies (Delhi Urban Environment and Infrastructure Improvement Project, 2021, as quoted in the Economic Survey of Delhi, 2007–8, p. 178).

This trend continues today, as urban development caters to the upper and elite classes through the building of apartment complexes, shopping malls, multiplexes, parks, recreational, sports and other facilities, creating huge divides between the rich and the poor (Unni, 2009, p. 78). Delhi has among the highest per capita incomes in the country. However, the problems Delhi faces – livelihoods, water and power – are not due to overall shortages, but because of distributional inequities (Economic Survey of Delhi, 2007–8). 'Inequality is the fastest-growing sector of India', says Sainath, in a recent article (Hardikar, 2011).

The preparations for Delhi's Commonwealth Games 2010 also led to massive evictions and resulted in a range of human-rights violations of the city's working poor, including the homeless, beggars, street vendors and construction workers – many of whom were women. The development of a 'world-class city' created infrastructure that did not benefit the poor in any way. A Housing and Land Rights Network study estimated that at least 250,000 people in Delhi have lost their homes since 2004 because of the games (Mishra *et al.*, 2010). In the context of this study, based on the lives of women who have been evicted and relocated from their original settlements, these statistics provide an alarming picture of violations of the right to the city.

Urbanization imposes huge costs on poor women. Although cities offer women some possibilities of work, they also place women at heightened risks of all forms of violence, restricting their mobility and keeping them in low-paying jobs in the informal sector and impeding access to life services (WHO and UN-HABITAT, 2010, p. 35). This is especially so for single women who head households and get limited access to food, health, child support and other public provisioning measures. Their overall safety is under threat in such circumstances (Rustagi *et al.*, 2009, p. 48).

A quick glance at the city's master plans of the last few decades illustrates exclusionary trends in urban development. One of the arguments put forward by Delhi's urban researchers and activists is that the growth of the slums in Delhi is a result of the master plan itself. The plan is based on an elaborate idea of 'zoning', where land is segregated as residential, commercial and industrial areas. From the first master plan for Delhi (MPD) in 1962 to the MPD of 2001, many displacements have occurred, including those due to de-industrialization and displacement of non-conforming industries (Roy, 2010). Another disconcerting feature of master plans is the gradual decline in living spaces for the poor. Whereas the 1962 MPD had provisions of 80 m^2 per plot per household, it was reduced to 40 m^2 during the massive resettlements of the 1970s, and to 25 m^2 per household by the MPD of 2001. In 2004, when forced evictions and relocations to the outskirts took place from Yamuna Pushta and other slum areas, the plot sizes allocated were a mere 12.5 m^2, thereby violating the norms laid out in the MPD. Services for residents too were diluted extensively over time. Studies indicate a shift towards provision of services to a group rather than to individuals. Most importantly, all recent resettlements have been without any secure tenurial rights (Banerjee and Pande, 2005, pp. 8–9). Thus, the poor have been further impoverished, and their participation in shaping city plans remains a distant dream.

Western, patriarchal and capitalist practices of urban planning and management have dominated the interrogation and re-creation of urban centres of the Global South – and this continues today. This conceptual frame for urban planning and management is dominated by a 'master plan' or 'strategic plan'. This plan segregates land uses and provides broad guidelines for land use, environmental protection and parks, infrastructure provision, transportation, community services, residential neighbourhoods and housing, industrial, commercial and retail zones, a central business district, etc. It defines cities as though there were no interconnectedness between the built form and its functions and users. Cities have a dynamic engagement of urban forces on multiple levels and multiple ways, and the master plans undervalue these.

Additionally, owing to the inequality faced by women in most societies, cities of both the Global North and the South have excluded women's daily lives and perspectives from informing urban forms and functions. Or, perhaps, it would be more accurate to say that undervaluation and segregation of women's needs and perspectives are what have shaped cities of the past and the master plans of today.

The master-plan lens is not suited to the lived reality of the majority of urban women and men in cities of the Global South, primarily owing to the vast differences in the socio-economic realities of the cities. For example, Delhi, as described above, is a city with a large informal sector and millions of low-income women and men living in informal and often illegal settlements or new areas post-evictions, without the services, infrastructure and segregated land uses described in master plans. The efforts to transform cities such as Delhi into New York or London and to conform to conventional notions of master plans often mean ignoring or overriding the lived realities of the majority of its residents.

This is not to say that urban planning in itself is wrong or irrelevant; this chapter argues that the time to change the urban-planning lens is long overdue. It would be useful, instead, to consider city planning and management from the perspective of the majority of its urban residents – poor women and men and their families and communities. It is high time urban planning and management were informed by a gender- and poverty-sensitive analysis.

The Action Research Project on Women's Rights and Access to Water and Sanitation in Asian Cities

Introduction to the action research project

The action research project was undertaken in two JJ relocation colonies in Delhi – Bawana and Bhalswa. Jagori worked in Bawana, and Action India, the co-partner, in Bhalswa. Overall research and technical support was provided by Jagori and WICI. Jagori also partnered with the

Centre for Budget and Governance Accountability (CBGA), One World Foundation, the Kriti team and the Women's Feature Service to support community and advocacy efforts (see WICI and Jagori, 2011).

Bawana and Bhalswa, Delhi

Bawana is situated in the north west of Delhi, towards the Haryana border, and is a site for the relocation of thousands and thousands of evicted slum-dwellers. Residents living in JJ colonies/slums from Yamuna Pushta, Dhapa colony, Banuwal Nagar, Saraswati Vihar, Deepali Chowk, Vikaspuri, Nagla Machi, Jahangirpuri, etc. were evicted to this site, about 35 km from their homes. Evictions and relocations from different parts of Delhi continue today. The plots in Bawana were assigned only to those who could prove their identity and had proof of residence. People who lived in Delhi before 1990 were allocated 18 m^2 plots, whereas those who had lived in Delhi between 1990 and 1998 were allocated a plot of 12.5 m^2.

To date, one of the key issues creating constant insecurity for residents is that rights to tenure in these relocation colonies are unclear. Residents were given a 'licence' for plots for either five, seven or nine years and they had to pay Rs7,000 for these plots. Without security of tenure, they are continuing to invest their hard-earned and meagre savings to make the space more liveable. They could be evicted again.

The second site, Bhalswa, is located in north-east Delhi, next to the Bhalswa landfill. Most people residing here were evicted from the north and east of Delhi, from communities such as Yamuna Pushta, Gautampuri, Barapulla, Nizamuddin, ITO and Rohini, about 10–20 km from their original homes. They were moved here in 2000 and they too were allocated plots of either 12.5 m^2 or 18 m^2, based on their years of residence in Delhi. Today, Bhalswa has roughly 2,600 plots, with an approximate population of 22,000–25,000 residents.

In recent evictions, Delhi witnessed a huge upheaval. Over 60,000 poor working families were uprooted from the Yamuna Pushta and other places, in the name of beautification and development of a 'world-class city'. They were evicted to the remote areas of Bawana and Savra Gheda, where no basic facilities were provided. The Yamuna Pushta housed around 35,000 working-class families, who had lived there for more than three decades; many of them were daily wage workers, domestic workers, hand-cart pullers, head loaders and rag pickers (Menon-Sen and Bhan, 2008). Seen as illegal migrants preying on the city's limited resources, 'dirtying the landscape' and engaging in criminal activities, they were thrown away like heaps of garbage. A traumatised Munni Ben from Bawana and a member of the *Mahila Nigrani Samiti* (Women's Monitoring Committee) supported by Jagori, said at a national workshop, 'we were seen as dirty garbage and filth to be thrown far away'.[5]

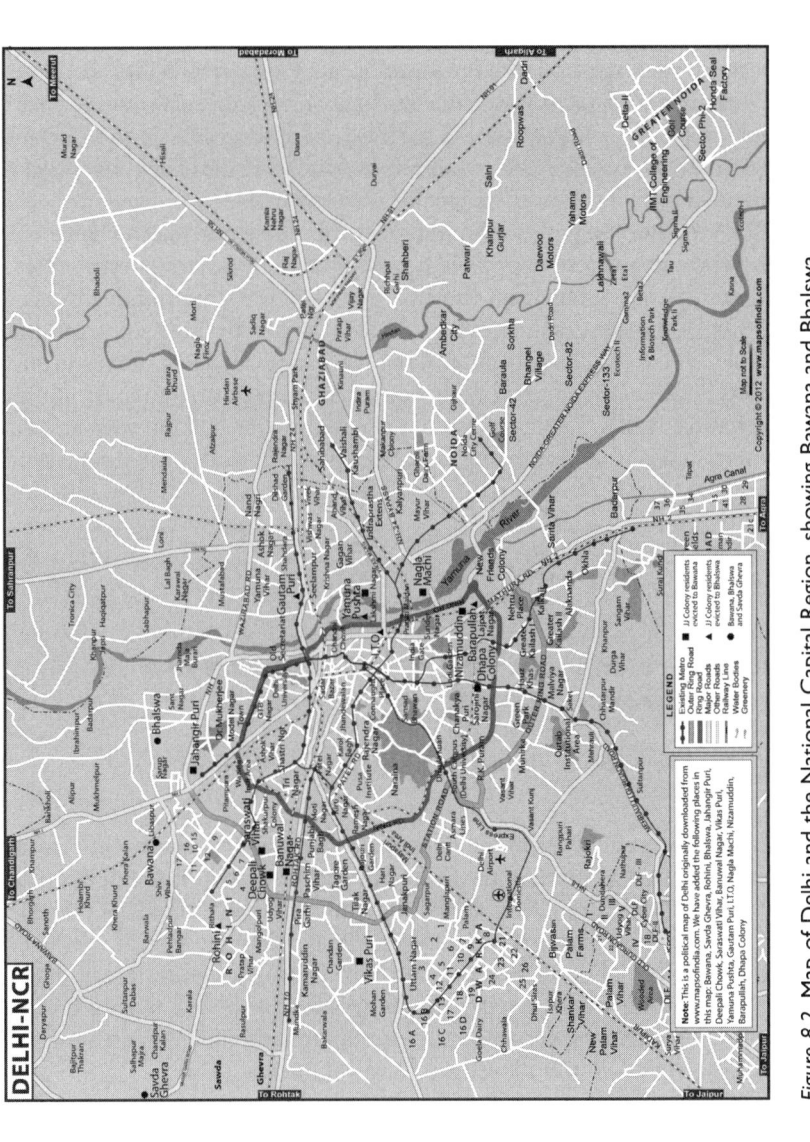

Figure 8.2 Map of Delhi and the National Capital Region, showing Bawana and Bhalswa
Source: Customized by expert cartographers from MapsofWorld.com

The action research process

The WSA, developed in the field of women's safety in urban settings, is a participatory tool that has been effectively utilized in a number of countries. It aids with identifying factors that increase women's vulnerabilities and assists in generating solutions to address these vulnerabilities. The process empowers women and aids in the development of partnerships between women's groups and local governments. It is a way of encouraging local governments to see communities as partners in finding solutions to urban problems, and it provides the communities and organizations with entry points for engagement with their local governments.

The WSA methodology was adapted for use in relocation and resettlement colonies before it was tested, applied and modified in the two communities. The research process included the use of a gender situational analysis, focus-group discussions, stakeholder and key informant interviews and the safety-audit walks in different parts of Bawana and Bhalswa. Focus-group discussions were held separately with women, men, boys and girls. Although the safety audit walks began predominantly with women, soon women and men, young and old, all joined in to accompany the walk or intervened as the walk progressed. From this research, a handbook on safety audits for low-income communities and for infrastructure and services has been developed for use by both civil-society organizations and local governments (see Mehrotra Tandon, 2010).

Infrastructure and essential services of everyday life in Bawana and Bhalswa

Toilets and sanitation: violation of dignity and basic human rights

There are no sewerage pipes in the relocation colonies and thus no provision for toilets in the home. Instead, the Delhi State government, through its land-development agency, the Delhi Development Authority, chose to provide community toilet complexes (CTCs). The toilet blocks have septic tanks, and often these are broken and overflowing into the surrounding areas. Each CTC has forty toilet stalls, twenty on the women's side and twenty on the men's side. Owing to the terrible state of maintenance and repair, some of them have been closed and locked up for a number of years.

Both communities have similar systems for the use and management of CTCs. For example, in Bawana women pay Rs2 for use of the toilets until 12 noon, and after that there are no charges. In Bhalswa, they have to pay every time they need to use the toilet. Charges for bathing and washing clothes vary between Rs5 and Rs7. Men pay Rs1 every time they use the toilet. There are no charges for children; however, in both Bawana and Bhalswa, children under six years of age are not allowed in unless their mothers pay, as the caretakers do not want to be responsible for cleaning the toilets and providing water. These children use the shallow drains outside their homes as toilets.[6] All residents complain that the CTCs are often dirty, as the cleaning is irregular and inadequate. Services are disrupted during power failures. Both women and men use open spaces for defecation, because the CTCs are either too dirty, too expensive or closed, or the location is inconvenient. In Bhalswa, more men than women use the CTCs for bathing. Girls and women can only use open areas for defecation later in the night. They live in fear and worry about the constant threats of sexual harassment and assault. Women have been raped in both communities when attempting to use the open areas. Incidences of sexual harassment and assault are not reported to the police. Women and girls now go out in groups. Schoolgirls report that the school toilets too are filthy and they avoid using them. For menstruating girls, this means they often miss school.

The CTCs are not open throughout the day and night. In most blocks, the CTCs are open from 5 a.m. to 10.30 or 11.30 p.m. In Bhalswa, the toilets shut at 10 p.m. After these hours, residents use open areas for defecation. In Bawana, owing to the growth of the settlement, the open areas are almost

Figure 8.3 Woman in a community toilet complex
Source: Jagori

non-existent now. Thus, women often also use newspapers to defecate on, or defecate in the drains late in the night. There are few or no dustbins in the CTCs, making menstrual-waste disposal impossible. Women in Bhalswa often dumped their menstrual waste in the toilet complexes that were locked up. Others buried it in the ground.

Women and girls have been subject to sexual harassment, assault and abuse, whether in the CTCs or while obtaining water and going to defecate in the open. The CTCs have an open roof that allows men and boys to peep into the women's section of the CTCs. In Bhalswa, boys of neighbouring homes have kept their pet birds on the roofs of the CTC and therefore are often on the rooftops. Further, in both Bawana and Bhalswa, latches and doors in the toilets and washing areas are broken or missing. Large numbers of boys play cricket next to the CTCs or stand in groups commenting or singing lewd songs or playing cards with the caretaker. Their constant presence violates the privacy that girls and women need when using the toilets and when bathing.

In both Bawana and Bhalswa, 30–40 per cent of households have now constructed home-based toilets at their own expense. For the vast majority, this investment is an effort to protect the females in the family from harassment and assault. Many families fear that, if their daughters are sexually abused, they will be unmarriageable. This has prompted some of them to marry their daughters off in their late teens. All the young women we spoke to would have liked to go to college rather than be married at that young age.

The CTCs are under the jurisdiction of the Municipal Corporation of Delhi, but the management of the toilets has been privatized, and these individuals in turn subcontract to others. The privatization and subcontracting make it difficult to achieve accountability for proper management of the CTCs.

Water supply: loss of time and health

In both Bawana and Bhalswa, no household water connections were provided by the government, even though the area was designated for relocation. Instead, standpipes were installed at set locations in the lanes. In Bawana in 2009, at the beginning of the research, many of these original standpipes were not working; instead, pipes were sticking out of the drains and along the drains next to waste water. The taps were either stolen or damaged, and, in many places, residents had connected rubber hoses to the pipes sticking out of the ground and out of the drains. The piped water is untreated ground water and it is consumed by residents without any treatment or filtration. Some residents complain about the foul smell and taste of the water, while others think it is good water.

The hand pumps installed at the time of relocation have run dry, as the water table has fallen considerably. Residents also source water from a temple about 1 km away from the main road of the relocation site. In Bawana, water is released into the pipes three times a day. After the women collect the water they need, there is no way to shut off the water, as there are no taps, and so often water is wasted, which adds to the settlement's problems of overflowing drains and muddy lanes.

The water supply in Bhalswa was very limited. At the start of the project in 2009, piped water was almost non-existent, and only three blocks received untreated piped water from a nearby industrial area. Most residents relied on tankers that came to the area once every seven to ten days. Tanker water was delivered at the behest of the informal political leadership in the community. With huge demand and crowding to get to the water first, women and girls faced problems of physical and sexual harassment. Owing to the intensity of the fighting, boys and men from the family were often sent to get water. On many days, both men and women were forced to bring drinking water from their workplaces in south and central Delhi.

Some residents set up water pumps for domestic use. As the ground water has been contaminated by the landfill, what they pump up is leachate.

Figure 8.4 Muddy streets in all seasons
Source: Jagori

Figure 8.5 Girls fetching water from a water tanker in Bhalswa
Source: Women's Feature Service

Leachate is used for bathing and washing clothes and dishes and sometimes even for drinking. Jaundice, kidney stones, skin problems, stomach upsets, headaches and nausea are common health problems that result.

In Bhalswa, the engagement of young women and men and older women with this project has seen some remarkable organization in the community and negotiations with elected officials with some outstanding results. Today, all the households receive sufficient water, either through piped water for a couple of hours three times a day, or via tankers that come to the lanes twice a week. Furthermore, women have set up lane committees in each of the lanes to monitor service delivery and quality.

Drainage

The drainage system in both Bawana and Bhalswa is localized, with no connections to any city drainage system. In the blocks that were initially inhabited, the drains were constructed after people started living there. In other areas, they were planned and constructed prior to the relocation of people. Drains in both the communities are usually clogged with solid waste. In Bawana, the drains in the older blocks were so badly built that the water flows back into the lanes and the houses. Owing to faulty design and construction, waste water does not flow from drains in the inner lanes to drains in the outer lanes. This means the lanes are often muddy with pools of stagnant and filthy water. There is an uneven response to cleanliness. Some residents take the trouble to clean the drains in front of their homes, whereas others end up blocking them by throwing solid waste into the lanes, without giving much thought to their neighbours. The large drains open into nearby fields, creating terrible smells from standing pools of waste and water that breed mosquitoes and flies, further adding to the ill health of residents.

The design and maintenance of drains running alongside the homes is another cause of concern. If the drains do get cleaned by the sanitary workers, the wet garbage gets dumped alongside the drains, to be collected only after it has dried out. However, in the interim period, it spills into the drains and causes clogging all over again. Such drains, overflowing with decaying solid waste, breed mosquitoes and flies and impede movement in the narrow, muddy lanes. For both women and men, it is a constant struggle to maintain some sense of cleanliness and hygiene in their daily living environments (see Figure 8.6).

Owing to the small plot sizes, women try and use the space beyond their doorstep to wash clothes and dishes and to cook (see Figure 8.7). These daily chores have to be done in this unhygienic and filthy environment.

The poor maintenance of drains increases sexual harassment. The faulty designs of the drains and messy lanes with stagnant pools of water and wet garbage make it difficult to walk and provide an excuse for boys and men to brush past the girls walking in the lanes.

Figure 8.6 Man cleaning the drain outside his home, Bhalswa
Source: Jagori

Figure 8.7 Woman cooking outside her home on her 'veranda' over the drain, Bawana
Source: Jagori

Solid-waste management

There are demarcated areas for disposal of solid waste in Bawana, but they are located quite far away, and the residents end up throwing their garbage away in empty plots and other open spaces, including parking areas and street corners. Recently, owing to the impact of the action research project, negotiations took place between the women, youth and service providers to create a more effective mechanism for removal and disposal of solid waste in five blocks of Bawana. Without official figures, it is estimated that these five blocks have a population of about 150,000 residents. In Bhalswa, following interventions by Action India, a woman's group in Delhi working on issues of displacement, right to health, education and ending violence against women and girls, negotiations were undertaken at a community meeting with elected representatives to create a system for solid-waste collection from the lanes. A small, motorized vehicle rings a bell in each of the larger lanes, and residents have to come out to deliver their garbage to the collector. This is a limited service, but better than no service at all. This is the first time in the ten years of Bhalswa's history that there has been any system of solid-waste collection.

Gender and the opportunity cost of water

The action research underscored what is commonly known – that women and girls are primarily responsible for managing households; however, it highlighted that the inadequate infrastructure in the relocation colonies increases demands on women's time and unpaid labour. Women spent a considerable amount of time in queues, either to collect water or to use the toilets. For instance, in Bawana, women and girls spent one or two hours per day standing in queues and filling containers to fetch water. Given the irregular supply of water, they cannot always collect the amount of water they require for their daily usage. Some schoolgirls reported that, owing to this demand on their time in the mornings, they did not get a chance to eat prior to going to school. As mentioned above, when there is a water shortage, water is brought from a temple some distance away, and young girls are not sent there on their own. Instead, they wait for a male family member to accompany them.

For many years, women and men in Bhalswa had limited access to potable water. They could obtain water from the tankers when they came to the community, which was infrequently, and they would have to bring water from outside the settlement on their way home from work. They were heckled while carrying this water on the bus, as it would take up space on the bus. It is also exhausting to carry heavy bottles of water home. Collection of water takes anywhere from two to three hours, and, as mentioned earlier, women in most cases, and sometimes men and boys, have to fetch it from a distance of 2–3 km. This is time taken off from their other crucial and productive tasks. Some women were concerned that it interfered with their livelihood options and activities.

Inadequate and inappropriate infrastructure and limited access to these services put additional burdens on girls compared with boys. The gender division of labour and the fact that the care economy – unpaid work within the domestic sphere – is mostly the work of women and girls underline this. Women and girls bear the unequal burden of the social and economic costs of water.

As part of this action research project, and in an effort to deepen women's knowledge about how they could make visible their labour and to track the trail of public funds for services meant for poor communities, Jagori partnered with the CBGA in Delhi. The aim was to engage with the issues of safety and security of women and essential services by conducting two gender-responsive budget initiatives (GRBIs) in the urban water and sanitation sector.

The first gender-responsive budget study was an opportunity cost of water study (Bist-Joshi, 2011). It was conducted through the use of structured interviews in a purposive random-sampling method, in selected areas of Bawana and Bhalswa. For Bawana, the data are for the amount of time women spent going to get water, waiting for water and bringing it back home from public standpipes and from a block with no access to public water. The residents without access to public water obtained water from private sources, natural sources or bore wells. In all cases, the time was also estimated based on the number of trips the women made to get water. For both sets of data, the opportunity cost of the time needed to obtain water is based on rates of pay for unskilled, semi-skilled and skilled workers, as per the government's daily-wage guidelines. The rates are provided in Table 8.1.

Tables 8.2 and 8.3 show the calculations for the opportunity cost of water for Bawana and Bhalswa.

Table 8.1 Prevailing wage rates, 2 January 2008

Category	Rates from 1–2–2008 (in Indian rupees and US dollar equivalent; conversion rate: US$1 = Rs39.42)	
	Per month	Per day
Unskilled	Rs3,633.00 (US$92.16)	Rs140.00 (US$3.55)
Semi-skilled	Rs3,799.00 (US$96.37)	Rs146.00 (US$3.70)
Skilled	Rs4,057.00 (US$102.91)	Rs156.00 (US$3.96)

Note: The exchange rate was Rs39.42 for US$1 on 2 January 2008 (http://indiaassuperpower.blogspot.com/2008/01/vs-rupee-january-2008-trends.html)
Source: Government of NCT of Delhi, 2008

Table 8.2 Bawana: the opportunity costs for water from public standpipes

Category	Rate/hour (8 hours work)	Opportunity cost/year
Unskilled	Rs17.5 (US$0.44)	544 hrs Rs9,520 (US$239.36)
Semi-skilled	Rs18.25 (US$0.46)	544 hrs Rs9,928 (US$250.24)
Skilled	Rs19.5 (US$0.49)	544 hrs Rs10,608 (US$266.56)

Source: Bist-Joshi, 2011

Table 8.3 Bawana: the opportunity costs of water without the provision of public water

Category	Rate/hour (8 hours work)	Opportunity cost/year
Unskilled	Rs17.5 (US$0.44)	237.25 hrs Rs4,151.8 (US$104.39)
Semi-skilled	Rs18.25 (US$0.46)	237.25 hrs Rs4,330 (US$109.13)
Skilled	Rs19.5 (US$0.49)	237.25 hrs Rs4,626 (US$116.25)

Source: Bist-Joshi, 2011

Table 8.4 Bhalswa: the opportunity costs of tanker supply

Category	Rate/hour (8 hours work)	Opportunity cost/year
Unskilled	Rs17.5 (US$0.44)	110 hrs Rs1,925 (US$48.40)
Semi-skilled	Rs18.25 (US$0.46)	110 hrs Rs2,007.5 (US$50.60)
Skilled	Rs19.5 (US$0.49)	110 hrs Rs2,145 (US$53.90)

Source: Bist-Joshi, 2011

Table 8.5 Bhalswa: the opportunity costs of pumps pumping leachate

Category	Rate/hour (8 hours work)	Opportunity cost/year (for one cycle)
Unskilled	Rs17.5 (US$0.44)	420 hrs Rs7,350 (US$184.80)
Semi-skilled	Rs18.25(US$0.46)	420 hrs Rs7,665 (US$193.20)
Skilled	Rs19.5 (US$0.49)	420 hrs Rs8,190 (US$205.80)

Source: Bist-Joshi, 2011

For Bhalswa, the calculations were based on the amount of time it took to get to a water tanker, to get to the pumps pumping leachate, to wait in line and to walk back with the filled containers. In addition, the annual time dedicated to this was also compared with the rates of pay for unskilled, semi-skilled and skilled workers, as per the government's daily-wage guidelines. The annual opportunity cost of water is shown in Tables 8.4 and 8.5.

The research indicates that, for women in Bawana who obtain their water from standpipes, the opportunity cost of water in terms of lost wages is Rs9,520/year (US$239.36) for unskilled labour, Rs9,928/year (US$250.24) for semi-skilled labour and Rs10,608 (US$266.56) for skilled labour.

For the women who obtained their water without having access to public water, the opportunity cost of water in terms of lost wages is Rs4,151.80/year (US$104.39) for unskilled labour, Rs4,330/year (US$109.13) for semi-skilled labour and Rs4,636/year (US$116.25) for skilled labour.

In Bhalswa, the opportunity cost of water in terms of lost wages for women who accessed water from tankers is Rs1,925/year (US$48.40) for unskilled labour, Rs2,007.50/year (US$50.60) for semi-skilled labour and Rs2,145/year (US$53.90) for skilled labour.

For women who obtained their water, i.e. leachate, from water pumps, the opportunity cost of water in lost wages is Rs7,350/year (US$184.80) for unskilled labour, Rs7,665/year (US$193.20) for semi-skilled labour and Rs8,190/year (US$205.80) for skilled labour.

The study reinforces the importance of time savings associated with better access to water and the disadvantage suffered in terms of loss of time and income.

Only the results of the study are described above. The detailed process of examination and calculation of women's activities and time is elaborated in the larger study. The second gender-responsive budget study analysed the urban water and sanitation policies and schemes of the Central and Delhi State governments and the Municipal Corporation of Delhi as they pertain to low-income settlements in the north-west district of Delhi. Both studies can be obtained from Jagori's and CBGA's websites (see www.jagori.org and www.cbgaindia.org).

Safety and inadequate infrastructure and services in daily life

Women and girls face violence, including sexual assault, in many aspects of their daily life, including in the home and at work, and from family members as well as colleagues, employers and strangers. This is a daily reality for millions of women around the world.

Community women and girls participating in the safety audit walks said that they had not thought about associating certain aspects of harassment with inappropriate services. It also prompted men and boys to reflect, become more aware and break their silence on issues of violence against women and girls in their communities.

The action research project has amply demonstrated that inadequate and inappropriate infrastructure, facilities and services in low-income urban communities contribute to violence against women and girls and violate the rights of women and girls to live in safety and security. The creation of inclusive and equitable cities will need to deal with this issue substantially, as the lack of safety and security for women and girls compromises their ability to exercise their other rights.

Conclusion

For many poor women and men, young and old, the right to live in the city with dignity, safety and security remains out of reach. Delhi, like many other cities of the world, has seen a growing divide between richer and poorer residents and a reshaping of the geography of the city based on an inequitable distribution of land, housing and essential municipal services.

The research presented here shows that a gender analysis of infrastructure, facilities and services is critical to understanding women's and men's daily life in slums, relocation colonies post-eviction, resettlement colonies, unregularized slums and other settlements of the poor, be they legal or illegal. Gender-neutral infrastructure and services have a greater impact on the lives of women and girls than men and boys, owing to their responsibilities in household management and the provision of domestic services. Evictions have meant the loss of employment for many women and a gap in the education of both boys and girls. Generally speaking, women spend more time in the low-income settlements than men. Usually, employment permitting, men leave the settlements for work, as do some women. However, women are left in the settlements in greater numbers to sustain daily living and to raise children.

The results from the action research described here demonstrate explicit links between gender, infrastructure and poverty in both Bawana and Bhalswa. With an average family size of six, many residents in both communities are living on less than a dollar a day. An improvement in the infrastructure and services of water, sanitation, drainage, solid-waste management, electricity and housing and tenure, as per the needs and demands of women and girls, will reduce the poverty of everyday living in terms of access to, and affordability of, services and could increase livelihood opportunities for some.

The results of the action research project also illustrate the importance of women's safety and security when women are engaged in their daily activities and responsibilities. Violence against women is not only defined by violence against women in the home and at work, but also in terms of their daily functions of going to the toilet, to bath, to wash clothes and to collect water in public and collective facilities. It underlines the need for gender- and poverty-sensitive urban governance and planning, if cities are to truly be inclusive.

Notes

1   The authors would especially like to acknowledge the work of Dr Surabhi Tandon Mehrotra in compiling the research findings used in this chapter. They also want to gratefully acknowledge Sarita Baloni, Kailash Bhatt, Chaitali Haldar, Radha Khan, Juhi, Rani, Shruti and Mahabir from Jagori; Gouri Chowdhury, Anubha Singh, Murti, Uma and Veermati from Action India, and Kathryn Travers and Adil Ali from Women in Cities International, for their work on the project. Special

thanks are due to the women leaders from Bawana and Bhalswa, Delhi, for their participation in the research.
2 www.ccre.org/docs/charte_egalite_en.pdf
3 www.urbanreinventors.net/3/wsf.pdf
4 www.cities-localgovernments.org/committees/cisdp/Upload/general_docs/charter_agenda_en_june_2010_def.pdf
5 Presentation at the Daughters of Fire, India Court of Women on Dowry and Related Forms of Violence against Women, Vimochana, 2009.
6 Information from Chaitali Halder, Jagori.

References

Banerjee, M. and Pande, S. (2005) *The Context of Public Accountability and Community Action. Ensuring public accountability through community action. A case study in East Delhi*. New Delhi: Institute of Social Studies Trust.

Bist-Joshi, S. (2011) 'The Opportunity Cost of Water – Bhalswa and Bawana', in WICI and Jagori, *Gender and Essential Services in Low-income Communities: Report of the Action Research Project Women's Rights and Access to Water and Sanitation in Asian Cities*, pp. 131–47.

Economic Survey of Delhi (2007–8) See: www.delhiplanning.nic.in/Economic%20Survey/ES2007-08/ES2007-08.htm, accessed 4 June 2011.

Forskargruppen för det nya vardagslivet (1987) *Veier till det nye verdagslivet (Ways to the new everyday life)*. Oslo: Nord.

Giddens, A. (1984) *The Constitution of Society*. Cambridge: Polity Press.

Giddens, A. (1990) *The Consequences of Modernity*. Cambridge: Polity Press.

Gilroy, R. and Booth, C. (1999) 'Building Infrastructure for Everyday Lives', *European Planning Studies*, 7, 3, 307–24.

Government of NCT of Delhi (2008) *Delhi Gazette Extraordinary, Part IV*. Delhi: Labour Department, Government of NCT.

Hardikar, J. (2011) 'Bomb drops on India Country Side', *New Internationalist*, Issue 440. Permalink, UK. See: www.newint.org/features/2011/03/01/india-inequality/, accessed 7 June 2011.

Harvey, D. (2008) 'The Right to the City', *New Left Review*, 53, 23–40.

Hashim, S.R. (2009) *Economic Development and Urban Poverty. India: Urban Poverty Report*. New Delhi: OUP.

Healey, P., Gilroy, R. and Norwood, P. (1997) 'Social Life: The State of the Borough', *CREUE*. Newcastle, UK: Department of Town and Country Planning, University of Newcastle.

Horelli, L. (2002) 'Gender Mainstreaming Urban Planning and Development – Experiences of Women S Place Based Politics.' Paper presented at the Conference Genero y Urbanismo: infraestructuras para la vida cotidiana. Escuela Tecnica Superior de Arquitectura, Madrid, 27–28 May 2002.

Jarvis, H. with Kantor, P. and Cloke, J. (2009) *Cities and Gender*. London and New York: Routledge.

Kapur, N. (2010) *Everyday Equality – Be the Change*. South Asia: United Nations Development Fund for Women (UNWomen).

Lefebvre, H. (1968) *Le droit à la ville*. Paris: Anthopos.

Lefebvre, H. (1996) *Writings on cities*. Oxford: Blackwell.

Mehrotra Tandon, S. (2010) *A Handbook on Women's Safety Audits in Low-income Urban Neighbourhoods: A Focus on Essential Services*. New Delhi: JAGORI, in collaboration with Women in Cities International. See: www.femmesetvilles.org/pdf-general/idrc_hanbook_wsalow-income.pdf, accessed 16 June 2011.

Menon-Sen, K. and Bhan. G. (2008) *Swept Off the Map: Surviving Eviction and Resettlement in Delhi*. Delhi: Yoda Press/Jagori.

Ministry of Housing and Urban Poverty Alleviation, Government of India and United Nations Development Programme (2009) *India: Urban Poverty Report Summary*. See: http://data.undp.org.in/poverty_reduction/IUPR_Summary.pdf, accessed 1 June 2011.

Mishra, S., Chaudhry, S. and Kothari, M. (2010) *The 2010 Commonwealth Games: Whose Wealth? Whose Commons?* Fact Sheet 4: p2. New Delhi, India: Housing and Land Rights Network – South Asia Regional Programme and Habitat International Coalition.

Roy, D. (2010) 'City Makers and City Breakers', in *Celebrating Delhi*. New Delhi: Penguin Books India and Ravi Dayal Publisher.

Rustagi, P. Sarkar, S. and Joddar, P. (2009) *Gender Dimensions of Urban Poverty in India: Urban Poverty Report*. New Delhi: OUP.

Sainath, P. (2011) 'Census Findings Point to Decade of Rural Distress', *The Hindu*, 25 September 2011, Mumbai. See www.thehindu.com/opinion/columns/sainath/article2484996.ece, accessed on 6 October 2011.

UN-HABITAT (2010) *State of the World's Cities 2010/2011, Bridging the Urban Divides*. UK: Earthscan, pp. 10, 55.

Unni, J. (2009) *The Unorganized Sector and Urban Poverty: Issues of Livelihood in Urban Poverty Report*. New Delhi: OUP.

WHO and UN-HABITAT (2010) *Hidden Cities: Unmasking and Overcoming Health Inequities in Urban Settings*. Geneva, Switzerland.

WICI and Jagori (2011) *Gender and Essential Services in Low- Income Communities. Report on the Findings of the Action Research Project Women's Rights and Access to Water and Sanitation in Asian Cities*. Canada: Women in Cities International. See http://womenincities.org/pdf-general/idrc%20final%20internet.pdf, accessed 17 December 2011.

Part III
Tools

Chapter 9

From gender mainstreaming to intersectionality

Advances in achieving inclusive and safe cities

Anita Lacey, Rebecca Miller, Dory Reeves and Yardena Tankel

Introduction

Multiple approaches to engendering safer and more inclusive urban spaces for women now exist, with city governments, planners and urban citizens across the world advocating for and adopting initiatives to create new urban paradigms where urban spaces are inclusive of the diverse needs and aspirations of all citizens. The importance of gender-specific approaches to urban spaces has evolved from a dominant and problematic approach to urban safety that has historically left women's needs off local and international agendas. Spatial and urban planning, as one particular approach to safe cities, has often disadvantaged women because of a failure to recognize that women and men have different needs and experiences in cities, as well as different concerns about how these needs are met. Liberal approaches to women in cities have seen the development, in the last twenty years, of numerous progressive and varying approaches to the public-policy fields of urban transport and planning, for example. Gender mainstreaming is one such approach developed to address women's concerns, although it engenders significant criticisms that question the extent to which using gender as a single axis of oppression can be truly transformative of women's everyday and diverse experiences of exclusion.

This chapter addresses the contributions and shortcomings of liberal mainstreaming approaches and explores intersectionality as a potential framework with which to understand and develop initiatives and policies that are shaped by, and work with, multiple and intersecting social, physical, political and economic aspects of individuals' lives, not limited to gender. The use of intersectional approaches in programmes for safe and inclusive cities would facilitate understanding of why cities exclude women. Exploring intersectionality as a framework for safe and inclusive cities for women, as this chapter seeks to do, provides for complex and nuanced understandings of women's diverse needs, recognizing that women experience city life in multiple capacities, not solely contra to men.

Intersectionality is one methodological and theoretical approach that addresses the shortfalls of gender mainstreaming by explicitly addressing the many different needs of women (and men). The examples in the chapter on participatory budgeting and gender-impact assessments (GIAs), which have been hallmark approaches in the safe-city movement, demonstrate the significance of bringing gender to the fore of urban debates and are further explored through an intersectionality framework to demonstrate the importance of moving beyond gender as the single identity marker for women. Intersectionality is a means of seeing the ways in which many different aspects of what determines our lived experiences – including gender, race, class, age and ability – need to be taken into account in analysis, planning and programming. This chapter does not seek to offer prescriptive approaches of how intersectionality can be enacted, though it does promote that, in order for an intersectionality framework to be transformative and achieve social justice-oriented spaces of inclusion (Lacey, 2005), it needs to be participatory of stakeholders and of the diverse populations in cities. Rather than a completely new approach to women's rights, this chapter explores intersectionality as a flexible framework that can inform safe-city discourse, policy and practice.

The chapter begins with a brief genealogy of both gender mainstreaming and intersectionality and provides a background to the substantial contributions made in engendering women's rights broadly, and how they have been applied and further developed to create more inclusive cities. It then sets out to explore potential frameworks, rather than to offer policy prescriptions, and the examples provided demonstrate ways in which approaches can be utilized to work towards gender-aware inclusivity and social justice. The examples explored in this chapter are a sample of the wide-ranging international adoption of gender-mainstreaming and intersectional frameworks and provide further evidence as to why context-specific initiatives and tools need to be developed that recognize the multiplicity of women's experiences in cities. They are examples that reflect some of the authors' own areas of research expertise and therefore reflect interests and experiences, rather than seeking to be all encompassing.

Unitary approach of gender: gender in safe-cities approaches

The adoption of gender as a principle and single axis in inclusive-cities strategies through which to understand oppression or exclusion of women from city life and public spaces was shaped by two distinct and interrelated areas of work – violence against women and women's safety (Shaw and Andrew, 2005). Work on violence against women in cities focused largely on violence by intimate partners in the domestic and private sphere, and issues of victimization. Women's safety, however, took a more proactive approach to the prevention of violence in public spaces, largely through a range of policies, tools and strategies to create safer cities for women and girls (Shaw and Andrew, 2005; Whitzman, 2007). Participatory tools, such as safety audits and walks, have been used to develop recommendations for urban planning, transport and housing design, and to lobby for increased support and services at the local level. Safe-cities initiatives were developed in Canadian cities, such as Montreal and Toronto, and became more widely adopted in Melbourne (Australia), Gothenburg (Sweden) and Dar es Salaam (Tanzania) (Shaw and Andrew, 2005; Whitzman et al., 2009). As these two streams of work evolved, gradual acknowledgement by policymakers and practitioners of the inequalities experienced by women and girls in cities and their public spaces occurred. The focus on women-specific policies and programme strategies (common in women and development approaches) to reduce violence against women and promote women's safety began to shift towards a more comprehensive analysis of gendered power relations and rights (Shaw and Andrew, 2005; Whitzman, 2007). As notions of gender and gender inequalities emerged, attention turned to the impact of policies on both women and men, and to the power relations between women and men. In this context, gender mainstreaming emerged as a policy approach for framing the issue of gender equality (Shaw, 2002; Rees, 2005; Squires, 2005; Walby, 2005).

The emergence of gender mainstreaming

In 1997, the United Nations (UN) adopted gender mainstreaming as the approach to promote gender equality between women and men, and it was to be used in all plans, policies and programmes. Governments and non-governmental organizations soon followed by adopting gender mainstreaming as a tool for integrating gender concerns in sectors ranging from health to transport (e.g. Status of Women Canada, 1995; World Health Organisation, 2002; UN-HABITAT, 2008; also see Moser and Moser, 2005).

Gender mainstreaming was envisioned as a transformative process to promote gender equality and women's empowerment. As an approach, it has the potential to identify the different needs and priorities of women and men and to address gender bias in policies, programmes and budgets. Gender mainstreaming is designed to make gender issues visible by putting gender equality at the centre of policymaking (Tiessen, 2007). Mainstreaming gender, however, is more than the integration of gender concerns into the status quo; it also has the potential to challenge institutionalized norms and practices and address ongoing constructions of gender inequalities (Tiessen, 2007). When executed effectively, gender mainstreaming can enable a more nuanced understanding of gender inequalities in diverse settings and situations, which can then translate into effective and targeted policies and planning.

International organizations, ranging from the UN to the European Union, gradually adopted mainstreaming as a gender-equality strategy. Gender-impact statements are now included in funding requirements, grant applications and recruitment policies (Woodward, 2008). Gender mainstreaming is also part of the regular policymaking processes for a number of local- and state-level governments. For example, the City of Graz in Austria is committed to mainstreaming gender, as well as the promotion of equality of women and men in all public policies and areas of administration, and, in 2001, gender mainstreaming was identified as a managerial tool of organizational development in order to change the structures and processes of local-level government. A number of measures were introduced, including changes to services, new recruitment processes and gender-equality targets.[1] Gender equality is seen as compulsory in all aspects of policy design (City of Graz, n.d.). The measures have led to changes in the structure and culture of the public sector as a whole. Departments are expected to use tools (discussed further in the next section) such as gender budgeting to ensure a fairer distribution of funding and subsidies in all policy areas, as well as GIAs to evaluate their services. The implications in the City of Graz, especially in terms of women's safety, were far-reaching. A GIA of policies on poverty and social exclusion revealed the relationship between domestic violence and homelessness, as well as a lack of services for women. The City of Graz developed a comprehensive strategy to build safer and more inclusive communities for these marginalized women. Working in partnership with local organizations, the city created 300 places for homeless women, expanded council housing and provided transitional shelters (City of Graz, n.d.).[2] In this regard, gender mainstreaming meant that women's safety issues were taken into account separately from men's in the policies and interventions developed.

Tools of gender mainstreaming

As gender mainstreaming became a more dominant approach in safe and inclusive city initiatives, planners and practitioners began to develop tools and strategies to translate principles into practice. GIAs, safety audits and gender budgeting became important tools to formulate gender-sensitive policies. Public authorities, including the Greater London Authority and Plymouth City Council in the United Kingdom (Mackie *et al.*, 2001; Mackie, 2002; Reeves, 2002, 2005) and the government of Ireland (McGauran, 2005), as well as transport agencies such as the Strathclyde Passenger Transport (SPT), have used GIAs to ensure their strategies and programmes are meeting the different needs of women and men (RTPI, 2003; Reeves and Davies, 2007). GIAs work best with a systematic checklist of questions. For instance, in the context of safe cities, the questions might be: does the policy or plan address the different needs and experiences of women and men? What are the implications of these differences for the delivery of safe places? Will the policy deliver outcomes that promote equality as well as reduce inequalities? How will implementation ensure that these goals are achieved? And, finally, how will outcomes be measured? The different experiences of women and men can be identified through careful project design and use of survey methods. In this way, for example, Plymouth and SPT were able to identify the very specific needs, for example, of particular groups of women in relation to public toilets (RTPI, 2003; Reeves and Davies, 2007).

Mainstreaming gender in cities has also involved building the results of gender-safety audits into policy to indicate the need for specific improvements to the public realm (RTPI, 2003). For example, the Women's Design Service, based in London, UK, has developed Making Safer Places processes in Bristol, Wolverhampton, London and Manchester, using an exercise called a 'fear-o-meter' to find out what makes women afraid (Women's Design Service, 2005). Using highly participatory tools, women conduct audits of their local neighbourhood, estate or park to identify features of the physical environment that need improving, such as moving or removing vegetation, rerouting paths or installing fences (Women's Design Service, 2005).

Gender budgeting, which assesses the impact of revenue raising and expenditure on equality between women and men, has also been widely used to mainstream gender (Rees, 2005). First pioneered in Australia in 1984 (Budlender and Sharp, with Allen, 1998), gender budgeting broadens notions of transparency and accountability to include the impact of gender in budget processes and macro-level policies. It is also seen as an effective mechanism for promoting gender equality. Since 1995, more than eighty countries have used gender budgeting as a tool for assessing the impact of national and local spending on the needs of women and men, boys and girls and, in many countries, has developed using participative techniques (Women in Cities International and Jagori, 2010). It is particularly useful in ensuring that safety issues are not only recognized in policy, but explicitly assigned the necessary resources to realize positive safety outcomes.

Challenges of gender mainstreaming

Although gender mainstreaming has the potential to alter organizational norms and practices, its limitations in moving towards deeper, meaningful and more transformative understandings of women's diverse experiences are becoming widely recognized. In spite of positive examples, there is little consensus on the overall benefits of gender mainstreaming (Moser and Moser, 2005). Gender mainstreaming is not always well understood, and planners as well as practitioners have struggled to translate principles into practice. Most strategies are technocratic, and, as such, they fail to bring about meaningful and transformative institutional changes (Meer, 2005). As Moser

(2010) points out, gender mainstreaming is criticized on a number of fronts. Some believe that gender mainstreaming shifts the focus away from women's rights, as well as the financial and institutional targeting of resources to meet the needs of women (e.g. Rao and Kelleher, 2005; also see Tiessen, 2007). More vocal critics maintain that gender mainstreaming has failed because it is seldom implemented, or, when it is, women's interests, needs and priorities are subsumed into those of communities as a whole, which, in turn, neutralizes the transformative nature of the gender-mainstreaming agenda (e.g. Miller and Razavi, 1998; Porter and Sweetman, 2005). Finally, women and men are often treated as homogenous groups, and such a notion falls short of providing a more nuanced understanding of women's lives in particular. Accordingly, gender mainstreaming needs to be reconceptualized to account for elements of difference, such as age, class, race, ethnicity or sexual orientation and the intersections among them (e.g. Squires, 2005; Verloo, 2006; Whitzman, 2007), as will be discussed further with the concept of intersectionality. Policy and planning tools have also been developed to accommodate gender as well as other aspects of individuals' lives. These tools, including equality-impact assessments (EQIAs) and participatory budgeting, although not explicitly intersectional in approach, emerged from the broad critiques of gender mainstreaming. They are explored below as a demonstration of attempts to move beyond a binary gendered view of identity, before a more comprehensive examination of the potentials of an intersectionality approach is presented.

Multi-stranded tools

Equality-impact assessments

EQIAs have developed in recent years as a means of dealing with multiple aspects of people's lives. These tools are designed for use by public authorities to examine whether and how policies and projects can better address the promotion of equality between women and men and among different equality categories. EQIAs were developed in response to the need to tackle issues of discrimination across a range of groups of people currently protected by human rights and equality legislation, and are tools that work explicitly with a rights-based approach to difference. Internationally, Northern Ireland (NI) has been at the forefront of the use of EQIAs since 1998 (Reeves Associates, 2006, 2007), when they were enshrined in Section 75 of the Northern Ireland Act of 1998 following the Good Friday Agreement (Northern Ireland Act, 1998). In the case of NI, categories of equality included: gender, marital status, sexual orientation, age, disability, race, dependence, religion and political opinion. EQIAs were soon adopted by local- and state-level governments across the United Kingdom, and London boroughs such as Lewisham adopted a more integrative EQIA approach, rather than undertake separate race-, disability- and gender-impact assessments to match the separate pieces of equality legislation operating in the mainland United Kingdom (Lewisham Borough Council, 2007). Following devolution in Scotland and Wales, EQIAs also became a feature of public policy, including in the transport arena (Reeves, 2008).

The process of undertaking an EQIA of the Scottish local government Strathclyde Partnership for Transport's draft strategy for 2007 illustrates the stages involved where the likelihood of a policy addressing the needs of safety and security can be tested, and the policy can be adjusted accordingly. This process is illustrated in the summary of the EQIA schedule in the box below.

The EQIA process highlights a number of issues relating to safety and security that would otherwise not receive attention, including in a gender mainstreaming framework, and that have implications, not only for transport plans, but also urban design and spatial/urban planning. These include the need to re-site existing bus stops that no longer meet the needs of travellers because of redevelopment and to ensure that customer-feedback surveys and patronage data are disaggregated by equality categories. In this case,

---

Summary of the EQIA schedule

Title: Name of policy, programme or sub-strategy.

Aims: What are the main aims of the policy, programme or sub-strategy?

Proposed outcomes: What proposed outcomes does it hope to deliver?

Evidence of likely impacts: What are the potential impacts (both negative and positive) of the policy, programme or sub-strategy on each of the equality groups listed? How will they help promote equality and good relations?

Potential for promotion of equality and good relations: Are there any opportunities within the policy, programme or sub-strategy for promoting equality and good relations? When implementing the policy, programme or sub-strategy, are there ways in which the process could be used to promote equality?

Adjustments to policy/strategy/intervention: Does the policy, programme or sub-strategy need adjusting, and should these adjustments be consulted on?

Performance indicators and monitoring arrangements: How do you propose to monitor the impacts of the policy, programme or sub-strategy on equality groups? What performance indicators should be used to assess these impacts?

(Source: Reeves, 2008)

the transport agency did not follow through and carry out an EQIA of the transport-project budget. This would have highlighted whether and how the issue of safety had been addressed in the operational budgets. The approach of participatory budgeting goes a step further than an EQIA budget audit and involves the allocation of city funds to communities who then decide where and how they will be spent.

Participatory budgeting

Participatory budgeting allows citizens to play a role in determining local-government-resource allocations and priorities for capital projects and encourages a more transparent and accountable model of local-government spending. It provides the opportunity for those often marginalized, such as elderly women, children and poor communities, to have a more direct impact on the decision-making process and subsequent outcomes. Although budget allocation is not a task undertaken by planners, community decisions on spending priorities have a direct impact on the projects planners are responsible for. For example, citizens may choose more public housing over pavements. The results of these decisions then have a direct impact on the shape and form of the built environment and how it is experienced.

Participatory institutional mechanisms gained momentum at the time of the emergence of gender mainstreaming in the international arena, most notably in Brazil, in the city of Porto Alegre (de Sousa Santos, 2008). Born out of a long lineage of urban reform and urban popular social movements (Dagnino, 2003), what became known as the 'participatory budget' in the 1990s was an institutional innovation that sought to guarantee popular participation in identifying and defining investment priorities for the municipal budget and how resources would be allocated and distributed (de Sousa Santos, 2008, p. 310). It has since been adopted in towns and cities across Latin America and Europe, and in projects in Africa (Rusimbi et al., 2000).

Cornwall and Coelho (2007, p. 11) have critiqued participatory budgeting as 'invited spaces' and 'spaces of power, in which forms of tacit domination silence certain actors or keep them from entertaining at all'. As decentralized civic and participatory spaces, they still require an in-depth gender analysis into whether women have the acknowledged agency and opportunity to participate in the meetings, and whether their diverse and specific needs are being met. In recognition of such shortcomings, Coordenadoria da Mulher (Women's Coordination Group of Brazil) introduced three initiatives in 2002 aimed at increasing women's participation in budgeting meetings at a local level to ensure that their issues were heard. First, mobile play areas were taken to meeting locations and installed. These allowed women with childcare responsibilities to bring children and attend the meetings. Second, information about the participatory budgeting process was distributed in areas where meetings were to take place, in order to encourage women to participate. Third, meetings between government officials and women's groups were held to discuss how to encourage women to participate. One of the outcomes of this initiative was the creation of a thematic forum on women, specifically looking at issues for women in communities (Oxfam, 2005).

We need to consider how inclusive and receptive to women's diverse experiences and needs these policy spaces are, and to consider the extent to which mainstreaming and participatory strategies and tools compel policymakers and practitioners to deconstruct normative assumptions of women's experiences. Rather than seeking to understand why cities and their public spaces are unsafe for particular women, liberal gender approaches, such as gender mainstreaming and women's safety audits, assume that it is women's relation with space that contributes to insecurity. These approaches, while providing the means for integrating gender into policy and practice, may not recognize women's diverse and changing needs, or the oppressions and privileging of women. The limits of such frameworks can be analysed when looking at broader issues of identity, power, equality and inclusivity. EQIAs and participatory budgeting can be seen as representing intermediate steps towards intersectionality. Although both take a multi-stranded approach, they are still in danger, however, of constituting a dualistic perspective of individuals, that is, women–men, young–older, disabled–able bodied, and so on. Intersectionality has the potential to address these disadvantages.

Intersectionality as a more inclusive approach

Intersectionality offers a framework for considering gender as part of a complex and dynamic series of social divisions, identities and structures that shape individuals' singular and collective experiences (Lacey, 2012). It is a framework that offers a means of transcending the potential unidimensionality of much gender analysis. Although gender mainstreaming takes a singular and binary unit of analysis that is gender, intersectionality deliberately and explicitly works with complex, multilayered and intersecting points of analysis. Intersectionality allows for recognition of simultaneous difference, identity, power, disadvantage and privilege, not only individually, but also for relative, collective social experiences and interactions. Some of these points of difference, identity, power, disadvantage and privilege focus on ethnicity, race, class, gender, sexuality, faith and religion, age and ability. Furthermore, gender itself is not seen in an intersectionality framework as a binary category, rather it is seen as more fluid and open, a feature that is particularly pertinent if we are to work with gender as socially constituted (Lacey, 2012). In tracing the origins and dynamics of intersectionality scholarship, the potential for, and benefits of, intersectionality as a framework and method of analysis for planning for safe cities for women will be explored in the following section.

In an attempt to locate and work with simplicity, it would be easy to see intersectionality as a framework that invokes a simple addition of aspects of identity, be they class, gender, sexuality, race, ethnicity or age. The danger is that such an approach leads to the reifying of the limited binary-bound understandings of these categories of analysis. Instead, intersectionality can offer a means of situating these points of analysis as lived experiences (Lacey, 2012). For example, rather than gathering disaggregated data according to various social, legal and identity categories of women, Anthias and Yuval-Davis (1983, 1992), Brah (1996), Maynard (1994) and Yuval-Davis (2006) call for recognition of intersecting and interlocking social divisions. These social divisions are 'about macro axes of social power' and have 'organizational, intersubjective, experiential and representational forms' (Yuval-Davis, 2006, p. 198). Intersectionality allows for the recognition and working through of cumulative and different intersubjective experiences of power (Lacey, 2012). It is a clear break from generalizations and assumptions about, for example, gendered impacts.

Intersectionality as a methodological and/or analytical framework has a rich genealogy, combining activist and academic roots, as well as feminist, anti-racist and social-justice derivations (see, for example, Combahee River Collective, 1977; Davis, 1981; Lorde, 1984; Crenshaw, 1989; Collins, 1990). A common momentum, regardless of emphasis or point of origin, is a desire to work with diversity and difference. The words of Sojourner Truth, a newly free black woman in the mid-nineteenth-century United States, capture this desire and also a prominent goal of intersectionality – to move beyond the dominance of one understanding of who it is to be a woman and who it is to call for social justice.

In genealogies of intersectionality, Sojourner Truth's words and the spirit they capture are sometimes overlooked in favour of more recent formulations and applications:

> I think that 'twixt the negroes of the South and the women at the North, all talking about rights, the white men will be in a fix pretty soon. But what's all this here talking about?
>
> That man over there says that women need to be helped into carriages, and lifted over ditches, and to have the best place everywhere. Nobody ever helps me into carriages, or over mud-puddles, or gives me any best place! And ain't I a woman? Look at me! Look at my arm! I have ploughed and planted, and gathered into barns, and no man could head me! And ain't I a woman? I could work as much and eat as much as a man – when I could get it – and bear the lash as well! And ain't I a woman? I have borne thirteen children, and seen most all sold off to slavery, and when I cried out with my mother's grief, none but Jesus heard me! And ain't I a woman?
>
> (1851, in Brah and Phoenix, 2004, p. 77)

What is worth establishing with a revisiting of this speech, made at the Women's Convention in Akron, Ohio, United States, is the explicit reference to overlapping and multiple points of difference and oppression and therefore possible ways of moving beyond disadvantage and hierarchies. Her words and determination provided a powerful inspiration for many generations of activists and academics, who have sought to struggle against one or many interlocking oppressions (hooks, 1981), and have been echoed or expressed anew by many others. In 1904, for example, Mary Church Terrell, the first president of the National Association of Colored Women, wrote, 'Not only are colored women ... handicapped on account of their sex, but they are almost everywhere baffled and mocked because of their race. Not only because they are women, but because they are colored women' (King, 1988, p. 42). Again, we hear a call for recognition that it is not one aspect of people's lives, be it gender or race, that determines experiences and social structures, but multiple layers of identities and experiences. Because of the nature of the overlapping and/or intersecting identities and experiences, which may shift depending on contexts, they may not be captured using simple matrices and disaggregated data. Rather, intersectionality can act as a means to ask questions and probe policymakers, activists and programme personnel to go further than static or potentially unidimensional matrices. It is a rich framework precisely because of its complexity.

The purpose here is to convey, albeit briefly, the rich background of this concept (for a more detailed history, see Brah and Phoenix, 2004). The idea of attempting to look beyond one category of analysis when trying to understand, work with and overcome oppression and/or privilege is clearly not new, nor is explicitly working with our own subjectivities. Intersectionality can offer a way to work with multiplicities of experiences and identities in cities and communally inhabited spaces, spaces that are defined by their own complexity. Cities are simultaneously sites of privilege and oppression, and, as demonstrated below, an intersectionality approach can be used to understand these dynamics. It is a framework, however, rather than an explicit set of policy prescriptions, and relies heavily on inclusive and participatory modes of consultation and delivery in order for it to translate to social-justice policies and programmes.

Intersectionality is a conceptual rather than an assessment tool; however, it can help us move beyond the problems created by looking at identities from a binary perspective. As a term, it was introduced by Kimberlé Crenshaw in 1989 in a piece published by the University of Chicago Legal Forum, in which Crenshaw contrasts the dominant, single-axis analysis of black women's experiences, which she argues is dominant in anti-discrimination law and anti-racist and feminist scholarship and politics, with the multidimensionality of their experiences (Crenshaw, 1989). Crenshaw calls for theories and strategies that incorporate both black communities' experiences and, simultaneously, women's experiences, while explicitly working with sexism and patriarchy, racism and privilege.

The calls made by Crenshaw in the late 1980s for an embracing of the intersection (1989), echoing those made perhaps less explicitly by feminists and anti-racists for many years prior to that, were taken up by fellow academics, activists and policymakers with considerable zeal. Nira Yuval-Davis (2006) succinctly traces the employment of intersectional frameworks and methodologies, both prior to and after Crenshaw's coining of the term, and in doing so is able to offer insights into the potential for intersectionality to simply further exacerbate analysis that does not take account of complexity. It would be easy to look to the work of Crenshaw, for example, and deduce that there are only two – albeit important – categories of analysis: gender and race. Concurrent and preceding intersectional critiques did, however, take into account multiplicities and did so in an explicit attempt to develop theories and methods that challenged dominant and narrow understandings of feminism, and what some referred to as imperial feminism (Anthias and Yuval-Davis, 1992, p. 101).

A black, lesbian, feminist collective, the Combahee River Collective, in Boston, US, released a ground-breaking statement in 1977 that grew from this group's recognition that what they were struggling against was 'racial, sexual, heterosexual and class oppression', and the group committed itself to the 'development of integrated analysis and practice based upon the fact that the major systems of oppression are interlocking' (Combahee River Collective, 1977). The collective's statement, influenced by other black feminists calling for recognition of multiple structures of oppression and privilege, was a radical charge at the time against a singular focus on race, sexuality or gender, and the collective argued that white feminists were fixated with gender alone. It was also one of the first explicit developments of analysis that facilitated recognition of simultaneous and multidimensional oppressions (Combahee River Collective, 1977; Davis, 1998). It is important, then, to recognize applications of an intersectional approach, even when the moniker is not used.

'Doing' intersectionality: intersectionality and safe cities

'Doing' intersectionality comes with particular theoretical and methodological challenges and commitments. In attempting to locate and analyse particularities, rather than so-called 'average' experiences that replicate dominant positioning, an intersectional method works with as many facets of social division as the subject divulges. Assumed categories of analysis may not in fact speak to people's experiences, and dialogical processes are key. An example comes from a workshop on gender and cities in Port Moresby, Papua New Guinea, where a Canadian tool (Simpson, 2009) was used to explain intersectionality to the group of civil-society members, government workers and academics working on women's safety in the city. The tool, developed in a Canadian context, refers to race rather than ethnicity, and it quickly became apparent that participants in Port Moresby, when asked to think about their unique life experiences and circumstances, did not see race as immediately applicable to their lives, whereas ethnicity – missing from the intersectionality wheel diagram – was central (Lacey *et al.*, 2011). This discursive exercise revealed further key insights into the benefits of an intersectionality framework and methodology, as it confirmed the importance of recognizing and working with different social divisions intermeshing in unique ways for individuals, in particular locations and contexts, depending on specific social, political and economic processes, and along with individuals' specific identities and political values (Yuval-Davis, 2006, p. 200). Intersectionality thus allows for analysis of particularities, even within a macro framework, in this case a diverse and fluid city.

An intersectionality approach, in contrast to gender mainstreaming, allows for context-specific programmes and policies to be developed that reflect the nature and multiple identities of women within particular urban spaces and at particular times. There has been, as Valentine (2007) concedes, a deficit within feminist geography of intersectionality; however, as Sandberg and Tollefsen (2010) demonstrate in the Swedish context, such an approach to complex spatial relations can deepen conversations and research on issues such as fear of violence in public space.

Rather than assuming that women are marginalized solely because of gender inequality and in relation to inequality with men, intersectionality broadens the lens to include how differences among women influence how women experience cities in particular ways and engage in public and participatory domains (Tankel, 2011), such as in the participatory examples previously discussed. In opposition to liberal mainstreaming approaches to gender, Wekerle (2000) suggested that adopting a notion of pluralistic citizenship would allow for an analysis of how women participate or are excluded in various areas of community life. This analysis is informed by the diverse identities women embody in the city. Intersectionality challenges mainstreamed and essentialized beliefs that cities are the same for men and women, and that women experience cities in a singular capacity. This in no way diminishes the way in which women are often marginalized; it recognizes the differences among women and the multiple identities that shape their experiences of city life. What some women identify as safe or unsafe, for example, will vary depending on their different experiences in the city and their degrees of mobility and autonomy relating to their socio-economic standing, age, physical ability, race or sexuality (Tankel, 2011).

MacDowell Santos's (2005) account of women's police stations in Brazil has become a policy and practice hallmark of approaching women's safety and supports the need to shift towards intersectional rather than gender-mainstreaming frameworks. Using the example of how police officers at women's police stations operate, she shows how the processes privilege the 'paradigmatic' complaints by women of domestic violence above women who have suffered from racial violence (MacDowell Santos, 2005).

Similarly, in developing a gender-analysis guideline for the South Australian and Western Australian state public sectors, Bacchi and Eveline (2009) demonstrate how the term 'gender' created a number of challenges and concerns for Aboriginal and Torres Strait Islander women relating to the privileging of gender as an analytical category. There was an implicit understanding that gender privileged male–female relations and was measured as a challenge to their 'social analysis of racialisation' (Bacchi and Eveline, 2009, p. 4). The case of South Australian Aboriginal and Torres Strait Islander women also shows how women's apprehensions were not solely predicated on 'gender' and/or addressing concerns of Aboriginal women, but on a desire to increase the status of the whole community (Bacchus and Eveline, 2009, p. 11). This situation is not dissimilar to the Canadian context, where Kirkness (1987–8) has employed the phrase 'discrimination within discrimination' to describe the process of prejudice towards indigenous women, not only shaped by gender, but through their marginalization maintained by racism and colonialism (Dhamoon, 2011, p. 232).

As suggested by Bacchi and Eveline (2009), both mainstreaming and diversity are contested concepts; however, through use of a diversity approach, contestation of identity categories and such complexities are in fact encouraged and embraced. Intersectionality encourages and demands us to develop such a diversity approach, utilizing complex and flexible context-specific frameworks, which allow us to ask appropriate questions about women's diverse experiences. Such an approach has long framed the work of women's and feminist organizations in cities throughout the world, through an unpacking of what safety for women in that particular city means, and how women's multiple positionings influence their relation to the city socially and spatially, and the extent to which they participate in decision-making and activism (Tankel, 2011).

Deep-rooted legacies of unequal power relations in cities contribute to determining whether people have the capacity and acknowledged agency to contribute in participatory forums, such as participatory budgeting meetings. By making such spaces gender inclusive, we cannot assume that other domains of power and inequality will not be silenced; it is problematic to imagine that the inclusion of women will provide a diverse range of women an avenue to participate in such decision-making processes. An intersectional approach would open space to question, for example, who is sitting at the table and who is excluded? Which women are there? And which women aren't? Beyond gender inclusivity, which women inform the policies and which women are these policies shaped for? This process of questioning would engage policymakers and practitioners to ask what spaces these methods of enquiry open for underrepresented people.

Bacchi and Eveline suggest that 'the decision to stop using the language of gender mainstreaming is a political one' (2009, p. 6). This decision can break through static confines and provide space and dialogue 'determined by common political emancipatory goals' (Yuval-Davis, 2006, p. 206). By embracing the complexity and shifting nature of identity, we can stimulate opportunities for great social change (McCall, 2005, p. 1777). Such an approach can furthermore encourage recognition of the agency individuals exercise in different spaces and the ways in which women are also empowered and may exercise resistance in multiple communities where they are positioned and with which they identify. Just as forms of violence and exclusion intersect on continuums, so do multiple axes of identity that render women vulnerable to diverse exclusionary practices, as well as providing the means to contest them (Tankel, 2011).

Conclusion

The chapter has demonstrated some of the contribution gender mainstreaming has made to ensure that women are on the agenda of policies relating to building safer cities and more inclusive cities. Further, it has explored the challenges and shortcomings in implementing what was originally designed as a transformative framework, but can be criticized for exacerbating existing binary conceptions and implementations of gender. Participatory budgeting and equality audits have made important contributions to inclusive dialogical processes and policy and programme outcomes in efforts to foster safe and inclusive public spaces and cities. EQIAs can represent an intermediate step towards intersectionality, as EQIAs take a multi-stranded approach to individuals and their needs. However, as a tool, EQIAs are in danger of constituting a dualistic perspective, that is, women–men, young–older, disabled–able bodied, and so on. The idea of working with multiplicity is central to intersectionality, which emerged from a desire to recognize the intersections between gender, race, ethnicity, class, ability, age and sexuality, and how these lived experiences and identities shape oppression as well as privilege. As a conceptual tool, intersectionality offers an approach that addresses the weaknesses of gender mainstreaming; it seeks explicitly to engage in complex understandings, rather than binary categories, of social, political and economic lives and experiences and responds to this complexity. Coming from a grass-roots social-justice tradition, the more inclusive approach of intersectionality has the potential to become accepted by all stakeholders to plan for and generate safe and inclusive public spaces and cities.

Notes

1 See www.graz.at/; also see http://unpan3.un.org/unps/Public_NominationProfile. aspx?id=492
2 See the Women in Cities International (2010) report entitled *Together for Women's Safety. Creating Safer Communities for Marginalized Women and Everyone*, for examples of how partnerships between community-based organizations, municipal governments and other key stakeholders can improve the safety of women and girls in cities.

References

Anthias, F. and Yuval-Davis, N. (1983). Contextualizing Feminism: Gender, Ethnic and Class Divisions. *Feminist Review*, 15, 62–75.
Anthias, F. and Yuval-Davis, N. (1992). *Racialized Boundaries: Race, Nation, Gender, Colour and Class and the Anti-Racist Struggle*. London: Routledge.
Bacchi, C. and Eveline, J. (2009). Gender Mainstreaming or Diversity Mainstreaming? The Politics of 'Doing'. *Nordic Journal of Feminist and Gender Research*, 17(1), 2–17.
Brah, A. (1996). *Cartographies of Diaspora*. London: Routledge.
Brah, A. and Phoenix, A. (2004). Ain't I A Woman? Revisiting Intersectionality. *Journal of International Women's Studies* 5(3), 75–86.
Budlender, D. and Sharp, R. with Allen, K. (1998). *How to Do a Gender-Sensitive Budget Analysis: Contemporary Research and Practice*. Canberra: Australian Agency for International Development and London: Commonwealth Secretariat.
City of Graz (n.d.). Gender Mainstreaming Happens in a Town! Retrieved 11 July 2011 from: http://unpan3.un.org/unps/Public_NominationProfile.aspx?id=492
Collins, P.H. (1990). *Black Feminist Thought: Knowledge, Consciousness, and the Politics of Empowerment*. New York: Routledge, Chapman and Hall.
Combahee River Collective (1977). *The Combahee River Collective Statement*. Retrieved 30 March 2011 from: http://historyisaweapon.com/defcon1/combriver coll.html
Cornwall, A. and Coelho, V.S.P. (2007). Spaces for Change? The Politics of Participation in New Democratic Arenas. In A. Cornwall and V.S.P. Coelho (eds), *Spaces for Change? The Politics of Participation in New Democratic Arenas* (1–29). London: Zed Books.
Crenshaw, K. (1989). Demarginalizing the Intersection of Race and Sex: A Black Feminist Critique of Antidiscrimination Doctrine, Feminist Theory and Antiracist Politics. *University of Chicago Legal Forum*, 138–67.
Dagnino, E. (2003). Citizenship in Latin America: An Introduction. *Latin American Perspectives*, 30(2), 211–25.
Davis, A.Y. (1981). *Women, Race and Class*. New York: Random House.
Davis, A.Y. (1998). Reflections on Race, Class and Gender in the USA. In A.Y. Davis and J. James (eds), *The Angela Y Davis Reader* (307–28). Malden, MA: Blackwell.
de Sousa Santos, B. (2008). Participatory Budgeting in Porto Alegre: Toward: a Redistributive Democracy. In B. de Sousa Santos (ed.), *Democratizing Democracy: Beyond the Liberal Democratic Canon* (307–76). London and New York: Verso.

Dhamoon, R.K. (2011). Considerations of Mainstreaming Intersectionality. *Political Research Quarterly*, 64(1), 230–43.
hooks, b. (1981). *Ain't I A Woman?: Black Women and Feminism*. Boston: South End Press.
King, D.J. (1988). Multiple Jeopardy, Multiple Consciousness: The Context of a Black Feminist Ideology. *Signs*, 14(1), 42–72.
Kirkness, V. (1987–8). Emerging Native Women. *Canadian Journal of Women and Law*, 2, 408–15.
Lacey, A. (2005). Spaces of Justice: The Social Divine of Global Anti-capital Activists' Sites of Resistance. *Canadian Review of Sociology and Anthropology*, 42(4), 403–20.
Lacey, A. (2012, under review). Biopolitical Governmentalities of Women's Lives: Security, Development and Population in Solomon Islands.
Lacey, A., Reeves, D., Tankel, Y. and Underhill-Sem, Y. (2011). *Gender Policy and Research in Cities: Report of Workshop Held at the National Research Institute, Port Moresby, Papua New Guinea, 7–8 February 2011*. Retrieved 6 May 2011 from: www.arts.auckland.ac.nz/webdav/site/arts/shared/Departments/development-studies/documents/Gender%20Policy%20and%20Research%20in%20Cities%20Workshop%20Report%20PNG%202011.pdf
Lewisham Borough Council (2007). *People, Prosperity and Place, Lewisham's Regeneration Strategy 2007–2020: Equality Impact Assessment*. Retrieved 30 April 2012 from: www.lewisham.gov.uk/SiteCollectionDocuments/RegenStrategyFullEIA.pdf
Lorde, A. (1984). *Sister Outsider*. Trumansberg, NY: Crossing Press.
McCall, L. (2005). The Complexity of Intersectionality. *Signs*, 30(3), 1771–801.
MacDowell Santos, C. (2005). *Women's Police Stations: Gender, Violence, and Justice in São Paulo, Brazil*. New York: Palgrave Macmillan.
McGauran, A.-M. (2005). Plus ça change . . .? Gender Mainstreaming of the Irish National Development Plan, *Studies in Public Policy*, 15. Dublin: Policy Institute, Trinity College Dublin.
Mackie, M. (2002). Mainstreaming Gender Equality in the Local Planning Process: The Gender Audit of Plymouth City Council's Revised Local Plan: Creating Sustainable Urban Environments: Future Forms for City Living. Unpublished.
Mackie, M., Lloyd-Tomlins, S., Woodward, V. and Reeves, D. (2001). *The Plymouth Gender Audit: A Gender Audit of the Local Plan for Plymouth*. Plymouth City Council: Department of Planning.
Maynard, M. (1994). 'Race', Gender and the Concept of 'Difference' in Feminist Thought. In H. Afshar and M. Maynard (eds), *The Dynamics of 'Race' and Gender*. London: Taylor and Francis.
Meer, S. (2005). Freedom for Women: Mainstreaming Gender in South African Liberation Struggle and Beyond. In F. Porter and C. Sweetman (eds), *Mainstreaming Gender in Development: A Critical Review* (36–45). Oxford: Oxfam.
Miller, C. and Razavi, S. (eds) (1998). *Missionaries and Mandarins: Feminist Engagement With Development Institutions*. London: Intermediate Technology Publications in association with United Nations Institute for Social Development.
Moser, C. (2010). Safety, Gender Mainstreaming and Gender Based Programmes (Trans. G. Marman and P. Matta, with collaboration of R. Burgess and A. Cahoon). In A. Falu (ed.), *Women in the City on Violence and Rights* (77–95).

Retrieved 26 May 2011 from: www.redmujer.org.ar/pdf_publicaciones/art_40.pdf#page=159

Moser, F. and Moser, A. (2005). Gender Mainstreaming Since Beijing: A Review of Success and Limitations in International Institutions. In F. Porter and C. Sweetman (eds), *Mainstreaming Gender in Development: A Critical Review* (11–22). Oxford: Oxfam.

Northern Ireland Act (1998). London: The Stationery Office Ltd. Retrieved 26 May 2011 from: www.legislation.gov.uk/ukpga/1998/47/contents

Oxfam (2005). *Bringing Budgets Alive: Participatory Budgeting in Practice*. Oxford: Oxfam. Retrieved April 25 2011 from: www.participatorybudgeting.org.uk/documents/Bringing-20budgets-20alive.pdf.

Porter, F. and Sweetman, C. (eds) (2005). *Mainstreaming Gender in Development: A Critical Review*. Oxford: Oxfam.

Rao, A. and Kelleher, D. (2005). Is There Life After Gender Mainstreaming? In F. Porter and C. Sweetman (eds), *Mainstreaming Gender in Development: A Critical* Review (57–69). Oxford: Oxfam.

Rees, T. (2005). Reflections on the Uneven Development of Gender Mainstreaming in Europe. *International Feminist Journal of Politics*, 7(4), 555–74.

Reeves, D. (2002). Mainstreaming Gender Equity: An Examination of the Gender Sensitivity of Strategic Planning in Great Britain. *Town Planning Review*, 73(2), 197–214.

Reeves, D. (2005). *Planning For Diversity*. London: Routledge.

Reeves, D. (2008). *How Equality Impact Assessments Can Promote Equality*. Paper presented at ACSP/AESOP, Chicago.

Reeves, D. and Davies, W. (2007). *Good Practice Note 7 Gender and Spatial Planning*. London, Royal Town Planning Institute (RTPI). Retrieved 27 May 2011 from: www.rtpi.org.uk/download/3322/GPN7.pdf

Reeves Associates (2006). Independent Audit of Compliance Section 75 of the Northern Ireland Act 2007, for the Equality Commission in Northern Ireland. Retrieved 27 May 2011 from: www.equalityni.org/archive/pdf/AuditofCompliance 231107.pdf#search='Reeves Associates 2007 Independent Audit

Reeves Associates (2007). Assessing the Impact of Section 75 of the Northern Ireland Act on Individuals, Belfast, ECNI. Retrieved 27 May 2011 from: www.equalityni.org/archive/pdf/AssessingImpactsIndividuals.pdf

RTPI (2003). *Gender Toolkit*. London: RTPI. Retrieved 27 May 2011 from: www.rtpi.org.uk/download/765/Gender-Equality-and-Plan-Making-Mainstreaming-Toolkit.pdf

Rusimbi, M., Budlender, D., Shayo, R. and Pehrsson, S. (2000) *Checklist for Mainstreaming Gender into the Government Budget*. Prepared for the Ministry of Finance, Dar es Salaam.

Sandberg, L. and Tollefsen, A. (2010). Talking About Fear of Violence in Public Space: Female and Male Narratives About Threatening Situations in Umea, Sweden. *Social and Cultural Geography*, 11(1), 1–15.

Shaw, J. (2002). The European Union and Gender Mainstreaming: Constitutionally Embedded or Comprehensively Marginalised? *Feminist Legal Studies*, 10(3), 213–26.

Shaw, M. and Andrew, C. (2005). Engendering Crime Prevention: International Developments and the Canadian Experience. *Canadian Journal of Criminology and Criminal Justice*, 47(2), 293–316.

Simpson, J. (2009). *Everyone Belongs: A Toolkit for Applying Intersectionality*. Ottawa, ON: CRIAW/ICREF. Retrieved 12 October 2010 from: www.oaith.ca/assets/files/Publications/Intersectionality/EveryoneBelongs.pdf

Squires, J. (2005). Is Mainstreaming Transformative? Theorizing Mainstreaming in the Context of Diversity and Deliberation. *Social Politics*, 12(3), 366–88.

Status of Women Canada (1995). *Setting the State for the Next Century: The Federal Plan for Gender Equality*. Retrieved 5 March 2010 from: http://publications.gc.ca/collections/Collection/SW21-15-1995E.pdf

Tankel, Y. (2011) Reframing 'Safe Cities for Women': Feminist Articulations in Recife. *Development*, 54(3), 352–7.

Tiessen, R. (2007). *Everywhere/Nowhere: Gender Mainstreaming in Development Agencies*. Bloomfield, CT: Kumanrian Press.

UN-HABITAT (2008). *Gender Mainstreaming in Local Authorities: Best Practices*. Retrieved 30 May 2011 from: www.un.org/womenwatch/ianwge/member_publications/gender_mainstreaming_in_local_authorities.pdf

Valentine, G. (2007). Theorizing and Researching Intersectionality: A Challenge for Feminist Geography. *Professional Geographer*, 59(1), 10–21.

Verloo, M. (2006). Multiple Inequalities, Intersectionality and the European Union, *European Journal of Women's Studies* 13(3), 211–28.

Walby, S. (2005). Gender Mainstreaming: Productive Tensions in Theory and Practice. *Social Politics* 12(3), 321–43.

Wekerle, G.R. (2000). Women's Right to the City: Gendered Spaces of a Pluralistic Citizenship. In E.F. Iisn (ed.), *Citizenship and the Global City* (203–17). London and New York: Routledge.

Whitzman, C. (2007). *The Handbook of Community Safety, Gender and Violence Prevention: Practical Planning Tools*. London: Earthscan.

Whitzman, C., Shaw, M., Andrew, C. and Travers, K. (2009). The Effectiveness of Women's Safety Audits. *Security Journal*, 22(3), 205–18.

Women in Cities International (2010). *Together for Women's Safety. Creating Safer Communities for Marginalized Women and Everyone*. Montreal: Women in Cities International.

Women in Cities International and Jagori (2010). *Third International Conference on Women's Safety: Building Inclusive Cities*. November. Retrieved 24 May 2011 from: www.womenincities.org/pdf-general/Final%20Conference%20Background.pdf

Women's Design Service (2005). Brunswick Estate, Women's Community Safety Audit. Retrieved 27 May 2011 from: www.wds.org.uk/www/download%20documents/MSP/Brunswick_Estate_Interim_Report_final_090205.pdf

Woodward, A. (2008). Too Late for Gender Mainstreaming? Taking Stock in Brussels. *Journal of European Social Policy*, 18(3), 289–302.

World Health Organisation (2002). *WHO Gender Policy: Integrating Gender Perspectives into the Work of the WHO*. Retrieved 30 May 2011 from: www.emro.who.int/somalia/pdf/WHO%20Gender%20policy.pdf

Yuval-Davis, N. (2006). Intersectionality and Feminist Politics. *European Journal of Women's Studies*, 13(3), 193–209.

Chapter 10

Safer discursive space

Artistic interventions and online action research

Melanie Lambrick

A great deal of the actions and theory associated with the safe cities for women movement focus on women's equal right to the city and, in particular, public space. Yet definitions of what constitutes public space are often contested and vary based on the history, physical composition and socio-political context of any given space (see Davis, 1990; Lefebvre, 1991; Mitchell, 2003). Also of particular note and with reference to the safe cities for women movement, the line between public and private space can at times be blurred or non-existent (see Haskell and Randall, 1998; Koskela, 1999; Viswanath and Mehrotra, 2007; Whitzman, 2007).

Consequently, it is very difficult to define a space as entirely public at any point in time. Instead, it appears that many public spaces could be considered discursive, that is, fluid and expansive (sometimes public, sometimes private, sometimes semi-public), depending on the positions, strategies and relationships of users. When the publicness of a space is considered to be discursive rather than static, the potential for expanding access to the city can also be considered discursively. Thus, it is important to examine how public space is constituted, both in terms of its subjectivity in relation to the safe cities for women movement and in terms of its potential for the advancement of the objectives of the safe cities for women movement.

This chapter examines two approaches in which space is discursively constituted as public within the safe cities for women movement: through artistic intervention and through online action research. In the first approach, artistic intervention is used to draw attention to the level of public access in city spaces, while inviting women and other passers-by to engage with the topic of women's safety and the composition of public space itself. In the second approach, the virtual space of the Internet is utilized for public debate and information-/experience-sharing around the topic of women's safety and inclusion in city life, with strong references to physical public spaces in several cities across the globe. By constituting the Internet as an international forum for people to engage directly with one another and with the safe cities for women movement, it is argued that the virtual realm provides important opportunities to expand women's and girls' active use of public space writ large. In both of these approaches, it is important to note that the publicness of certain spaces is challenged and reframed through women's and girls' creative reconstitution of traditional or expected parameters of experiencing the city. Often, this creative reconstitution involves confrontation with problematic 'private' attitudes, behaviours and beliefs within a setting that is accessed by a wide range of urban citizens on a day-to-day basis.

To illustrate these ideas in depth throughout the chapter, the chapter draws on Leonie Sandercock's concept of narrative as the act of meaning-making in everyday life:

> In order to imagine the ultimately unrepresentable spaces, lives, and languages of the city, to make them legible, we translate them into narratives. The way we narrate the city becomes constitutive of urban reality, affecting the choices we make and the ways we then might act.
> (2010, p. 18)

In particular, this chapter draws upon Sandercock's assertion that the act of producing narratives can generate opportunities for reconciliation and reformulation of power relations (Sandercock, 2010, p. 21). The chapter argues that actors within the safe cities for women movement use artistic intervention and online action research to engage with the nature of public space and women's role within it. They are effectively using narrative to heal past exclusionary practices within the urban environment, while at the same time opening up new opportunities for the generation of safe and inclusive city space.

Artistic intervention and safer discursive space: 'Tek it to dem an rise up wi community', 'Berri-UQAM: *Accessibilité universelle*' and '*Mujeres por la Cuidad*'

Traditional approaches to the creation and distribution of public art have been problematic in many cities. This is because art, as with space itself, cannot be divorced from the sociopolitical context in which it is generated. Public art is created to add a particular symbolic meaning to a given space. It is created with reference (and possibly resistance) to prevailing cultural norms – the intended message and import of a piece of art cannot be communicated unless viewers/participants understand its symbolic references. The meaning of a piece of public art, therefore, is not only generated by the piece itself but by the public or semi-public space in which it is situated.

Within city spaces that are commonly considered public or semi-public, it is rare that art, especially large-scale or fixed pieces of art, are created or installed without approval from urban decision-makers such as city councils, arts councils, neighbourhood associations, urban planners or architects. Thus, when we encounter public art in cities, we are often encountering a message about the space we are in that is carefully selected by those in traditional positions of power. This means that most times, the message we receive from a piece of public art is linked to the values and beliefs of those who manage and control urban spaces, and, what is more, the message we receive is usually coded in a symbolic language that requires a certain level of cultural literacy to understand (Miles, 1997, p. 16; Rendell, 2000, p. 23). By this very process, it is likely that the values and beliefs of urban citizens who are not usually represented in traditional positions of decision-making power will also not be represented by a great deal of their city's public art (Hall and Robertson, 2001, p. 19). Thus, public art, as part of the public culture of a city, has the power to include or exclude people, both through the symbolic language that is chosen to convey its message and through the message that itself is meant to be conveyed (Zukin, 2005, p. 137; Adamek and Lorenz, 2008, p. 57). Women, as a group who have been historically excluded from many traditional forms of urban decision-making power, are therefore less likely to find their experiences accurately represented in public art (Miles, 1997, p. 32).

Although public art cannot be viewed as a neutral part of the urban environment, it can be viewed as an opportunity to engage viewers/participants in debate over contentious topics related to the specific sociopolitical context in which the piece of art is situated. The opportunity for the creation of this kind of art often comes from outside the realm of official urban decision-making; alternative art, by its very nature, is not likely to be supported by the mainstream adjudication processes mentioned above. Rather, this kind of art, often termed 'guerilla art',[1] is created or installed without official sanction and, for this reason, tends to be smaller in scale and more ephemeral than traditional public art.

When thinking about alternative interpretations of public space through art, one should also consider the power that viewers/participants have to destabilize the meaning of a particular space or piece through their own individual interpretation of what they encounter:

> While historical meanings are encoded in urban form, perception is also the active process of decoding and employing these meanings in practice. A person's experience of the city triggers memory, but it does not compel them to relate to it in a specific fashion. People's incidental engagements with urban artifacts mean that memory and meaning (and hence, social conventions) are themselves also encountered in a state of distraction, and it becomes possible to recognize, question and dislocate these conventions.
>
> (Stevens, 2007, p. 15)

The artistic interventions presented in this chapter represent forms of 'alternative' public art. Each intervention uses art in public space to draw attention to what is usually ignored or overlooked by most everyday users of the space. The primary topics addressed by these interventions (women's safety and pervasive forms of gender-based violence and exclusion) are not topics that are normally explicitly referred to in the physical make-up of the public spaces in which the interventions occur, nor are they necessarily referred to within the common symbolic meaning attached to the spaces. None of the artistic interventions is very large scale or permanent, and all are created by women acting outside traditional realms of urban decision-making power. In each of these artistic interventions, the nature of public space is contested and reframed through a lens that challenges assumptions about the nature of gender relations in the city and, in particular, in the city's public spaces.

'Tek it to dem an rise up wi community' – Sistren Theatre Collective, Kingston, Jamaica

Sistren Theatre Collective was established in Kingston, Jamaica, in 1977. The collective's mission is to 'provide consistent popular theatre that will reflect socio-economic issues as they relate to gender roles in an entertaining and educational atmosphere that influences society to change' (Sistren Theatre Collective, n.d.(a)). In 2008, Sistren Theatre Collective initiated the three-year project 'Tek it to dem an rise up wi community'.[2] The project was developed in response to baseline research indicating that, in two inner-city communities in Kingston, Hannah Town and Rockfort, high levels of violence (notably shootings, murders and violence against women) are having a community-wide impact (Tafari-ma, n.d., p. 22). The goals of 'Tek it to dem an rise up wi community' are to: provide women and girls with the tools to empower themselves and their communities to take action to prevent violence against females; target an intergenerational sample of female survivors/victims and young men in the 15–25 age group who are at risk of becoming both perpetrators and victims; and to tackle the issue of physical abuse and psychosocial ill health in women and girls who have been exposed to multifaceted violence as part of their daily existence (Sistren Theatre Collective, n.d.(b)). In order to reach these goals, Sistren Theatre Collective is using a three-part outreach strategy in both Hannah Town and Rockfort: behaviour-change communication; psychosocial healing; and collective creations[3] (Sistren Theatre Collective, n.d.(b)).

The Sistren Theatre Collective's third strategy, collective creations, is an example of an artistic intervention in public space in which actors create a community narrative that challenges norms about gender-based violence. Collective creations are often manifested as street-theatre performances, with actors performing disturbing scenes of community and/or domestic violence. In a recent video of such a performance posted on the Sistren Theatre Collective website, viewers can watch a scene in which a young girl is forced to choose between fulfilling her family duty, by going to the store to purchase food for supper, and her fear of the store owner, an older man who eventually sexually assaults her. In the following scene, a younger male, presumably a member of the girl's family, confronts the store owner and instigates further violence as retribution for the sexual assault. This kind of theatre does not provide easy entertainment. Rather, it directly confronts the audience with the painful experiences that women and men undergo as they relate to each other within a scripted set of sociocultural standards about gender and the normalcy of violence. Borrowing from the work of Dunstan and Sarkissian (1994), Sandercock notes that narratives such as this are an essential part of the collective reinvention process that occurs when historically disenfranchised people are allowed to create their own vision of the city and its social landscape:

> Some tragic core stories need to be transformed by an explicitly healing process or else the core story will be enacted again and again. Renewal and redemption are possible ... New 'chapters' can be written if there is the collective will to do so. The first is a public telling of the story in a way that accepts its truth and acknowledges its power and pain.
> (2010, p. 23)

What is particularly interesting is that collective creations bring this kind of confrontational messaging into the streets and into public space. The audience is implicated in the action without choice – they simply encounter a performance and must at once decide to engage or disengage with what is happening. What is more, by addressing the continuum of violence between the public and private spheres and between gender roles and expectations, 'Tek it to dem an rise up wi community' draws out subject matter that is typically hidden beneath layers of normative discourse and humiliation/pain – effectively airing the community's dirty laundry for all to see. In so doing, project actors renegotiate the boundaries between public and private space, while, at the same time, emphasizing the typical lack of publicness attached to discourse around violence and gender.

'Berri-UQAM: Accessibilité universelle' (Berri-UQAM: Universal Accessibility) – Conscience Urbaine, Audiotopie and Action des Femmes Handicappées (Montréal)

The 'Berri-UQAM: Accessibilité universelle' (Berri-UQAM: Universal Accessibilty) project was a collaborative artistic intervention that occurred in 2010 in Montreal, Canada. It was realized by three local organizations: Conscience Urbaine, Audiotopie and Action des Femmes Handicappées (Montréal) (AFHM).[4] 'Berri-UQAM: Accessibilité universelle' featured an audio-guided tour and photographic exhibition in the central downtown area of Montreal, around the Berri-UQAM metro station. The purpose of the project was to develop a greater consciousness among the urban population of the accessibility and safety issues faced by women with disabilities in public spaces.

Audio-tour participants were invited to download an audio commentary from the Audiotopie website on to a personal portable listening device. The commentary featured the stories of nine women living with disabilities in Montreal, told in their own words. Participants were then invited to listen to the commentary while following a guided tour around the Berri-UQAM area. On the tour, several large-scale photographs of the women featured in the commentary were displayed in public spaces – on lampposts, street signs and the like. These photographs visually situated the women and their experiences within the immediate physical environment, to be recognized by both passers-by and audio-tour participants.

In her essay 'Whose Culture, Whose City?', Sharon Zukin points out that, in an increasingly fragmented and transitory world, the creation of images within the urban environment has potentially greater power than in the past:

> The cultural power to create an image, to frame a vision, of the city has become more important as publics have become more mobile and diverse, and traditional institutions – both social classes and political parties – have become less relevant mechanisms of expressing identity. Those who create images stamp a collective identity.
>
> (2005, pp. 137–8)

Certainly, the act of displaying photographs of women with disabilities in prominent public places in the city (places more usually reserved for commercial advertising or for official municipal signage) represents a definitive stamping of another, often overlooked identity upon the urban landscape. The inclusion of the audio commentary represents a further reclaiming of the sensory urban landscape, with the voices of the featured women usurping the common Montreal public soundscape. What is notable here is that, while the 'Berri-UQAM: Accessibilité universelle' intervention may appeal to a mobile and diverse urban population, the issue at hand is one of lack of mobility and lack of diversity (in terms of possible experiences) due to inaccessible and potentially unsafe public spaces. Thus, when these women's experiences of public space were marked upon the physical city itself, participants and viewers were asked to consider how their own identity and their own bodies do or do not relate to the vision that is presented before them. At the same time, by both visually and aurally manifesting representations of women with disabilities in the public spaces of downtown Montreal, the personal and creative expressions of those women were elevated to a public status normally reserved for those with more traditional forms of power. Fanie St-Michel, founder and director of Conscience Urbaine, observes that the effectiveness of such artistic interventions is twofold:

Art provides opportunities to touch other communities outside of those groups who already work to end violence, and it allows us to broaden our level of impact to sensitize more people. Also, importantly, art provides opportunities to creatively express what women need.

(Personal communication, 4 May 2011, translation provided by author)

'Mujeres por la Ciudad' (Women in the City) – Latin American Women and Habitat Network and Agency Go

The Latin American Women and Habitat Network (RMH) was founded in 1989 and is comprised of both women's organizations and individual women committed to promoting women's rights and to greater gender equity in the area of human settlements (CISCSA, n.d.). The 'Mujeres por la Cuidad' (Women in the City) project developed from RMH's 'Ciudades sin Violencia hacia las Mujeres, Ciudades Seguras para Tod@s' (Regional Programme for Safe Cities without Violence against Women, Safe Cities for All), which has been operating in six Latin American countries since 2006.[5] 'Mujeres por la Ciudad' began with a competition organized by RMH in which the organization solicited advertising agencies to submit proposals for innovative campaigns encouraging the community to engage with the issue of gender equality in the city. Agency Go, based in Uruguay, won the bid and has been working with RMH on the 'Mujeres por la Ciudad' project in nine cities since 2010.[6]

In each participating city, the 'Mujeres por la Ciudad' project has been developed in three stages. In the project's first stage, large, white statues of women figures were installed in well-used public spaces. Local governments and community organizations worked together in each city to determine the exact location for the installation. The figures were not accompanied by any signs indicating their intended use or purpose. They were simply left so that the public could interact with them, while the process of this interaction was recorded. In most cases, the women figures were modified and/or mistreated, with graffiti and various negative phrases and insults being inscribed on their surfaces (see Figure 10.1). While some figures were damaged or even destroyed, other figures were decorated with positive messages about gender and community. In the project's second stage, signage was installed with the figures, revealing the motivation behind 'Mujeres por la Ciudad'. The signage also encouraged viewers/participants to join in a public event meant to 'win back women'; the event included a number of interventions by local artists, community women and women's organizations. In the final stage of the project, the women figures were recovered and celebrated by the community through ceremonies in which local artists redecorated the figurines using positive symbolism – a process that represents the restoration of integrity to every woman (see Figure 10.2). Following the recovery process, the figures

Safer discursive space 169

were re-installed more permanently in important public spaces, such as cultural centres and district centres. This re-installation of the recovered figures symbolizes the city's commitment to the safe and equal inclusion of women in public city life.

Soledad Quadri, a member of CISCSA/RMH, emphasizes the fact that the 'Mujeres por la Ciudad' project extends beyond traditional awareness-raising

Figure 10.1 Defaced woman figure in Rosario, Argentina
Source: 'Mujeres por la cuidad' Campaign, Latin American Women and Habitat Network

Figure 10.2 Several recovered women figures in Rosario, Argentina
Source: 'Mujeres por la cuidad' Campaign, Latin American Women and Habitat Network

or community education to actively repossess urban space for visioning and for publicly debating the status of women:

> The project hit the streets, reclaimed the streets as a space for encounter, dialogue, consensus and above all participation, not only by women but by society as a whole. The project challenged people to create safe public spaces for everyone in a way that is not passive, but active – we need people to be aware of how they see and experience and use the spaces they travel daily.
> (Personal communication, 10 May 2011, translation provided by author)

Returning to Sandercock's discussion of narrative, one can view the 'Mujeres por la Ciudad' project as particularly remarkable because of the freedom it provided to the public to generate its own story about women in public space. The interactions between the public and the women figures were not prescribed in any way, although they were invited by the presence of the clean, white surfaces of the figures. This kind of invitation and opening up of dialogue can be contrasted to many traditional forms of public art, which are not necessarily designed and installed in a way that encourages interaction and possibly defacement. This subversion of both the experience of public art and of public representations of women (in which normally hidden acts of gender-based violence were revealed quite plainly) was accompanied by opportunities for engagement and reaction. As was the case with the 'Tek it to dem and rise up wi community' intervention, the initial narrative generated by 'Mujeres por la Ciudad' was not necessarily positive, but rather was illuminating, implicating the public as co-producers of both negative and positive experiences of city space.

This direct implication of urban citizens as co-producers of public space and the public body expands both concepts beyond the realm of the physical into the realm of values and beliefs. What is more, by illustrating the level of gender-based violence that exists in public space, 'Mujeres por la Ciudad' draws attention to the fact that women are not able to experience the city without experiencing violence or the threat of violence. Finally, by allowing for a recovery process, the intervention once again provides the public with agency – this time in redrawing the boundaries of public space through inclusive actions and positive ceremony.

Online Action Research and Safer Discursive Space: *The Stop Street Harassment* and *Hollaback!* websites and *Blank Noise*

We now live in a global context where access to the Internet is increasingly considered a fundamental right rather than a privilege. The interpretation of the Internet as a fundamental right indicates that it can be considered a worldwide public good, to be accessed equally by all. For the purposes of this chapter, then, the Internet will be considered a primarily public entity. At the same time, the Internet functions as a kind of space in the sense that it is a constitutive element of cyberspace, which is defined by the Merriam-Webster dictionary as 'the online world of computer networks and especially the Internet'. Therefore, by these criteria, the Internet will be treated here as a potential type of public space. This chapter cannot attempt to address the many and varied arguments that analyse the Internet's quality or level of publicness or spatiality. Rather, it will focus on how the safe cities for women movement engages with the Internet as a potential public space through online action research, which is related and refers to various other public spaces in the physical world. In this way, it is hoped that links can be drawn between the creative online tactics employed by actors within the safe cities for women movement and the generation of discursive understandings of public space and its relation to gender.

Even within the limited and simple definition of the Internet as public space used here, it is important to remember that, as with other types of public space, the Internet does have limits in terms of access. Moreover, the line between what constitutes public and private in the virtual world (in terms of both use and content) is extremely difficult to define. Harrison and Barthel point out that the invention of Web 2.0[7] has enabled more dynamic and participative interactions between Internet users (2009, p. 157). They also point out that:

> Web 2.0 applications demonstrate that, regardless of their levels of technical expertise, users can wield technologies in more active ways than had been apparent previously to traditional media producers and technology innovators ... This burgeoning phenomenon suggests that users are gratified in significant ways by the ability to play an active role in generating content, rather than only passively consuming that which is created for them by others.
>
> (Harrison and Barthel, 2009, p. 157)

The new opportunities afforded by Web 2.0 indicate greater access for Internet users in terms of defining and authoring (in effect, engineering) the public spaces of the Internet. At the same time, the authors note that, for many Internet users, the tools used to engineer these spaces are still largely controlled by software developers, who design popular applications such as Flickr or YouTube (Harrison and Barthel, 2009, p. 162). Of course, it is also important to remember that physical access and ability to use the Internet are also limited throughout the world, with an estimated 71 per cent of the population having access in developed countries, and 21 per cent of the population having access in developing countries (UN News Centre, 2010).

When considering the possibilities that the Internet affords for activism and action research associated with the safe cities for women movement, and particularly the three examples given here, it should be noted that there are also limits to the extent individual actors can use the Internet to influence women's safety and inclusion in physical public spaces. That is, although the Internet provides a place for users to come together, discuss and create interventions that address women's safety and inclusion in cities, the Internet does not appear to provide a public space which, on its own, allows users to create new narratives of public space that easily apply to multiple, geographically specific communities of varying sociopolitical, cultural and historical make-up. Rather, in the examples referred to here, the Internet offers opportunities for users to develop shared understandings of women's safety and inclusion in cities, as well as of the nature and parameters of public space. These shared understandings are then diffused through a series of context-specific actions and investigations within various physical (as opposed to virtual) locales. Thus, although it appears possible to develop a common narrative among Internet users, the translation of that narrative to the people and spaces within specific cities may require the coordinated support of activities performed in the 'real world'.

Finally, it should be noted that, although the Internet is presented here as a potentially fertile ground for women's empowerment, activism and attainment of rights, it is also a space where misogynist sentiments and actions (including harassment, stalking and hate speech) are regularly enacted and publicly supported. Jessica Valenti, co-founder and editor of the popular online community for feminists, feministing.com, has commented that:

> While no one could deny that men experience abuse online, the sheer vitriol directed at women has become impossible to ignore ... It's all very far from the utopian ideals that greeted the dawn of the web – the idea of it as a new, egalitarian public space, where men and women from all races, and of all sexualities, could mix without prejudice.
>
> (Valenti, 2007)

Although this chapter does not specifically address misogyny on the Internet, it does acknowledge its existence. Just as the case studies above illustrate the potential transformative power of action taken within public spaces that are not always safe or inclusive for women, the case studies below seek to illustrate how online action can reconfigure potentially hostile online space in an empowering and gender-sensitive way.

The Stop Street Harassment and Hollaback! websites

This section will refer to two online action research projects – the *Stop Street Harassment* website and the *Hollaback!* websites. Both of these projects use the Internet and, in particular, a blog format to create an ongoing dialogue about sexual harassment. Both projects invite women and LGBTQ individuals to publicly post narratives about their experiences of sexual harassment on the Internet, and, once stories are posted, both the *Stop Street Harassment* website and *Hollaback!* websites provide the opportunity for other users to respond to narratives with their own ideas, strategies and experiences. For example, on 20 May 2011, the story of an anonymous woman from Detroit, USA, was published on the *Stop Street Harassment* blog:

> I was walking down the street and a man driving passed, slowed down and started yelling, 'Hey Sexy, Hey Sexy hey sexy, come here let me talk to you.' I showed no interest and started walking faster. He then sped up and drove around the corner and came back around and yelled out the window, 'Bitch!'.
>
> (*Stop Street Harassment*, 2011)

Despite similarities, the *Stop Street Harassment* and the *Hollaback!* websites have different histories and overall strategic approaches. The *Stop Street Harassment* website was founded in 2008 by Holly Kearl. It evolved out of her 2007 Master's thesis research on women's use of the Internet as a tool for responding to street harassment. At the time, Kearl noted that some of the websites used for this purpose were disappearing, and she decided to create a new online space to fill the void. The *Stop Street Harassment* website offers users a variety of resources and opportunities to share through its blog component, resources and advice sections, and 'Ideas for Action' section. In addition, a 'Male Allies' section has recently been added to the site, which provides information on educating men and boys, 'how to talk to women' and bystander tips. In 2010, Kearl published the *Stop Street Harassment* book, based on the information and experiences of *Stop Street Harassment* website users.

The *Hollaback!* websites were founded by a group of young women and men in New York City who were inspired by an incident in 2005 when a woman, Thao Nguyen, published a photo on the Internet of a man masturbating in front of her on a subway train. The *Hollaback!* approach is framed in activist rhetoric as 'a movement dedicated to ending street harassment using mobile technology' (*Hollaback!*, n.d.). The first *Hollaback!* website focused specifically on sharing and opening up for debate experiences of street harassment in New York City. However, the movement has grown, and currently *Hollaback!* websites now exist for over thirty-eight cities/ regions/countries worldwide. Each *Hollaback!* website is managed by a local team, with support from the entire *Hollaback!* community. The diversity of identities represented by local team leaders (44 per cent LGBTQ, 26 per cent people of colour, 76 per cent under the age of 30 internationally) speaks to the cross-cutting appeal of the *Hollaback!* approach. The foundation of each *Hollaback!* website is a home page that features user-submitted narratives about experiences of street harassment. The websites also offer information about resources, upcoming events related to the movement, and opportunities for further involvement/activism. Moreover, many local teams organize or participate in events and actions within their cities, communities and neighbourhoods in order to raise awareness and mobilize community members around the issue of street harassment.

Holly Kearl notes that, although websites such as *Stop Street Harassment* and *Hollaback!* are located in online public space, the focus of action is still mainly in the offline realm (personal communication, 20 April 2011). She points out that having online space for discussion, information and strategizing can be extremely valuable for this kind of action research and activism in terms of users' time commitment, opportunities for international networking and anonymity:

> A huge advantage to the online space is that people can participate when they have time and they can participate from anywhere in the world ... Also, these are sensitive topics and so I think sometimes people may feel more willing and able to share stories online than they might face-to-face since they know it can be anonymous and they don't have to look at anyone while they share.
> (Personal communication, 20 April 2011)

Emily May, one of the co-founders and current Executive Director of *Hollaback!*, echoes this sentiment, pointing out that virtual space provides an entirely new medium when it comes to creating collective narratives:

> With the Internet as our new campfire, women and men around the world are standing up, standing together, and telling their stories. Together we are transforming street harassment from something that was isolating, to something that's sharable ... Working in virtual space gives us access to new ways to tell our stories, and new audiences as well.
> (Personal communication, 27 April 2011)

It is particularly interesting to note that, as a new form of public space, the Internet has the potential to remove some of the barriers to participation that women and other marginalized individuals may experience in offline public space, as Shir Ben-Or, Director of *Hollaback! Israel* points out:

> I think the World Wide Web has a lot of advantages for women. Interactions with others can be safer than the AFK (away from keyboard) world. And when you have these terms, you can start thinking

differently. You can start asking other questions. Why do I have more freedom online? Why do I feel more safe online? I always felt that online I can be myself. Without wasting energy on appearance, I could just speak and find my place. My words stay online, and I choose places where I can edit, change or remove them completely. It gives me freedom of action physical, 'real world' spaces cannot give.

(Personal communication, 3 May 2011)

In this sense, the *Stop Street Harassment* and *Hollaback!* websites use the Internet to provide the opportunity for users to reframe negative experiences of public space in a way in which they are active and empowered participants, capable of certain kinds of agency, authorship and even creative licence:

People say that history is written by the victor – generally, rich and powerful men. But with crowd sourcing technology like that which *Hollaback!* uses, every woman has the chance to speak out and write history. The site also gives women who have been harassed something to do rather than just be silent about it. As a result, women who have experienced street harassment aren't just victims anymore; *Hollaback!* allows us to re-imagine these 'victims' as agents who provide on-the-ground, relevant information, that we will use to urge legislators to take concrete action to make the streets safer for all women.

(Aisha Zakira, *Hollaback! Mumbai* founder, personal communication, 24 April 2011)

At the same time, there are certainly limitations to working in virtual space. For instance, Lauren Alston, Director of *Hollaback! Alberta*, points out that the Internet, as an open and publicly accessible space, has the potential to open up channels for negative messaging from anonymous users (personal communication, 24 April 2011). Thus, incoming comments require careful moderation. Also, online forums such as blogs do not necessarily allow for the level of engagement needed to fully to dissect the complex issues of street harassment:

It's not always possible to have a good conversation around these issues. Sometimes there will be good discussions in the comments section of posts but often there is not. I think this is why it is good to also have offline groups at the same time – that is what I'm doing when I work in collaboration with *Hollaback! DC* in my community, the Washington, DC area.

(Holly Kearl, personal communication, 20 April 2011)

Like Holly Kearl, Emily May also emphasizes that online action must be accompanied by offline action for greatest impact:

The Internet is a powerful tool, and can inspire a global movement, but real change must have an on-the-ground component as well. Our site leaders hold events, film screenings, meet with legislators, perform safety audits, and participate in public art projects, bringing the movement to end street harassment alive in their communities.

(Personal communication, 27 April 2011)

The complementary nature of on- and offline action in the cases of the *Hollaback!* and *Stop Street Harassment* websites provides insight into how online action research in the safe cities for women movement functions to broaden and reconstitute the possibilities for engagement and activism in public space. In particular, it appears that the extension of action into the virtual realm surmounts some common barriers to participation and action in physical spaces. Simultaneously, the act of connecting online action with community events and networks situates the work more strongly in geographically based, rather than identity-based, communities.

Blank Noise

Blank Noise was founded in 2003 in Bangalore by Jasmeen Patheja. It began as a student project, with a series of nine workshops on the subject of sexual harassment (*Blank Noise*, 2005). Today, *Blank Noise* exists as an online hub with multiple awareness-raising and action campaigns, sexual harassment and feminist resources, and a blog. In addition, there is a strong offline component to *Blank Noise*, with local chapters organizing street interventions in nine different Indian cities.[8] One example of a *Blank Noise* campaign that exists on- and offline is the 'I Never Asked for It' campaign. As part of this campaign, *Blank Noise* website users are invited to mail in articles of clothing that they were wearing when they experienced sexual harassment. *Blank Noise* organizers also hold clothing drives to collect items from women and girls personally. The aim is to collect 1,000 articles of clothing with which *Blank Noise* will create an installation, to be displayed in public spaces in India's major cities. At the same time, articles of clothing received by *Blank Noise* are photographed and displayed on the website, accompanied by the message 'I never asked for it'. The *Blank Noise* website urges visitors/participants to 'discard the clothes worn at the time you were sexually harassed on the streets. This collective building of an installation of clothes seeks, primarily, to erase the assumption that you "asked for it" because of what you were wearing' (*Blank Noise*, 2001).

Another example of a *Blank Noise* campaign that exists on- and offline is the 'Blank Noise This Place' campaign. In this campaign, women and girls are invited to photograph places where they have been sexually harassed or have feared sexual harassment. Photographs are then displayed on an online gallery, often accompanied by text describing the experience. For example, a photograph posted on 15 September 2009, entitled *Action Hero Tani. Calcutta. Lake Gardens*, depicts a dark, narrow sidewalk between a wall and two parked trucks. Text that is superimposed on the photograph reads, 'mama always told us not to walk here . . . she thought someone would pull us into his truck. Nothing ever happened though . . . but we always walked on the road instead' (*Blank Noise*, 2009).

Blank Noise also conducts campaigns that are entirely offline, such as the 'Y R U Looking at Me' campaign. This campaign is comprised of a series of interventions where volunteers (termed action heroes by *Blank Noise*) wear T-shirts bearing letters on the chest that, when combined, create the phrase 'Y R U Looking at Me' (see Figure 10.3). The action heroes gather at busy intersections and assemble themselves so that drivers can read the message when they are stopped at a traffic light. When the light turns green, the action heroes separate and disappear into the crowd. Other action heroes stay close at hand to distribute information about sexual harassment to passers-by. According to *Blank Noise*, this campaign is designed to challenge the traditionally all-powerful male public gaze: 'Often when challenged by a frank and fearless female gaze, onlookers tend to look away or feel embarrassed; thus the ubiquitous male gaze is countered and an interest is generated which allows for dialogue to open up' (*Blank Noise*, 2001).

In a series of ten posts entitled 'Beyond the Digital', blogger Maesy Angelina from the HIVOS-CIS Digital Natives Knowledge Programme provides an analysis of the *Blank Noise* approach. Angelina noted that:

> *Blank Noise* recognizes that the issue is not as straightforward as it may seem. While some actions like groping are clearly a form of harassment, other forms such as looking or verbal taunting are not as obvious. Therefore, rather than offering a rigid guideline to what is or is not street sexual harassment, *Blank Noise* attempts to build a definition of 'eve teasing' through public polls, both online on its blog and on the streets. *Blank Noise* does not advocate for any specific, tangible solution either. It is not proposing for a new legislation or service provision. Many youth experts would say that it is a sign of youth's decreasing trust to the state, but actually this is an extension of *Blank Noise*'s acknowledgement of the ambiguity of street sexual harassment.
>
> (2010, paragraphs 7–8)

As with the other interventions and projects mentioned in this chapter, it appears that the primary focus of *Blank Noise*'s work is not necessarily to reformulate public space as safe and inclusive using a prescriptive approach. Instead, *Blank Noise* encourages users/viewers/participants to develop a stronger experiential relationship with public space, both through the explicit recognition of the traditional discourses that make up the space, as well as through the recognition of possibilities for alternative discourses that can be

Figure 10.3 Y R U LOOKING AT ME, *Blank Noise* action heroes
Source: © Jasmeen Patheja

Figure 10.4 'Mohini. Age 19. A stranger rubbed himself against me', *Blank Noise* action heroes
Source: © Jasmeen Patheja

developed on- and offline. To accompany this encouragement, *Blank Noise* offers users/viewers/participants a series of options for generating alternative discourses, each of which requires a different level of exposure or engagement. The provision of such options, accompanied by resources and discussion forums, showcases the way in which action and research can be combined to illuminate the various narratives that influence our experience and perception of gender and public space. Furthermore, this approach draws attention to the myriad of possibilities (both in terms of interventions and publics) that actors have to demonstrate, record and analyse their own understandings of gendered-city life and fear.

Final notes on creating and maintaining safer discursive spaces for women and girls

A key component of safe cities for women work is its focus on how public space is experienced, both physically and socially. Cities that are safer and more inclusive for women and girls must be created in response to the specific needs of women and girls, in all of their diversity. Answering this call requires a sensitive and flexible understanding of what public space is and can be to urban citizens; it requires a discursive approach. Such an approach, it is argued here, has been achieved within the safe cities for women movement by researchers, artists and activists working in a variety of different contexts and media, including street theatre, photography, installation work, blogging and performance art. In each of the case studies presented, public space has been constituted (or perhaps reconstituted) as fluid, expansive and open to interpretation. Furthermore, in each case study, the actors involved have engaged other public-space users in the generation of urban environments that are more representative and responsive in some way to the experiences of women and girls.

A great deal of this work has been done through the public recognition and articulation of the fears, violence and exclusion that women and girls experience in a normally 'private' way. This recognition and articulation fulfils a dual purpose: it creates experiences of public spaces that physically, emotionally and symbolically reflect realities that were previously excluded, and it creates an awareness of, and responsibility towards, the attainment of women's human rights among the urban citizenry. In a sense, this work breaks space open and allows the ideas, stories and histories that are inherent in any location to be understood by its users. Physical locales become experiential realms, where different ways of being in the world can be supported or challenged.

There can be no prescription for creating safer discursive spaces because, by its definition, discursive space cannot be delineated or defined – it is constantly changing and open to interpretation. However, an understanding of space as malleable and responsive to user experience can aid actors working within the safe cities for women movement in their approaches to community engagement and change-making. When space is understood as discursive, and when our work engages with this characteristic of space, we recognize both the individual and collective realities of the women around us. Our strategies must be as varied as the experiences that we seek to represent, and our tactics, to be successful, must find innovative and engaging ways to weave our narratives into the fabric of our cities, our neighbourhoods and our common lives.

Notes

1 In her book *The Guerilla Art Kit*, Keri Smith defines guerilla art as not necessarily outside the law, but rather, as a form of personalized engagement with the urban environment:

> I would like to expand the concept and define guerilla art as any anonymous work (including but not limited to graffiti, signage, performance, additions, and decoration) installed, performed or attached in public spaces, with the distinct purpose of affecting the world in a creative or thought-provoking way.
>
> (2007, p. 11)

2 The Sistren Theatre Collective project 'Tek it to dem an rise up wi community' is funded by the United Nations Trust Fund in Support of Actions to Eliminate Violence against Women.

3   Collective creations are 'a process of community cultural communications which blend education, life skills building, community organizing/mobilization, group processes and the arts' (Sistren Theatre Collective, n.d.(b)).
4   Conscience Urbaine is an arts- and culture-based organization that connects fine arts, social sciences and landscape architecture in order to develop a greater understanding of public space (Conscience Urbaine, n.d.). Audiotopie is an artist cooperative that develops experiential tools for urban projects, blending new media, landscape architecture and electro-acoustic music (Audiotopie, n.d.). AFHM is a feminist non-profit association that defends and promotes the rights, interests and personal goals of women living with disabilities (Action des Femmes Handicapées (Montréal), n.d.). The 'Berri-UQAM: Accessibilité universelle' project was funded by the Canada Council for the Arts.
5   The 'Mujeres por la Cuidad' project was developed with the support of UN Women and the Spanish Agency for International Development Cooperation.
6   Rosario, Argentina; Lima, Peru; San Salvador, El Salvador; Talca, Chile; Guatemala City, Guatemala; Bogotá and Medellin, Colombia; Mexico City, Mexico; and Tegucigalpa, Honduras.
7   Tim O'Reilly defines 'Web 2.0', a term that he coined, by the following characteristics: use of the web as a platform (as opposed to a self-contained entity); harnesses collective intelligence; features Internet applications that use specialized databases; features software that is delivered as a service rather than a product; uses simple/lightweight programming models; can be used on multiple devices (in addition to personal computers); provides rich user experiences (O'Reilly, 2005).
8   Calcutta, Mumbai, Bangalore, Hyderabad, New Delhi, Chennai, Lucknow, Chandigarh and Jaipur.

References

Action des Femmes Handicappées (Montréal) (n.d.) 'Mission and Objectives', www.afh-montreal.org/afhm/qui-sommes-nous/, accessed 26 April 2012.
Adamek, M. and Lorenz, K. (2008) '"Be a Crossroads" Public Art Practice and the Cultural Hybrid', in C. Cartiere and S. Willis (eds), *The Practice of Public Art*, New York, Routledge, pp. 56–65.
Angelina, M. (2010) 'Beyond the Digital: First Things First', 10 December, http://blog.blanknoise.org/2010/12/beyond-digital-first-things-first.html, accessed 13 April 2011.
Audiotopie (n.d.) 'Profil', http://audiotopie.org/profil, accessed 20 May 2011.
Blank Noise (2001) 'Interventions and Techniques', http://blog.blanknoise.org/2007/09/interventions-and-techniques.html, accessed 19 April 2011.
Blank Noise (2005) 'Frequently Asked Questions!', http://blog.blanknoise.org/2005/03/frequently-asked-questions.html, accessed 19 April 2011.
Blank Noise (2009) 'BLANK NOISE SITE IDENTIFIED's photostream', www.flickr.com/photos/blanknoisethisplace, accessed 20 May 2011.
CISCSA (n.d.) 'The Latin America Women and Habitat Network', www.redmujer.org.ar/eng/home.html, accessed 21 May 2011.
Conscience Urbaine (n.d.) 'Conscience Urbaine', www.facebook.com/conscienceurbaine.mtl?sk=info, accessed 20 May 2011.
Davis, M. (1990) *City of Quartz: Excavating the Future in Los Angeles*, London, Verso.

Dunstan, G. and Sarkissian, W. (1994) 'Goonawarra: Core Story as Methodology in Interpreting a Community Study' in W. Sarkissian and K. Walsh (eds), *Community Participation in Practice. Case Book*, Perth, WA, Institute of Sustainability Policy.

Hall, T. and Robertson, I. (2001) 'Public Art and Urban Regeneration: Advocacy, Claims and Critical Debates', *Landscape Research*, vol. 26, no. 1, pp. 5–26.

Harrison, T.M. and Barthel, B. (2009) 'Wielding New Media in Web 2.0: Exploring the History of Engagement with the Collaborative Construction of Media Products', *New Media and Society*, vol. 11, no. 1–2, pp. 155–78.

Haskell, L. and Randall, M. (1998) 'The Politics of Women's Safety: Sexual Violence, Women's Fear and the Public/Private Split [The Women's Safety Project]', *Resources for Feminist Research*, vol. 26.3, no. 4, pp. 113–49.

Hollaback! (n.d.) 'About', www.ihollaback.org/about/, accessed 22 May 2011.

Koskela, H. (1999) '"Gendered Exclusions": Women's Fear of Violence and Changing Relations to Space', *Geografiska Annaler. Series B, Human Geography*, vol. 81, no. 2, pp. 111–24.

Lefebvre, H. (1991) *The Production of Space*, D. Nicholson-Smith (trans.), Oxford, Blackwell Publishing.

Miles, M. (1997) *Art, Space and the City: Public Art and Urban Futures*, London, Routledge.

Mitchell, D. (2003) *The Right to the City: Social Justice and the Fight for Public Space*, New York, Guilford Press.

O'Reilly, T. (2005) 'What is Web 2.0', 30 September, http://oreilly.com/pub/a/web2/archive/what-is-web-20.html?page=1, accessed 22 September 2011.

Rendell, J. (2000) 'Public Art: Between Public and Private', in S. Bennet and J. Butler (eds), *Locality, Regeneration and Divers[c]ities*, Bristol, intellect, pp. 19–26.

Sandercock, L. (2010) 'From the Campfire to the Computer: An Epistemology of Multiplicity and the Story Turn in Planning', in L. Sandercock and G. Attili (eds), *Beyond the Flatlands: Multimedia Explorations in Urban Policy and Planning*, Vancouver, Springer, pp. 17–38.

Sistren Theatre Collective (n.d.(a)) 'About Sistren', http://sistrentheatrecollectiveja.org/about.htm, accessed 19 May 2011.

Sistren Theatre Collective (n.d.(b)) 'Tek it to dem an rise up wi community', www.sistrentheatrecollective.com/tek-it-to-dem-and-rise-up-wi-community/, accessed 19 May 2011 but no longer available.

Smith, K. (2007) *The Guerilla Art Kit*, New York, Princeton Architectural Press.

Stevens, Q. (2007) *The Ludic City: Exploring the Potential of Public Spaces*, London, Routledge.

Stop Street Harassment (2011) '"Sexy" One Minute, "Bitch" the Next', 20 May, www.stopstreetharassment.org/2011/05/sexy-one-minute-bitch-the-next/, accessed 22 May 2011.

Tafari-ma, I. (n.d.) *Tek it to dem an rise up wi community Baseline Report*, Kingston, Sistren Theatre Collective.

UN News Centre (2010) 'Number of Internet Users to Surpass 2 Billion by End of Year, UN Agency Reports', 19 October, www.un.org/apps/news/story.asp?NewsID=36492&Cr=internet&Cr1, accessed 21 May 2011.

Valenti, J. (2007) 'How the Web Became a Sexists' Paradise', *The Guardian*, 6 April, www.guardian.co.uk/world/2007/apr/06/gender.blogging, accessed 22 September 2011.

Viswanath, K. and Mehrotra, S.T. (2007) ' "Shall We Go Out?" Women's Safety in Public Spaces in Delhi', *Economic and Political Weekly*, vol. 42, no. 17, pp. 1542–8.

Whitzman, C. (2007) 'Stuck at the Front Door: Gender, Fear of Crime and the Challenge of Creating Safer Space', *Environment and Planning*, vol. 39, pp. 2715–32.

Zukin, S. (2005) 'Whose Culture? Whose City?', in R.T. Legates and F. Stout (eds), *The City Reader*, Third Edition, London, Routledge, pp. 136–46.

Chapter 11

How do we evaluate the safety of women?

Margaret Shaw[1]

> I understand the preoccupation of the organization [UNIFEM] to measure impact. I understand this perfectly. But at the same time, impact is not something easy to measure. There are many aspects [*caras*] of impact. It's not immediately visible. And results-based management includes planning also. And results-based management has very rigid limits, and requires us to work with these matrices that are an inferno in our life. They're like hell for us![2]

This quotation from a recent study by Lynne Phillips and Sally Cole (2009) of how feminism is shaping women's activism and movements in Latin America is taken from an interview with a staff member in a UNIFEM office in the region.[3] The authors of the study suggest that there are two main ways and places in which feminism has been, in their words, 'translated' in Latin America: through what they term 'the UN orbit' and through 'another world'. The first refers to the whole range of feminists (who used to be referred to as femocrats) working in UN agencies, or national state machineries, whose work is guided by international conventions. The authors see them as feminist activists working in institutionalized settings. The second group refers to those service providers, activists and advocates working in social movements at all levels, including locally.

Phillips and Cole provide an explicit account of the pressures being applied to staff in UN agencies in the region since the mid 2000s 'to demonstrate concrete results in order to attract more funding' (p. 195).[4] This includes what they term the technologies governing those agencies: calls for proposals, monitoring and logical frameworks with measurable results to be established at the beginning of projects. As one interviewee put it, 'You have a monitoring system and, because of it, it's impossible for the project to *end* as a failure' (p. 197).

The opening quotation is one that many women's organizations can also relate to, as in recent years donors have increasingly constructed their grant programmes around tightly structured matrices of inputs and outputs, with the intended aim of ensuring accountability and demonstrating the impact of money spent. Concerns about the use of results-based monitoring and evaluation approaches have been quite widespread for some years within the development field, especially among women's organizations, as the following quotation suggests: 'Social change organizations and activists are spending substantial amounts of time and energy filling in sophisticated LogFrames and compiling various kinds of data that are thought to effectively track change' (Batliwala and Pittman, 2010, p. 3).

In a very succinct resumé of the problems of donor-required monitoring and evaluation frameworks for capturing women's realities and change in the development field, Srilatha Batliwala and Alexandra Pittman (2010) have argued that the assumptions underlying these 'cause and effect' or theory of change approaches are not realistic and do not lead to understanding, learning from errors or adapting projects accordingly. The authors also acknowledge that many organizations do not possess 'a strong culture of assessment', which makes it difficult for them to meet the expectations of complex monitoring frames and project development.

However, it is a natural, logical and practical human expectation that we can learn from experience and improve the ways we respond to problems on the ground, and to want to expand approaches that work so that other people can also benefit. To do this, we usually look for evidence – information based on observations and tested in some way against a theory of how we expect things might work. This is no different for policy-makers and governments, and so evaluating projects and programmes is not an irrelevant and unnecessary process for organizations to undertake, but it is difficult.

This chapter looks at some of these issues in relation to the evaluation of policy and change in general and its political nature; at the wide range of schools of thought on how to evaluate; and conceptual and theoretical developments more specifically in relation to the field of women's safety and gender-based violence. It looks at them from the point of view of the 'competing' interests of policymakers (and donors), researchers, practitioners, including non-government organizations (NGOs), and individuals and communities on the ground (the beneficiaries of change projects). It concludes with a brief discussion of two current examples of evaluation strategies used in global programmes to promote the safety of women – GICP and SCGP.

Evaluation is a political (and difficult) process

> The idea of evidence for policy making has never had a firmer footing. A universal acceptance seems to suggest that policy needs to be smart, and the way to make it smart is to build it on a foundation of evidence.
> (Clear, 2010)

Evaluation comes with its own language and lexicon, which are never static and are always being modified and expanded. In his 2009 Presidential Address to the American Society of Criminology, Todd Clear acknowledged the centrality of evaluation in current mainstream policy-making. Evidence-based or knowledge-based policy and practice have become common phrases that are now used globally.

He also demonstrated that criticisms and concerns about the ability of results-based monitoring and evaluation to capture realities or innovation on the ground are not restricted to feminist analysis or to the field of development: they are common to many areas of social change, intervention and theory.[5] As Batliwala and Pittman note, they have also been voiced recently in relation to the limitations of measures of gross domestic product for evaluating change in national economies.[6]

Evaluation in policy development works at different levels. For governments, there is often a need to evaluate an overall programme, as well as to examine the effects at the individual and local level. Some projects may prove to be more effective than others, but the government (or donors) will want to know whether, on balance, there is more evidence that projects were effective than ineffective, and whether the approach should be replicated and, if successful, expanded (scaled up) to other areas, or discontinued.

It is clear that, for governments, policy evaluation is always a political process. Governments need to be able to show that their policies are having an effect on problems; that they are taking the right decisions and spending public money wisely. In order to do so, strong scientific 'proof' is seen as valuable. It has been argued that governments have increasingly sought to evaluate the impact of crime-prevention policies for two main reasons: the scientific case and the political case (providing accountability, a 'blueprint' for what to do next, and validation that this is desirable policy) (Hope, 2008). The need to have 'quick wins' (short-term evaluations that can demonstrate that things are on the right track) and for the evaluation needs *themselves* to shape the setting of priorities in project development are some of the less desirable consequences of this political and scientific context.

In the field of crime prevention and community safety, which provides part of the underpinning for work on women's safety, there has often been resistance to the imposing of evaluation requirements. Practitioners, whether they are police officers or youth workers, have tended not to see monitoring and evaluation as an important aspect of their work and do not necessarily have the time or the requisite skills to undertake it. It has tended to be added on to projects and has often been underfunded and underestimated. And yet, as Todd Clear notes in the quotation above, many governments are now strongly wedded to the idea that evidence from research is necessary for policy development. The widespread belief held by many academic researchers that 'we know what works' has been successfully communicated to policymakers. However, it has led to a failure to pay attention to the ways in which projects work and the qualities and basic necessities for good implementation. In other words, there has been less attention to 'how' projects work.

This has been well demonstrated in one of the biggest government-initiated crime-prevention programmes in the world, the £250 million Crime Reduction Programme (CRP), which was implemented in England and Wales from 1999 to 2002 (Homel *et al.*, 2004; Shaw, 2009). The CRP was seen as a knowledge-acquisition programme to ascertain what works through extensive investment in evaluation.[7] Based on some 25 years of accumulated research and evidence about reducing and preventing crime, it included significant funding for evaluation of both individual projects and the overall programme.[8] However, it illustrated many of the pitfalls of assuming that knowing 'what works' is all that is necessary, and it has been judged an example of major programme-implementation failure, as well as failing to find 'what worked'.

From scientific perfectionism to imperfect measures of human interactions

In addition to being a political process, evaluation is further complicated by the fact that there are many different and competing schools of thought and theory about how it should be accomplished. These schools disagree about the nature of evidence, how to create it and how to measure it. They range from those promoting scientific evaluation and randomized controlled trials, through approaches that aim to capture change in complex multiple interventions (Rosenbaum, 2002; Kelling, 2005), to those that argue that only qualitative methodologies, including participatory approaches, can truly capture the realities of change experienced on the ground. The latter includes the use of internal or self-evaluation, participatory and feminist evaluation processes that often place greater emphasis on the added value of qualitative measures than quantitative ones.

In crime prevention, the notion of a 'gold standard' for scientific evaluation has a long history and suggests that there is an ultimate method that scientifically proves beyond doubt that an action or intervention has resulted in a specific change. The use of randomized controlled trials, with before and after measures and control and experimental groups, represents the highest – the gold standard – level.[9] In the absence of fully randomized trials, quasi-experimental approaches represent the next level. However, in practice, it is much easier to demonstrate the effectiveness of a single intervention using randomized controlled trials, or, given time, an early childhood intervention programme, than a programme of community-based initiatives. Thus, scientifically measuring the impact of the introduction of street lighting on reducing crime, or following up changes in a specific cohort of children compared with a control group over twenty years, is (relatively) easy. On the other hand, measuring the impact of a comprehensive programme to reduce youth crime in a community, which may include opening youth clubs after school, improving public spaces and providing incentives for children to stay in school, or a public-education campaign to change attitudes, is far more complex.

Beyond these issues, mainstream scientific evaluation as it has developed has been largely gender blind, or at the most gender neutral. Pamela Davies (2008), for example, has shown how work on community safety has been largely gender blind in failing to take account of how risk is gendered in relation to victimization, offending and public/private spaces.

However, a further concern about the reliance on evidence-based policy is that it is inherently conservative and anti-innovation, as Todd Clear puts it:

> So we want to require evidence as a foundation for action, but we also acknowledge that a narrow construction of evidence – what has already been shown to work – can be too restrictive. [. . .] Evidence per se is inherently conservative as a standard. It imposes a discipline on action that, in the area of crime control, is decidedly unwelcome.
>
> (2010, pp. 7, 13)

Similarly, Phillips and Cole, in their analysis of the impact of UN results-based project management in Latin America, argue that it leaves many women's groups and 'non-experts' excluded and 'limits exploration of alternatives' (2009, p. 199).

The recent advent of 'developmental evaluation' and 'RealWorld evaluation' is an example of responses to these kinds of criticism and of the needs of organizations on the ground for more flexible ways of assessing change (Gamble, 2008; Patton, 2011; Bamberger et al., 2006).

Reviewing current developments in the evaluation of crime prevention and community safety internationally, the International Centre for the Prevention of Crime (ICPC) concluded, in 2010, that more flexible approaches are indeed now gaining some traction, including those that include participatory and context-related techniques (ICPC, p. 182):[10]

> The dominance of experimental methods akin to those used in the natural sciences has, to some extent, given way to a more flexible and plural understanding. Experimental approaches have been criticised for their inability to respond to the kinds of complex multi-sector and community-based programmes which are characteristic of contemporary prevention. They have tended to privilege evaluations of single interventions, ignoring the benefits and challenges of integrated community-based approaches, or those which attempt to change institutional cultures. The use of more flexible approaches, such as action and participatory research, the use of qualitative as well as quantitative data, and of a broader range of indicators of change beyond

crime or victimization alone is now more widespread. Thus the use of a range of evaluation methods, multiple sources of data and outcome measures and the engagement of stakeholders, all appear to be crucial to assessing the impact and effectiveness of prevention policies and informing future decision-making.

Evaluating gender violence, women's safety and other tails (or tales)

Thus, what used to be marginalized areas of work have begun to impact mainstream policy and programme evaluation. In 2002, it was noted that the international development field has shifted its focus, in three decades, from economic development to human-capital development, and then to empowerment and participatory development. It has also moved from talking about women to talking about gender (Bamberger and Podems, 2002). Many authors in recent years have reviewed, in some detail, the problems and evolution of thinking about evaluation in relation to gender issues, gender-based violence and women's safety.[11] Carolyn Whitzman has provided a detailed discussion of some of the problems of evaluating women's safety and some practical ways of building evaluation into local women's-safety planning (Whitzman, 2008).[12] The Geneva Declaration, in its review of future directions for work on violence against women, argues that contextual and participatory approaches to data collection and assessment need to be given much greater credence in the evaluation of initiatives (Milliken, 2011).

Concerns about gender violence, women's empowerment and the use of participatory and non-judgemental methods are central to this work, and a number of attempts have been made to capture realities better.

Some of the recent work on the use of gender budgeting and gender audits is discussed elsewhere in this book, but tools such as gender indicators have emerged to help set some benchmarks against which to measure progress in social change. Gender indicators have been one of the tools used to evaluate the UNIFEM regional programme in Latin America: 'Cities without Violence against Women: Safe Cities for All' (Falu, 2010). The Gender Equality Observatory, based in Santiago, Chile, and developed by the Economic Commission for Latin America and the Caribbean (ECLAC) and other international partners, has developed a series of indicators that have been applied to all countries in the region, together with a manual on using the observatory (ECLAC, 2010). There are a number of other guides to indicators that measure progress in work to reduce violence against women and on gender, although these too are not without their limitations (Bloom, 2008; Demetriades, 2007).

One of the most comprehensive practical guides to researching and evaluating violence against women, written by Mary Ellsberg and Lori Heise (2005), was published by the World Health Organization (WHO) in 2005. They demonstrate the use of WHO's public-health model for understanding and responding to violence against women and provide detailed guidance on the use of a variety of quantitative and qualitative approaches and tools, all of which can help to build the evidence base for guiding project development. They pay attention to ethical issues in terms of showing respect for all people involved in the research process, doing no harm and maximizing the benefits to participants; to capacity building and training of the research team; and to analysing the data and using the results. It is interesting to note that, in its extensive work on violence prevention, WHO describes its public-health-model approach as 'science driven'.

More recently, WHO has published a review of different types of evidence-based intervention to prevent intimate-partner and sexual violence against women (WHO, 2010; Shaw, 2010). It is based on research literature from high-income countries, primarily the United States, and interventions are categorized in terms of the strength of evidence of their effectiveness. This was largely because no published information on evidence-based practice was available from other regions of the world. There is, thus, some irony in the fact that the review, which covers many decades of research, found only *one* evidence-based practice that was judged to be effective in preventing intimate-partner violence (school-based curriculum programmes to prevent dating violence), and none that was judged to be effective in preventing sexual violence.

From a feminist perspective, Batliwala and Pittman (2010) acknowledge in their review that there have been some important gains made in recent years in understanding social change, and they discuss a number of the common problems found in 'required' evaluation frameworks (2010) including:

- the linearity of many tools, which they argue 'flatten' change processes into 'cause and effect' relationships;
- the political assumption of stable and equitable sociopolitical contexts that bear little relation to the realities of many post-conflict or low- and middle-income countries;
- the failure to track negative changes, reversals or backlash, which could in themselves provide valuable lessons;
- the use of false binaries and dichotomies such as qualitative/quantitative and 'success/failure', which are reductionist and create hierarchies;
- the disjuncture between change measures and (too-short) time frames that forces projects to produce 'results' in a three-year period; and yet short-term change and sustainable change are not necessarily achieved in the same ways.

Other problems they raise include donors' lack of understanding about work on women's empowerment, and the lack of 'genuine and on-going negotiation space' between some donors and NGOs on the monitoring and evaluation frameworks put in place.

In their search for approaches that reflect feminist concerns, they consider in detail the strengths and weaknesses of a number of tools and monitoring and evaluation frameworks (see box below). Not all of these are about evaluating the impact and outcomes of programmes. Some are concerned with programme planning; some with assessing the extent to which gender is integrated into an organization's practices; some with assessing advocacy or network strength, for example, but they do illustrate the flurry of activity that is attempting to improve and respond to gender-neutral and mainstream scientific-evaluation approaches.

Somewhat depressingly, Batliwala and Pittman conclude that, 'many current assessment methods are neither gendered nor feminist' (p. 16), and 'the ideal feminist monitoring and evaluation framework has yet to be created and ... no one among the wide repertoire of tools currently at our

---

Monitoring and evaluation frameworks reviewed by Batliwala and Pittman

Causal frameworks:

- logical-framework approach;
- results-based-management approaches;
- theory-of-change approach.

Contribution-focused frameworks:

- outcome mapping;
- participatory approaches.

Gender-analysis frameworks:

- the Harvard Analytical Framework or gender-roles framework;
- the Moser Gender Planning Framework;
- the Gender Analysis Matrix;
- the Women's Empowerment Framework;
- the social-relations approach;
- InterAction's Gender Audit.

Advocacy and network-analysis frameworks:

- measuring-advocacy strategies;
- assessing networks.

disposal can serve the assessment needs of every organization, intervention, and change process' (p. 19).

Perhaps the answer is that there can never be an ideal framework, as context, political, economic, cultural and environmental changes will always influence what is regarded as relevant or useful, and whose voices are heard. Social and economic transformation is by nature messy and unpredictable, and the best we can hope for is to work to provide imperfect measures of what has taken place, what the process was, and what might help to improve future interventions. And it is important that evaluation needs do not lead to the setting of priorities, and that we do not expect to live in a perfectly controlled universe.

The case of women's safety

Within the field of women's safety, there are a number of reasons why evaluation has been difficult to accomplish, as should by now be clear. Measuring change in gender-based violence has been described as one of four 'hard to measure' areas, along with poverty, empowerment and conflict (Esplen and Bell, 2007). Many projects have been developed by NGOs at the grass-roots level, often with very limited budgets and short timescales. There has been a lot of experimentation with methodologies, such as participatory women's safety audits. There have also been a lot of innovative action projects, as in the case of the non-profit organizations PUKAR in Mumbai[13] and Jagori in Delhi, India. A recent action research project on 'Women's Rights and Access to Water and Sanitation in Asian Cities' illustrates the range of data sources being used to assess outcomes and impact.[14] The project has focused on women's access to water and sanitation services in two resettlement communities in New Delhi, India, and has used a gender budget analysis, including rapid situational analysis, policy assessment and an analysis of budget adequacy, and a range of in-depth interviews, household questionnaires, focus-group discussions and participatory women's safety audits.

In some cases, there have been regional programmes that have enabled women's organizations to learn from each other's experiences as they develop action programmes on the ground around the safety of women. UNIFEM's regional programme on 'Cities without Violence against Women, Safe Cities for All' in Latin America and the Caribbean began in 2003, with funding for two women's organization in Rosario, Argentina, and Lima, Peru, and was subsequently expanded in 2007–8 to cities in Brazil, Chile, Colombia, Guatemala and El Salvador. Much of the output of the programme has been in the form of proactive initiatives on the ground, workshops, activities, advocacy, publications and tools. There have been a number of very specific achievements in terms of city and ministerial actions resulting from this work, and they continue to emerge.[15] The outcomes and impact of the programme have been measured by a range of factors, including levels of participation and involvement by local organizations and communities, understanding of problems of women's safety and how they might be addressed, as well as concrete changes in legislation or the use and design of public space.

Generally, however, individual NGOs have rarely had the resources or capacity to replicate across different cultures and countries, to scale up projects or to set up controlled experiments. To some extent, projects have also been developed in isolation from other fields. There has been relatively little cross-fertilization of knowledge in relation to evaluation, for example, between the community-safety field in general and women's safety. Finally, as there is a strong emphasis on women's right to be heard and to be included in governance issues, many projects have purposefully used participatory and qualitative methodologies and eschewed scientific approaches.

Given the very complex social, cultural and political roots of gender-based violence, it requires complex interventions, similar to those found elsewhere in community crime prevention (Falu and Segovia, 2008). A small intervention can show some immediate outcomes, such as a demonstrable increase in satisfaction with the process, lower levels of insecurity, a greater willingness of women to use public space, or greater empowerment in terms of engaging with local governments, and actual changes in physical infrastructures resulting from the project. It is much more difficult to show long-term and fundamental change in behaviours or attitudes among women or men, local populations or governments.

This problem was well demonstrated in a review of the use of women's safety audits internationally undertaken for UN-HABITAT (Lambrick and Travers, 2008). In a related article, the authors concluded:

> Through this study of six women's safety audit initiatives in three continents, we have shown that this tool can be effective in validating local women's experiences, developing partnerships with local governments and other key urban decision-makers, creating the impetus for spillover effects such as women's employment programs, or training for architects and planners, and making small but concrete improvements to places. The question of whether these improved built, social, and policy environments have, in turn, led to behavioural changes amongst women and other vulnerable groups, still remains under researched. Women's safety audits can thus be conceptualized as a promising tool not only in reducing violence and insecurity in public space, but as a mechanism for increased gender equality in urban planning, design, and governance.
> (Whitzman *et al.*, 2009)

By their very nature, grass-roots or locally developed programmes of intervention to reduce violence against women in either public or private space – as has been argued above – are going to involve a range of initiatives, in quite small spaces in cities, and will probably have limited funds and short timelines. Changing attitudes and behaviour takes time. There is unlikely to be funding available for the long-term evaluation of outcomes.

Thus, as is clear from the quotation at the beginning of this chapter, UNIFEM itself has not been immune from the trend towards results-based management, in common with all UN agencies. Increasingly, those countries, foundations or institutions donating funds for UN programmes have required international organizations to account for their spending.[16] And they in turn, as governments or international funders, have been required to give good accounts to their boards, shareholders or citizens. At the bottom of the chain, NGOs feel the weight, not only of these requirements to show impact, but also of the dominant discourses on the best evidence-led and scientific methods of evaluation. Two recent international programmes illustrate how flexible evaluation approaches are being developed and applied.

Recent developments and examples

UN Women's new strategic plan endorses the use of evidence-based advocacy and programming, including data collection, analysis and research, an approach that was endorsed in recent consultations.[17] Two current projects, the GICP, funded by the UN Trust Fund, and the UN Women SCGP, illustrate evolving attempts to develop meaningful evaluation strategies in the area of women's safety.

The GICP, which is discussed elsewhere in this book, is a three-year comparative-action project being administered by WICI, taking place in four cities: Dar es Salaam, Tanzania; New Delhi, India; Petrozavodsk, Russia; and Rosario, Argentina.[18] The project coordinator (Kalpana Viswanath) and project evaluator (Sohail Husain) have been involved from its planning stages and worked together closely with all the local organizations and their evaluators. Funded by the UN Trust Fund, and in each case involving a local women's organization, the project has been an opportunity to develop a monitoring and evaluation framework that is flexible to local conditions and cultures and combines data and qualitative material from a variety of sources. Tools have been developed collectively to provide comprehensive and reliable data that are both qualitative and quantitative. They include focus groups, street surveys, policy reviews and women's safety audits, which enable the project to map safety and insecurity, review local policies, legislation and initiatives, assess gaps and problems, and advocate for change.

In the first year, the data collection was designed largely to inform subsequent activities within each project. Although it generated a baseline, this is not a benchmark that will be used in the evaluation to measure change in terms of outcomes. Most of the evaluative work has focused on assessing the value of the tools used and the knowledge gained from the data generated.[19] Over the three years, the project involves engaging with local governments and specific sectors to effect change in pilot areas, or more widely, identifying and piloting good practices and building partnerships with municipal governments on women's safety.[20]

In part, the framework for the monitoring and evaluation of the programme has been established by the donors in terms of their requirements, using a logic model, but has allowed for some flexibility. The project evaluator and coordinator have maintained very close ties with each project, including through emails, monthly Skype conference calls, face-to-face meetings and visits, and they have worked with all the partners implementing the project to develop the tools used (Lambrick, 2010). Although comparisons between sites have been important, it has also been recognized that there are some major differences that make it difficult to make precise comparisons. Baseline findings from all the data collected in the first year have now been published and show the range of concerns and attitudes experienced in different cities in considerable richness and depth (Lambrick *et al.*, 2010). The project can also be seen as innovative in enabling some scaling-up of projects in two of the four cities (Lambrick, 2010). In the case of both Delhi and Rosario, the organizations involved have considerable previous experience of action and research on women's safety, in the former when launching a Safe Delhi campaign, and in the later as part of the UNIFEM regional programme on safe cities for women. In both cases, they have been able to combine some of their other resources and expertise to scale up their work. However, as the programme lasts for only three years, it will not be possible to undertake follow-on monitoring and impact evaluation of any changes that may result from the interventions taking place. That may only be possible if follow-funds are found.

UN Women's SCGP 2010–2015 was launched at the Delhi conference in November 2010. Like the GICP, which was a partial inspiration, along with the UNIFEM Latin American regional programme, it is grounded in the promotion of women's rights and gender equality and will be using a range of tools and quantitative, qualitative and participatory methods, including women's safety audits. As outlined elsewhere in this book, the programme will involve action projects in selected communities in five cities: Cairo, Delhi, Kigali, Port Moresby and Quito, with the overall aim of reducing violence against women, and specifically sexual violence, in urban public spaces (UN Women, 2010).

The evaluation strategy for the UN Women global programme, which has been in development since 2009, has been the subject of considerable discussion between the partners involved and included an evaluation meeting in Delhi in November 2010. It is a good illustration of the 'process of negotiation' over how best to measure action, which Batliwala and Pittman have urged should take place in relation to such programmes (2010, p. 4).

The project's impact-evaluation strategy is referred to as a 'living document' and reflects the attempt to provide a flexible approach (UN Women, 2011). It is based on the classic 'theory of change' model, but is also sensitive to contexts and local conditions and the difficulties of comparing very different cities and countries with different experiences and capacities. It is also alert to the need not to raise expectations too high about the extent and kinds of change that can be achieved, and is termed a 'work in progress': 'The Strategy does not impose a single evaluation design on individual projects but two main types of evaluation design have been considered: quasi-experimental and non-experimental' (UN Women, 2011, p. 10).

The impact strategy incorporates women's rights; the use of participatory techniques with the women and girls involved in the communities where the interventions will take place; the application of a 'mixed methods' approach; and the collection of before and after intervention baseline data, along with ongoing monitoring. Evaluation of each local project will be undertaken with a plan that responds to the local context and capacities, all with some common information to enable (it is hoped) the overall impact and replicability of the programme to be assessed. Overall, the strategy aims:

- to measure the impact of the intervention model(s);
- to assess which strategies have been successful and which have not;
- to show how the results were achieved; and
- to assess the circumstances or conditions that helped determine their effectiveness.

Both of these programmes pose huge evaluation challenges of the kind characteristic of developmental projects in terms of funding, time, data and political contexts (Bamberger et al., 2006), apart from their ambitious aim to create safer cities for women and girls. They are, nevertheless, good examples of more flexible and reflexive models of the monitoring and evaluation of complex projects involving women on the ground.

Towards less-imperfect measures of human interactions

The purpose of this chapter has not been to reject mainstream or orthodox scientific models of evaluation, nor to argue against the need for good evidence or accountability for resources spent, but to show the constant flux in understandings of what evaluation could or should do, and how it has evolved over time to meet the challenges posed by the development world, by people on the ground, by feminists and by critical academics. The purpose has also been to illustrate very briefly how this has applied to the field of women's safety and gender-based violence. We cannot expect to discover the pot of gold or the archetypal method – nor to respond to all the issues of discrimination and poverty in our small, carefully planned interventions – but we can continue to work towards ways of improving our abilities to reflect the change process on the ground and the realities of political and economic processes that help to shape them in comprehensive and sensitive ways.

Apart from 'developmental evaluation' and 'RealWorld evaluation', other more recent approaches and tools entering the ever-expanding lexicon on evaluation include 'knowledge translation', 'implementation science' and 'outcome mapping'.[21] In a sense, all of them can be seen as positive reactions to the static and tight linear models that so many women on the ground, women's organizations, feminists and femocrats have fought to humanize. They are also recognitions of the gaps between what people wish for themselves and their communities, what policymakers (and donors) hope for, what researchers and practitioners think they are doing, and the everyday and unanticipated events affecting how practitioners and those with whom they work are affected.

Notes

1 *Many* thanks are due to Sohail Husain for acting as a very thoughtful colleague and critic for this chapter, having declined the invitation to be a co-author owing to other work commitments. Any mistakes and misinterpretations are mine, not his.
2 Interview with a UNIFEM officer from a 2007–8 study undertaken in Brazil and Ecuador, from Phillips and Cole (2009, p. 197).
3 UNIFEM is now part of UN Women.
4 Other international donor organizations, such as the World Bank, began this process much earlier.
5 See also discussions on the transparency of aid by organizations such as Publish what you Fund, www.publishwhatyoufund.org, and the International Aid Transparency Initiative, www.aidtransparency.net
6 See discussion on the views of Joseph Stiglitz and Amartya Sen on the need for indicators of lifestyle and national well-being in Batliwala and Pittman (2010).
7 I am grateful to Sohail Husain for his insights on this point.
8 It has also been described as an attempt to 'scale up' that knowledge into everyday practice across the country; see Homel (2009).
9 For further discussion, see Sherman (2009); Hough (2010).
10 See Chapters 9 and 10 on evaluation in ICPC (2010).
11 For example, Lundgren *et al.* (2007); Bamberger and Podems (2002).
12 Whitzman (2008). See also UNODC (2010).
13 PUKAR (Partners for Urban Knowledge, Action and Research) undertook a Gender and Space project from 2003 to 2006, www.pukar.org.in; Jagori has been developing projects on women's and girls' safety in Delhi since the 1990s.
14 The 2009–11 project was undertaken by Women in Cities International and Jagori and funded by the International Development Research Centre, Canada. See WICI and Jagori (2011).
15 See, for example, Rainero, L. (2010) and Falu and Segovia (2008).
16 For example, UNODC has been subjected to much more stringent expectations in terms of accounting for funds in the evaluation of its programmes by donor

countries. A number of countries have also changed funding policies to provide funds only for specific programmes, reducing sustaining funding, a problem familiar to many NGOs.
17 See www.unwomen.org/about-us/executive-director. In the consultations on UN Women's first strategic plan, ending violence against women received the most universal support of all the focus areas, while capacity building for national governments and civil society, opening space for dialogue and gender mainstreaming were the most strongly supported programme strategies. There was also strong support for evidence-based advocacy and programming, including data collection and analysis and research.
18 See www.womenincities.org.
19 Personal communication, Sohail Husain.
20 See Viswanath and Husain (2011), and WICI (2010).
21 See for example Bennett and Jessani (2011); Outcome Mapping Virtual Learning Community, www.outcomemapping.ca; and the National Implementation Research Network www.fpg.unc.edu

References

Bamberger, M. and Podems, D.R. (2002) 'Feminist Evaluation in the International Development Context', *New Directions for Evaluation*, no. 96, Winter.

Bamberger, M., Rugh, J. and Mabry, L. (2006) *RealWorld Evaluation: Working Under Budget, Time, Data, and Political Constraints*, Sage Publications, California.

Batliwala, S. and Pittman, A. (2010) *Capturing Change in Women's Realities. A Critical Overview of Current Monitoring and Evaluation Frameworks and Approaches*, Association for Women's Rights in Development, Toronto, Cape Town, Mexico City.

Bennett, G. and Jessani, N. (2011) *The Knowledge Translation Toolkit. Bridging the Know-Do Gap: A Resource for Researchers*, IDRC, Ottawa.

Bloom, S. (2008) *Violence Against Women and Girls. A Compendium of Monitoring and Evaluation Indicators*, USAID, Washington, DC.

Clear, T. (2010) 'Policy and Evidence: The Challenge to the American Society of Criminology: 2009 Presidential Address to the American Society of Criminology', *Criminology*, vol. 48, no. 1, pp. 1–25.

Davies, P. (2008) 'Looking Out a Broken Old Window: Community Safety, Gendered Crimes and Victimizations', *Crime Prevention & Community Safety*, vol. 10, pp. 207–25.

Demetriades, J. (2007) *Gender Indicators: What, Why, How?* BRIDGE, Institute of Development Studies, University of Sussex.

ECLAC (2010) *User Manual for the Gender Equality Observatory for Latin America and the Caribbean*, ECLAC, Santiago.

Ellsberg, M. and Heise, L. (2005) *Researching Violence Against Women. A Practical Guide for Researchers and Activists*, World Health Organization, Geneva.

Esplen, E. and Bell, E. (2007) *Gender and Indicators. Supporting Resources Collection*, BRIDGE, Institute of Development Studies, Sussex.

Falu, A. (ed.) (2010) *Women in the City. On Violence and Rights*, Latin American Women and Habitat Network, Ediciones SUR, Santiago.

Falu, A. and Segovia, O. (ed.) (2008) *Living Together: Cities Free from Violence Against Women*, Latin American Women and Habitat Network10, Ediciones SUR, Santiago.

Gamble, J.A.A. (2008) *A Developmental Evaluation Primer*, The J.M. McConnell Family Foundation, Montreal.

Homel, P. (2009) 'Lessons for Canadian Crime Prevention From Recent International Experience', *IPC Review*, vol. 3, pp. 13–39.

Homel, P., Nutley, S., Webb, B. and Tilley, N. (2004) *Investing to Deliver: Reviewing the Implementation of the UK Crime Reduction Programme*, Home Office, London.

Hope, T. (2008) *Evaluation of Safety and Crime Prevention Policies. England and Wales*. Paper for the CRIMPREV Workshop on Evaluation, Bologna, 10–12 July.

Hough, M. (2010) 'Gold Standard or Fool's Gold? The Pursuit of Certainty in Experimental Criminology', *Criminology & Criminal Justice*, vol. 10, no. 1, pp. 11–22.

ICPC (2010) *International Report on Crime Prevention & Community Safety 2010*, International Centre for the Prevention of Crime, Montreal.

Kelling, G.L. (2005) 'Community Crime Reduction: Activating Formal and Informal Control'. In Tilley, N. (ed.), *Handbook of Crime Prevention and Community Safety*, Willan Publishing, Cullompton, UK.

Lambrick, M. (2010) *Creating Safer Cities for Women: Women in Cities International and the Gender Inclusive Cities Programme*. Paper given at the meeting on Gender Governance and Cities in the Arab World and the Mediterranean, Cairo, April.

Lambrick, M. and Travers, K. (2008) *Women's Safety Audits: What Works Where?* UN-HABITAT and Women in Cities International, Nairobi.

Lambrick, M., Viswanath, K. and Husain, S. (2010) *Learning from Women to Create Gender Inclusive Cities. Baseline Findings from the Gender Inclusive Cities Programme*, Women in Cities International, Montreal.

Lundgren, H., Downes, M. and Kennedy, M. (2007) 'Encouraging Effectiveness of Conflict Prevention and Peacebuilding Activities: Towards DAC Guidance', *OECD Journal of Development*, vol. 8, no. 3.

Milliken, J., with Gilgen, E. and Lazarevic, J. (2011) *Tackling Violence Against Women: From Knowledge to Practical Initiatives*, Geneva Declaration, Small Arms Survey, Geneva.

Patton, M.Q. (2011) *Developmental Evaluation: Applying Complexity Concepts to Enhance Innovation and Use*, The Guilford Press, New York, NY.

Phillips, L. and Cole, S. (2009) 'Feminist Flows, Feminist Fault Lines: Women's Machineries and Women's Movements in Latin America', *Signs: Journal of Women in Culture and Society*, vol. 35, no. 1, pp. 185–211.

Rainero, L. (2010) 'A Contribution to the Debate on the City, Public Space and Safety from a Feminist Perspective'. In Falu, A. (ed.) *Women in the City. On Violence and Rights*, Latin American Women and Habitat Network, Ediciones SUR, Santiago.

Rosenbaum, D. (2002) 'Evaluating Multi-agency Anti-crime Partnerships: Theory, Design and Measurement Issues'. In Tilley, N. (ed.) *Evaluation for Crime Prevention. Crime Prevention Studies*, vol. 14, pp. 171–225, Lynne Rienner Publishing, Boulder, CO.

Shaw, M. (2009) 'Lessons for Canadian Crime Prevention: Cultural Shifts and Local Flexibilities', *ICP Review*, vol. 3, pp. 81–6.

Shaw, M. (2010) 'A Note on What to do Now. Reflections on Preventing Intimate Partner and Sexual Violence Against Women', Women in Cities International, Montreal.

Shaw, M. and Carli, V. (eds) (2011) *Practical Approaches to Urban Crime Prevention*. Proceedings of the 12th UN Congress Workshop on Crime Prevention, Salvador, Brazil, 12–19 April 2010, International Centre for the Prevention of Crime, Montreal.

Sherman, L. (2009) 'Evidence and Liberty: The Promise of Experimental Criminology', *Criminology & Criminal Justice*, vol. 9, no. 1, pp. 5–28.

UNODC (2010) *Handbook on the Crime Prevention Guidelines. Making them Work*, United Nations Office on Drugs and Crime, Vienna.

UN Women (2010) *Safe Cities Free of Violence against Women and Girls*, Global Programme Document, March, www.unwomen.org.

UN Women (2011) *Impact Evaluation Strategy*. Safe Cities Free of Violence against Women and Girls Global Programme 2010–15, February, www.endvawnow.org/uploads/browser/files/safe_cities_ie_strategy.pdf.

Viswanath, K. and Husain, S. (2011) 'Gender Inclusive Cities'. In Shaw, M. and Carli, V. (eds) *Practical Approaches to Urban Crime Prevention*. Proceedings of the 12th UN Congress Workshop on Crime Prevention, Salvador, Brazil, 12–19 April 2010, International Centre for the Prevention of Crime and UNODC, Montreal.

Whitzman, C. (2008) *Handbook of Community Safety, Gender and Violence Prevention. Practical Planning Tools*, Earthscan, London.

Whitzman, C., Andrew, C., Shaw, M. and Travers, K. (2009) 'The Effectiveness of Women's Safety Audits', *Security Journal*, vol. 22, no. 3, pp. 205–18.

WHO (2010) *Preventing Intimate Partner Violence and Sexual Violence Against Women*, WHO, Geneva.

WICI (2010) *Learning from Women to Create Gender Inclusive Cities. Baseline findings from the Gender Inclusive Cities Programme*, Women in Cities International, Montreal.

WICI and Jagori (2011) *Gender and Essential Services in Low-income Communities*. Report on the Action Research Project Women's Rights and Access to Water and Sanitation in Asian Cities, Women in Cities International, Montreal.

Chapter 12

Conclusion

Women's safety and the right to the city

Fran Klodawsky, Carolyn Whitzman, Crystal Legacy, Caroline Andrew, Margaret Shaw and Kalpana Viswanath

Advancing the vision of safer and more inclusive cities for women and men, identifying tools and strategies to help move that vision closer to a reality, and further specifying what it means to experience a right to the city – these are the motivators for the work discussed in the preceding pages. While much remains to be done, it is also important to celebrate the considerable achievements of those who have persisted, despite considerable and sometimes growing odds. They have contributed significantly to the idea (and occasionally the reality) that places should support all residents' struggles to meet their daily needs, but also advance their dreams of recognition, representation and encounter – in other words, a right to the city. The goal of this final chapter is to provide an overview of the achievements to date that are highlighted in this volume, as well as the lessons learned, but, equally, to discuss the work that remains to be done and the voices that are not yet sufficiently audible. Finally, we also signal challenges and opportunities that lie ahead and suggest where more attention is required to advance the building of more inclusive cities worldwide.

Celebration/achievements

This edited volume was inspired by the 2010 Third International Conference on Women's Safety in Delhi, India, an event that attracted more than 270 participants from over forty countries, mostly from the Global South. The themes discussed and the initiatives highlighted in Delhi were a powerful statement of the myriad, innovative, place-based efforts, knowledge exchanges and wider collaborations that have contributed to the current state of the art on safer cities for women. These efforts are sometimes traced to the 1970s, but especially since the First International Conference on Women's Safety, in Montreal, Canada, in 2002. The chapters in this book reflect this progress. They combine sophisticated and nuanced analyses of how broad structural trends can have impacts on individuals' and groups' everyday experiences of living in cities, and how concrete measures, geared to the particular individuals, groups and relations that constitute each place, can make a significant and positive difference in those experiences. Broadly speaking, they help to clarify the meaning of, and distinctions between, three key concepts: safer public spaces, safe spaces and dialogic or deliberative discursive spaces (Whitzman, 2008).

Women's organizations, often in partnership with governments, have developed tools and other intervention methods to nurture safer public spaces. A particularly ambitious example of such activity is the GICP. Viswanath outlines the impressive suite of tools that has been adapted and cross-culturally tested to diagnose women' safety issues: street surveys, focus-group discussions and women's safety audits. Equally impressive is the action research project on Women's Right and Access to Water and Sanitation in Asian Cities, which began with the idea of adapting women's safety audits, but ultimately drew on a variety of participatory methods. Khosla and Dhar outline the motivations and range of tools that were used to examine gender gaps in safe access to basic infrastructure, such as water and sanitation services for women and men living in informal settlements in Delhi, and the often dangerous circumstances that women face in depending on public toilets and community water taps. The impressive outputs so far of these two particularly ambitious efforts are the culmination of learning that has emerged from myriad smaller initiatives and insights, identified in particular locales but then taken up, adapted and refined in other places. Two such insights are the value of peer exchange and grass-roots academies, as discussed elsewhere by the Huairou Commission among others (UN-HABITAT, 2009), and civic society–government partnerships, as discussed in this volume by Andrew and Legacy. Peer exchange and grass-roots academies have helped to transform tools that can meet needs within very different cultural and political contexts. One key example is the manner in which women's safety audits, which began in subway stations and a large park in Toronto, were subsequently adapted for use in a range of very different circumstances, often as a result of civil society–government partnerships (Women in Cities International, 2008). Related to such arrangements, Andrew and Legacy describe how policy-analysis tools originally used to mainstream 'women' as a simple category have been adapted to address marginalization based on recent migration, disability, indigenity and age, with the help of multi-sectoral partnerships that include gender as one aspect of unequal power relations. Whitzman's analysis of mobility contributes further insights, having to do with an explication of how land-use planning can be a key link between safer spaces and shorter distances between home, work, shops and leisure activities.

However, *safer public spaces*, although necessary, are not sufficient to advance the quality of life of diverse urban residents. As Klodawsky outlines, poor women's livelihoods are increasingly found in the informal sector, and this reality has impacts on both material well-being and access to safe places. When productive activities are carried out at the margins and in the midst of reproductive responsibilities, women's vulnerability tends to be high. The semi-public and semi-private places where informal livelihoods are performed multiply opportunities for exploitation, oppression and violence. Women in these circumstances can face potentially catastrophic impacts when authorities suddenly decide, for example, to clamp down on hawking, or when male partners use violence to steal earnings earmarked for basic necessities. A consideration of these issues leads to a broader recognition of what is required to create *safe places*. A safe place can be housing for a woman and her dependents that is free of threat from imminent eviction. As Escalante and Sweet outline, it can be as simple as a locked room for a domestic worker living in someone else's house in a foreign land, or a community-health or social-service agency that takes migrant women's distinct safety concerns seriously. Safe places are also about partnerships that work to address and respond to immediate needs, such as safe houses for refugee women, organizations that collectively strengthen street vendors' rights or websites where women can share stories of resistance to street harassment. Such initiatives in turn reveal the layers of social, economic, environmental and political factors that will need attention in order for such safe places to be thoroughly institutionalized everywhere.

Finally, the literature on the right to the city emphasizes the importance of dialogic or deliberative *discursive spaces*, where, as Lambrick elaborates, the notions of inclusion and partnership are worked out concurrently in widespread virtual and localized material places. Moving from 'unsafety' towards 'communities of opportunity', as Holtmann explains, requires developing widely understood visions of how all members of a locality can meaningfully find the preconditions for productive and dignified lives. This deliberative discourse depends, in turn, on equalized partnerships between diverse agents of civil society, including women's organizations, and various levels of government. It also involves a serious consideration, simultaneously, of the built, social and policy environments of a place. A genuinely inclusive city requires a constant effort to be inclusive of different voices, across gender, income, age, ethnicity, sexuality and abilities, as Lacey *et al.* elaborate upon in their examination of how intersectional approaches differ from those that focus on gender mainstreaming only. The necessity of participatory approaches, and public processes of inclusion and partnership that are modelled at various scales have been emphasized by numerous authors, who have together highlighted the contributions that such approaches can provide in a variety of contexts, from localized struggles to obtain access to basic infrastructure, to city-wide gender mainstreaming and equity auditing, to peer-to-peer knowledge exchange between local initiatives that connect locally, regionally and transnationally. Though certainly not a panacea, by any means, Shaw's reflections on the potential value of evaluation illustrates an opportunity to gather further evidence about the power of safer cities for women approaches and frameworks.

Remaining gaps/insufficient attention

Over the past twenty years, women's safety issues have moved from being virtually invisible in 'crime prevention' and 'community safety' discourses, to a status of limited inclusion. Gender is now a legitimate topic within some crime-prevention initiatives, but, disturbingly, and despite the continuing and widespread problem of gender-based violence, the preventative approach remains marginalized within a broader 'law and order' agenda. Elsewhere, a growing interest in 'difference' discourses sometimes enables gender-based violence to occupy a distinct silo, separate in theory, practice and funding stream from 'mainstream' crime and violence. The unfortunate reality remains that there still are very few places where gender and other differences have been fully incorporated within safer-communities discourses and implementation. Although this book does signify an important advance – in analysis and perhaps especially in knowledge exchange and tools – clearly there is much more to be done. The discussion in Lacey, Miller, Reeves and Tankel's chapter on the distinction between intersectional and mainstream gender analysis and in Holtmann's chapter on communities of opportunity are important examples of how current thinking and practices need further stretching to help shift thinking in ways that emphasize prevention and progress towards more inclusive places for all.

Even as the editors aspired to present the current state of the art as fully as possible, we fell short, despite our best efforts to include chapters with a focus on peer exchange and grass-roots academies, land-use planning, housing and masculinities. In each case, chapters were commissioned, but, for various reasons, often outside the control of the prospective authors, there was no follow-through. This was especially disappointing, given that, in most instances, these authors would have added voices from the Global South, where we recognize that our book also falls far short, especially in terms of an absence of voices from Latin America, West Asia, most of Africa and East and South East Asia. Women's safety will not move from margins into the mainstream globally until these voices are equal in theory and practice.

Thematically, despite the mention of land-use planning in the first part of the book, a chapter devoted to exploring questions of how and under what circumstances planners are able to incorporate strategies that promote inclusivity, and the extent of planners' capacity to contribute to inclusive cities, even under the best of circumstances, would certainly have strengthened the text. So too would a chapter on housing, given the immense negative impacts that accrue when housing is absent or dangerous, and, conversely, the positive implications of safe and secure housing. The absence of a chapter on masculinities has meant that our goal of gender mainstreaming was not met even in a minimal way – clearly, men's voices are muted in this text. As a result, men's perspectives on public violence and the strategies that are most effective in ameliorating its negative impacts have not even begun to be addressed.

Next steps

The world that is currently unfolding is one of less (perceived) certainty, but also less rigidity. Old assumptions about the categorical distinctiveness of 'public' versus 'private', 'domestic' versus 'foreign', 'here' versus 'there', are giving way to a greater acknowledgement of fluidity and the fuzziness of boundaries, albeit at the same time as inequalities are becoming more pronounced and consequential. If a woman is living on the street and is beaten by an intimate partner, is that public or private violence? If a woman is squatting in a field to defecate, does this private function have new public implications and responsibilities? How should one describe the living circumstances of a live-in nanny? When is she at home, and when is she at work? Safer cities, for women scholars and practitioners, are raising such questions and offering important theoretical insights and strategic responses that draw upon visions of more inclusive cities, as well as the practical experiences of trying to make them so.

Their contributions are grounded in myriad action research projects, some now approaching their second decade of experience and refinement, and they are also grounded in growing opportunities for knowledge exchange, both virtual and face to face, that have been a vital enabler for the growth of this movement. Local innovations have been shared widely through face-to-face opportunities such as the three International Conferences on Women's Safety and the Grassroots Women's Academies, piggybacked on to World Urban Forums. The opportunity to use cheap web-based technologies such as Skype to maintain close contact with specific initiatives, while also drawing on other knowledge and expertise in cases such as the GICP, has been invaluable. Access to the web to convey lessons learned to other places has allowed wide access to videos and other resources produced by WICI, Jagori, Mujer y Habitat and *Blank Noise*. Cheap and accessible long-distance communication has also facilitated the localized public education that takes place through street theatre and murals. At diverse scales, the networks facilitated by the web have opened up new opportunities for knowledge exchange between individuals, organizations, languages and cultures. The potential of web-based tools to contribute capacity to local organizations and to open up new action research opportunities has only begun to be articulated.

Some argue that governments, particularly national governments, appear somewhat less powerful in responding to global economic and cultural forces, whereas international corporations, but also international NGOs, are becoming increasingly powerful. The United Nations (and particularly UN-HABITAT and UN Women), as funders and facilitators of peer exchange, have been particularly significant drivers, helping to plant the seeds that ultimately enabled the projects described by Viswanath and Khosla and Dhar in this volume to come to fruition. These recent developments, exciting as they are, are also thoroughly beholden to the long-term work of numerous grass-roots organizations that have developed their own safe places to exchange knowledge, with various levels of support from national, regional and/or private funders. These observations raise questions that certainly need greater attention moving forward: To what extent do private–public partnerships allow grass-roots women to take on important roles: are they more or less likely to occur? To what extent does international aid funding override national and local policies in the Global South, and to what extent is that good or bad news for women's safety and the right to the city?

In line with the growing recognition of complexity, there is an emerging acknowledgement of the value of intersectionality and increasing understanding of the multiple layers and interactions that are women's and men's identities, extending to gender definition and certainly including the intersections of gender, age, ethnicity and class. The question of national identities and regional and international responsibilities underscores the discussions by Escalante and Sweet about the situations of migrant women and leads back to questions of how safe can cities be for women. Are indigenous women 'disappearing' in North and Central America because they are indigenous, women, or both? Does a safe community of opportunity for 'everyone' mean a safe community for women? Do dangers remain for women to get lost when gender mainstreaming becomes equity auditing?

Despite increasingly complex governance structures, individual identities, and understandings of safety and the right to the city, there is still a strong desire, among both initiatives and funders, to know that we are making a positive difference. Shaw describes both the politicization and the difficulties inherent in evaluation of women's safety initiatives. Like all of the phenomena described in this book, there have been considerable changes in the ways that women's safety has been evaluated over the past twenty years. From a somewhat simplistic understanding on behalf of funders (are you reducing crime in a city with a small and very time-limited programme?), refinements in thinking have acknowledged that the building of broad-based and resilient partnerships takes time, that the transformation of public spaces from exclusionary (very few women visible, day and night) to more inclusionary might be an aim in and of itself, and that fear of crime in public space is not a mistake on the part of women who do not recognize that they are assaulted more often by intimate partners, but a reflection of constant, low-level harassment in public space, as well as violence in the home.

Final thoughts

Women's safety scholars, particularly those from the Global South, are contributing new and valuable theoretical insights (Falu, 2010; Phadke et al., 2011) about this more complex world. This new theory has resulted in valuable insights about the gaps between what a right to the city would mean and the current limitations that mainstream understandings of women's 'place in the city' reveal. These theories have been informed by action research projects that are now entering their second decade in some cases. A suite of tools – most notably the women's safety audit – have been disseminated and translated into different economic, political and cultural contexts. Evaluation, while still in its infancy, is at last being given the serious consideration it deserves. Linkages have begun to be made between women's safety and economic resilience, and between women's safety and environmental sustainability. There is an unpacking of gender that goes beyond simplistic male–female, North–South binaries. A global community of research and practice is being developed.

There is no single vision of what a safe and inclusive city would look like, nor should there be. A safe and inclusive city would include basic access to livelihoods, housing and education, but also to leisure activities and the pursuit of happiness. There would be greater gender equality, but also lessened inequalities across a range of differences. Encounter with strangers would be taken for granted and not feared. There would be a sense of empowerment in relation to the shaping and inhabitation of public space, but privacy would be available to all. An understanding of rights, both of those formally accorded citizenship and of children, refugees and other people not accorded formal citizenship at present, would be more fully integrated into mainstream debates and policies. Women and men would not feel alone with their problems, and the pleasures of the city would outweigh the dangers. Where does this leave us in terms of ways forward? It is our hope that this book provides ideas, case studies and inspiration towards attainment of these elusive goals.

References

Falu, A. (2010), 'Violence and Discrimination in Cities'. In *Women in the City: On Violence and Rights*. Santiago: Women and Habitat Network of Latin America, 15–38.
Phadke, S., Khan, S. and Ranade, S. (2011), *Why Loiter? Women and Risk on Mumbai Streets*. Delhi: Penguin Books India.
UN-HABITAT (2009), *Not About Us Without Us: Working with Grassroots Organizations in the Land Field*. Nairobi: UN-HABITAT.
Whitzman, C. (2008), *The Handbook of Community Safety, Gender, and Violence Prevention: Practical Planning Tools*. London: Earthscan.
Women in Cities International (2008), *Women's Safety Audit: What Works and Where*. Montreal: Women in Cities International.

Index

Action des femmes handicappées de Montréal 97–100, 166–8
Action India 123, 133
Action Research Project on Women's Rights and Access to Water and Sanitation in Asian Cities 117, 123–4, 136, 192, 202
  see also Bawana and Bhalswa, Delhi
Agency Co., Uruguay 168–70
Ahn, S. 91
alcohol abuse 107, 108, 115 n2
Alston, Lauren 175
Angeline, Maesy 177
Anitha, S. 61
anonymity 42
Ansell, C. and Gash, A. 94
Anthias, F. and Yuval-Davis, N. 152
Anzaldúa, G. 53
apartheid system 104–5
artistic intervention 11, 162–5, 205
  Berri-UQAM: Accessibilité universelle 166–8, 181 n4
  Latin American Women and Habitat Network (RMH) 76, 77, 88 n4, 168–70, 169, 181 n5, 205
  Sistren Theatre Collective 165–6, 170, 180 n2, 181 n3
ASSOTSI (Associação dos Operadores e Trabalahdores do Sector Informal) 30
Audiotopie 166–8, 181 n4

Bacchi, C. and Eveline, J. 156, 157
Bachelet, Michelle 2
Batliwala, S. and Pittman, A. 185, 186, 190–2, 191, 195, 197 n9

Bawana and Bhalswa, Delhi 124
  drainage 131, 132, 137
  gender, and opportunity cost of water 133–6, 134–5
  solid-waste management 133, 137
  toilets and sanitation 126–8, 127
  water supplies 128–31, 129, 130, 133–6
  wave rates 134
  Women's Safety Audit 125, 126
Ben, Munni 124
Ben-Or, Shir 174–5
Berri-UQAM: Accessibilité universelle 166–8, 181 n4
'Beyond the Digital' 177
Biles, J. 21
Blank Noise 35, 176–9, 178, 179, 205
'Blank Noise This Place' campaign 176–7
Bogota, Colombia 1, 36
  public transport 44–8
Boston, US 154
Brah, A. 152
Brah, A. and Phoenix, A. 152
Bristol, UK 147
Brodie, J. 91
Brown, A. 26–7
Brown, A. et al. 30
budgeting 2, 3, 46, 98, 99, 145
  gender 5, 11, 146, 147, 189, 192
  participatory 77, 85, 144, 148, 150–1, 156, 157

Cacho, L. 57
CAFSU 75
Cairo, Egypt 195
Calcutta, India 21
Casa Segura, Chicago 63–4, 64, 67, 68 n4

Catholic Crosscultural Services 97–100
CCTV 40
Central Karoo, South Africa 104–10
  alcohol abuse 107, 108
  child neglect 108–9
  crime and poverty 107
  crime-violence cycle 107–9, *109*
  drawing methodology 106–7
  fragmented families 108–9
  migration 107
  sense of uselessness 108
  weapons 108
Centre for Budget and Governance Accountability (CBGA) 124, 134, 136
Chant, S. 23, 24
Chazan, M. and Whiteside, A. 31
Chicago, US 63–4
child neglect 108–9
Ciclovia programme 46
CISCSA 77, 84–5, 169–70
cities
  positive effects 11
  production of space 49
  safe and inclusive: a definition 207
citizenship 22, 35, 36, 44–5, 48
  pluralistic 155
City of Graz 146
'Civic and Citizens' Pact' 62
Clear, Todd 186, 188
climate change 10
clothing 176
Combahee River Collective 154
Commonwealth Secretariat 27
communities of opportunity 110–12, *111*, 204
  see also Bawana and Bhalswa, Delhi
community leadership 46–7
community safety planning (Whitzman) 94, 95
community toilet complexes 126, 127
Conscience Urbaine 166–8, 181 n4
Convention on Decent Work for Domestic Workers 59
Convention on Domestic Work 59
Coordenadoria da Mulher (Women's Coordination Group of Brazil) 150
Cornwall, A. and Coelho, V.S.P 150
Council of European Municipalities and Regions (CEMR) 118
Crenshaw, Kimberlé 153–4

Crime Reduction Programme, England and Wales 187, 197 n13
Curitiba, Brazil 46
cycling 37, 48

daily mobility 38, 39
Dakar, Senegal 6, 62
Dar es Salaam
  Gender Inclusive Cities Programme 77, 77–8, 79, 80, 81, 82, 83, 88 n4, 88 n6, 194
  police/policing 85–6
  Safer Cities Programme 78, 88 n6
Davies, Pamela 188
Dayif, A. *et al.* 38
Declaration on the Elimination of Violence Against Women (1993) 3
De Koning, A. 22
Delhi 1, 2, 25, 39, 76, 82, 119, 120, 137, 192, 194, 202
  Commonwealth Games (2010) 122
  Gender Inclusive Cities Programme 76–7, 77, 78, 79, 80, 81, 82, 83, 86–7, 88 n4, 89 n14, 194, 195
  Housing and Land Rights Network 122
  informalization 123
  master plan for Delhi (MPD) 122–3
  urbanization, and exclusion of the poor 121–3
  zoning 122
  see also Action Research Project on Women's Rights and Access to Water and Sanitation in Asian Cities; Bawana and Bhalswa, Delhi
Delhi conference *see* Third International Conference on Women's Safety: Building Inclusive Cities (2010)
Delhi Declaration 87 n2
Delhi Development Authority 126
Delhi Transport Corporation (DTC) 86–7
Department for Transport UK 44
Department of Education, Nairobi 112, *113*
Devenish, A. and Skinner, C. 29
Dhaka, Bangladesh 40, 43, 44
Dhavari, India 41
discursive safe spaces 49, 162–3, 179–80, 203

see also artistic intervention; Online Action Research
diversity 156, 167, 179
 and migrant women 55, 59
domestic violence against women 6–7, 57, 119
domestic workers 58–9, 65
drainage 117, 131, *132*, 137
Dunstan, G. and Sarkissian, W. 166
Durban, South Africa 20, 27–9, 30

Economic Commission for Latin America and the Caribbean (ECLAC) 189
economic empowerment 2
economic liberalization 23
Edinburgh, UK 39
Ellsberg, M. and Heise, L. 189–90
employment, gender-disaggregated 20–1
environment 10
equality-impact assessments (EQIAs) 148–50, *149*, 151, 157
Erman, T. and Turkyilmaz, S. 22, 25, 26, 30
EuroFEM 120
European Charter for Equality of Women and men in Local Life 118
European Union 104, 146
evaluation of women's safety 66–7, 206, 207
 common problems 190–2
 developmental evaluation 188–9
 donor-required monitoring 185
 evaluation frameworks 185
 feminist approach 184, 190–2, *191*
 future of 196–7
 a political process 185–7
 randomized control trials 187
 RealWorld evaluation 188–9
 resistance to 186–7
 scientific approach 187–8
 UN-HABITAT 193–4
 Women's Safety Audit (WSA) 193–4
eviction 8–9, 117–24, *125*, 137, 203

Falu, A. 22–3, 24, 53
farm labourers 58
femicide 4, 7, 23
feminism 184
feministing.com 172

feminization of responsibility 23, 24
Fenster, T. 42, 53
Fincher, R. and Iveson, K. 42, 49
First International Women's Safety Seminar: Making the Links (2002) 1, 13 n3, 201, 205
Flickr 171
Floro, M. and Pichetpongsa, A. 24
Foetal Alcohol Syndrome 108
Fonchingong, C. 24
Formar Ciudad 45
Forum of Women's Organizations of Burma 65
Fourth World Conference on Women (1995) 4
Freire, Paulo 63

Garber, J. 42
Garzon, Luis 48
Gatineau, Canada 97, 98, 99
gender
 as analytical category 156
 and discrimination 56
 emphasis on 204
 and opportunity of cost of water 133–6, *134–5*
 and power 49
 unpacking 207
gender auditing *see* Women's Safety Audit (WSA)
gender-based violence (GBV) 4, 170
 hard to measure areas 192–4
 and migration 9
gender budgeting 5, 11, 146, 147, 189, 192
gender equality 2, 3, 5, 6
Gender Equality Act (2007) 44
Gender Equality Observatory, Santiago 189
gender-impact assessments (GIAs) 144, 146–7
gender inclusion 76, 78, 156–7
Gender Inclusive Cities Programme 12, 43, 75–8, 185, 194–5, 205
 Dar es Salaam 77, 77–8, 79, 80, 81, 82, 83, 88 n4, 88 n6, 194
 Delhi 76–7, 77, 78, 79, 80, 81, 82, 83, 86–7, 88 n4, 89 n14, 194, 195
 findings 80–4, *82*, 88 n10
 focus-group discussions 79–80, 81, 202

partnerships and synergies 84–7
Petrozavodsk 77, *77*, 78, 79, 80, 81, 83, 86, 88 n4, 88 n7, 194
research tools 79–80, 88 n8, 88 n9
responses to sexual harassment *83*, 83–4
and right to the city 78
Rosario, Argentina 76, 77, *77*, 78, 79, 80, 81, 82, 83, 87, 88 n4, 195
street survey 79, 202
Tanzania 194
types of harassment *81*
Women's Safety Audit 78, 80, 202
gender indicators 189
Gender in Planning and Urban Development (Commonwealth Secretariat) 27
gender mainstreaming 4–5, 11, 13, 19, 143–4, 157, 204, 206
   challenges of 147–8
   equality-impact assessments (EQIAs) 148–50, *149*, 151, 157
   and public transport 44
   a transformative process 145–6
   Women's Safety Audit (WSA) 146
gender-responsive budget initiatives (GRBIs) 134, 136
gender-safety audits 147
Geneva Declaration 189
Giddens, A. 119
Gilroy, R. and Booth, C. 119–21
Global Charter-Agenda for Human Rights to the City 118
governance
   and partnerships 92–3, 94, 98
Graz, Austria 146
Greater London Authority 146
Grey, S. and Sawer, M. 91–2
Guardian (UK) 40
guerrilla art 164

Haifa, Israel 38
Hannah Town, Jamaica 165
Hanson, S. 29–30
Harrison, T.M. and Barthel, B. 171
Harvey, D. 84, 88 n12, 118
Healey, P. *et al.* 120
Hegel, G.W.F. 35
HIVOS-CIS Digital Natives Knowledge Programme 177
Hollaback! 172–6
housing 57

Huairou Commission 202
human rights 61, 65, 66
human-settlement growth 21–3
Husain, Sohail 194
Huxham, Chris 96, 98, 99
   'Theorizing collaborative practice' 93–4

Indian Census (2011) 121
'I Never Asked for It' campaign 176
informalization 20–1, *21*, 22–3, 31, 123, 202–3
Information Centre of the Independent Women's Forum (ICIWF) 78, 88 n4, 88 n7
infrastructure 202
   gender-neutral 137
   and right to the city 117–19, 137
   and safety 136
   and urban planning 119–21
   see also sanitation; water supplies
International Centre for Network and Information on Crime (ICNIC) Dar es Salaam 88 n4
International Centre for Network and Information on Crime (ICNIC) Tanzania 77–8
International Centre of the Prevention of Crime (ICPC) 188–9
International Day for the Elimination of Violence against Women 44
International Development Research Centre (IDRC), Canada 117, 198 n31
International Labour Organization 10, 56
   Bureau of Statistics Database 58
   Convention on Domestic Work 59
International Organization for Migration (IOM) 9
International violence against women survey (IVAWS) 7, 14 n22
Internet 162–3, 170–2, 205
   limitations to 175–6
   misogyny on 172
   as public space 171–2, 174
   and sexual harassment 172, 173–6
intersectionality 4, 143–4, 148, 204, 206
   applied 154–7
   inclusive approach 151–4
   and migrant women 54–5, 56

and multiplicity 157
and partnerships 95, 97, 100
intimate partner violence 6–7, 54, 56, 57, 144, 190, 205, 206

Jagori 13 n1, 19, 39, 44, 77, 88 n4, 89 n14, 117, 123–4, 134, 136, 192, 198 n30, 205
Jarvis, H. with Kantor, P. and Coke, J. 120
Jenson, J. 91

Kantor, P. 25–6
Kapur, N. 119
Kearl, Holly 173, 174, 175
Kigali, Rwanda 195
Kingston, Jamaica 165
Kirkness, V. 156
Knights of the Zebra 45
Kriti team 124

Labour and immigration Department, Manitoba 62
labour trafficking 9–10
Laforest, Rachel 92
Laingsburg 115 n2
land-use planning 25, 26–8, 29, 31, 202, 204
Latin American Women and Habitat Network (RMH) 76, 77, 88 n4, 168–70, *169*, 205
  'Mujeres por la Ciudad' (Women in the City) 168–70, *169*, 181 n5
Law, R. 37–8, 43, 49
leachate 129, 131, 135, 136
Le centre des ainés 97–100
Lefebvre, Henri 6, 48–9, 88 n12, 118
'Licence to rape' report 66
Lima, Peru 39, 192
Limbe, Cameroon 24
Lindblom, C. and Cohen, D. 95
Lindell, I. 29, 30
L'Isha, Isha 38
London 44, 147, 148
Loukaitou-Sideris, A. and Fink, C. 40
Lucknow, India 25

MacDowell Santos, C. 155
Machado, Ramírez 58
Mahila Nigrani Samiti (Women's Monitoring Committee) 124
Making Safer Places 147

Manchester, UK 147
Manila, Philippines 40
Maputo, Mozambique 30
maquiladoras 23
May, Emily 174, 175–6
Maynard, M. 152
McDowell, L. 37, 41
Meagher, K. 23
men/boys, attitudes and behaviour 11
Menjívar, C. and Salcido, O. 54, 61
Menon-Sen, K. and Bhan, G. 25, 27
menstruation 106, 112, 127, 128
Mestre, R. 56
Meth, P. 57
Metro Toronto Action Committee on Public Violence Against Women and Children (METRAC) 43
Mexico City 40, 118
Michaud, A. 80
migrant women 9–10, 107
  501-c3^2 status 63, 68 n2
  Casa Segura, Chicago 63–4, *64*, 67, 68 n4
  community-based responses 59, 62
  criminal justice responses 59, 60–1, 62
  and discrimination 56
  and diversity 55, 59
  domestic work 58–9, 65
  immigrant-rights approach 60–1
  and intersectionality 54–5, 56
  involuntary migrants 55–7
  mainstream national policies and strategies 59, 60, 62
  and mobility 57, 58
  programme approach 67
  Red Nacional de Trabajadoras del Hogar, Mexico 65, 67–8
  and right to the city 53, 59, 62
  voluntary migrants 55–6
  Women's League of Burma 65, 66, 67, 68
Miraftab, F. 22
mobility 36, 38, 155, 167, 202
  migrant women 57, 58
  and right to the city 36
Mockus, Antanas 45, 47, 48
monitoring *see* evaluation of women's safety
Montreal, Canada 1, 97, 98, 117, 145, 166, 167, 201
Moser, C. 147–8
Mumbai, India 40, 41, 50, 192

Nairobi, Kenya 111
Nairobi Council Education Department 112
National Association of Colored Women 153
National Institute for Women 7
National Sample Survey Organization (NSSO) 121
New Delhi *see* Delhi
New Everyday Life 119
New York 42, 44, 173
New York City Subway Safety Survey 39, 42
Ngunyumu School, Korogocho 111–12
Nguyen, Thao 173
Northern Ireland Act (1998) Section 75 148

One World Foundation 124
Online Action Research 162–3, 170–2
  Blank Noise 35, 176–9, *178*, *179*, 205
  Hollaback! 172–6
  Stop Street Harassment 172–6
O'Reilly, Tim 181 n7
Organization for Economic Cooperation and Development (OECD) 20
Ortiz, Lilia 63

Panelli, R. *et al.* 62
Paquet, Gilles 92, 98
Parson, N. 54
participatory budgeting 77, 85, 144, 148, 150–1, 156, 157
participatory planning, feminist approach 59
partnerships 11, 90–1, 115, 202, 203, 205–6
  case study 96–100
  collaborative 94
  common aims 93, 98–9
  as co-optation 91–2
  and governance 92–3, 94, 98
  inclusive 96
  and intersectionality 95, 97, 100
  knowledge and experience 94–5, 98, 99–100
  and leadership 94, 99
  membership structures 93–4, 96, 99
  outcomes 100
  and power 93, 99
  problem diagnosis 95
  and synergies 84–7
  theory and practice 92–6
  and trust 93, 99
  see also Central Karoo, South Africa
Partnerships for Urban Knowledge and Research (PUKAR) 41, 192, 198 n30
Patheja, Jasmeen 176
peace and security agenda 2
Peel, Ontario 97, 99
Penalosa, Enrique 45, 46, 48
Peters, D. 40, 43
Petrozavodsk: Gender Inclusive Cities Programme 77, 77, 78, 79, 80, 81, 83, 86, 88 n4, 88 n7, 194
Phadke, S. 40–1, 42
Phillips, L. and Cole, S. 184, 188
Piper, N. 55
pluralistic citizenship 155
Plymouth City Council 146, 147
police/policing 82
  Dar es Salaam 85–6
  Rosario, Argentina 84–5
  women's police stations 155–6
Pollit, Katha 42
Port Moresby, Papua New Guinea 154–5, 195
Porto Alegre, Brazil 46, 150
Programme for Addressing and preventing Gender-based Violence 88 n5
public art *see* artistic intervention
public transport 39–42, 49–50, 82, 86–7, 146–7, 149–50
  Bogota 44–8
  and gender differences 36–9
  and gender mainstreaming 44
  policy initiatives 43–4
  and right to the city 44–5, 48
  and sexual harassment 39, 40–1
  social logics of planning 49
  'tyranny of purpose' 41
  and urban planning 27, 37, 39
  women only 40
  Women's Safety Audit 43, 47
Pune, India 40
Pushta *see* Yamuna Pushta

Quadri, Soledad 169–70
Quito, Ecuador 46, 195

race/racism 152–6, 206
Rainero, L. 22, 24, 83
Red Feminista 7
Red Mujer y Habitat network 76, 77, 88 n4, 168–70, *169*, 205
  'Mujeres por la Ciudad' (Women in the City) 168–70, *169*
Red Nacional de Trabajadoras del Hogar, Mexico 65, 67–8
Reeves, D. *149*
Regina, Canada 97, 98
Regional Safer Cities for Women 46–7
RightRides for Women's Safety 44
right to the city 5–6, 84, 88 n12, 201, 203
  and Gender Inclusive Cities Programme 78
  and infrastructure 117–19, 137
  migrant women 53, 59, 62
  and mobility 36
  and public transport 44–5, 48
Rio de Janeiro, Brazil 40
risk engagement 42, 43
Robson, S. and Spence, J. 91
Rockfort, Jamaica 165
Rojas, Samuel 48
Rosario, Argentina 22, 43
  CISCSA 77, 84–5, 169–70
  defaced women figures *169*
  Gender Inclusive Cities Programme 76, 77, *77*, 78, 79, 80, 81, 82, 83, 87, 88 n4, 195
  Latin American Women and Habitat Network (RMH) 76, 77, 88 n4, 168–70, *169*, 181 n5, 205
  police/policing 84–5
Roy, A. 21, 23
Roy, A. and AlSayyed, N. 22

Safe Cities Free of Violence against Women and Girls Global Programme 185
Safe Delhi campaign 87, 195
safety and unsafety 104
safety audits *see* Women's Safety Audit (WSA)
Sainath, P. 122
Sandberg, L. and Tollefsen, A. 155
Sandercock, Leonie, concept of narrative 163, 166, 170
sanitation 8, 10–11, 38, 112, 117, 126–8, *127*, 137, 202

Santiago, Chile 189
Second International Women's Safety Seminar: Safer Cities (2004) 1, 13 n4, 46, 205
self-employment 21
  see also informalization
Self-help Women's Union (SEWU) 29
Sen, Amartya 197 n9
Sen, G. 24–5
Seoul, South Korea 40
sexual harassment/assault
  community toilet complexes 126, 127
  daily reality 136, 137
  definition 177
  and drainage 131
  effects of 166
  and the Internet 172, 173–6
  public transport 39, 40–1
  and water supplies 129
  women's responses to *83*, 83–4
Shan Human Rights Foundation (SHRF) 66
Shan Women's Action Network (SWAN) 66
Shaw, Margaret 66
Silbaugh, K. 37
Singh, R. *55*, 60
Sistren Theatre Collective
  collective creations 165–6, 181 n3
  'Take it to dem an rise up wi community' 165–6, 170, 180 n2
Skinner, C. 28–9
Smith, Keri, *Guerrilla Art Kit* 180 n1
social development 47
social transformation 103–4, 110–12
  methodology 104–10
  safe city for women *114*
  safe community of opportunity model 110–12, *111*, 113–14
  unsafe communities 111–12
  see also Central Karoo, South Africa
solid-waste management 117, 133, 137
South African Police Service (SAPS) 104, 105
space-time feasibility 19, 23, 24–7
Spanish Agency for International Development Cooperation 181 n5
Status of Women in Canada 97, 98
Stevens, Q. 164
Stiglitz, Joseph 197 n9
St-Michel, Fanie 167–8

'Stop Licence to Rape in Burma' campaign 66
'Stop State Violence against Women' campaign 66
Stop Street Harassment website 172–6
Strathclyde Passenger Transport (SPT) 146, 147, 149–50
StreetNet International 29, 30
street trading 26–30, 47
Sweet, E.L. and Ortiz Escalante, S. 23, 24, 55
systems view of community/society 110–12

Tanzania: Gender Inclusive Cities Programme 194
Terrell, Mary Church 153
Third International Conference on Women's Safety: Building Inclusive Cities (2010) 1, 2–3, 13 n2, 87 n2, 103, 113–14, 195, 201, 205
Thompson, D. 42
Tibaijuka, Anna 90
Tokyo, Japan 40
Toronto, Canada 39, 43, 97, 145, 202
Toronto Transport Commission 43
Town and Country Planning Office (TCPO) 121
trafficking 9–10, 56–7
Transmilenio 46, 47
transport *see* public transport
Transport for London 49
  Women's Action Plan 44
Truth, Sojourner 152–3

UNDP 13 n4
UN-HABITAT 8, 10, 13 n4, 20, *21*, 78, 88 n6, 89 n14, 193–4, 205
UN-HABITAT Safer Cities Nairobi 112
UN-HABITAT Safer Cities Programme 78, 88 n6
  'The Global Assessment on Women's Safety' 90
UNIFEM 13 n4, 184, 194, 195, 197 n3
  'Cities without Violence against Women: Safe Cities for All' 189, 192
United Cities and Local Governments (UCLG) 118

United Nations Office on Drugs and Crime (UNODC) 56, 57, 198 n36
Global report on trafficking in persons (2009) 10
United Nations (UN) 145, 146, 205
Universal Declaration of Human Rights (1948) 5
University of Chicago Legal Forum 153
UN Trust Fund 12, 194
UN Trust Fund to End Violence against Women 76, 88 n3
UN Women 2, 7, 13 n5, 47, 181 n5, 194, 197 n3, 198 n37, 205
UN Women Regional Programme on Safer Cities 76, 77, 84
UN Women Safe Cities Free of Violence against Women and Girls Global Programme 194, 195–6
UN Women South Asian office 87
urban design 47, 83, 113–15, 149
urbanization 8, 118
  and exclusion of the poor, Delhi 121–3
urban planning 11, 31, 143, 149–50
  conceptual models of everyday life *120*, 120–1
  and infrastructure 119–21
  and public transport 27, 37, 39
  zoning 122
Usme, Colombia 46

Valenti, Jessica 172
Valentine, G. 155
Vangen, S. and Huxham, C. 94
Victoria Charter of Human Rights and Responsibilities 62
violence, cultural acceptance of 5

walking 37, 39, 48, 49
Walton-Roberts, M. 60
war/conflict 7, 56
Warwick Junction, Durban 27–8, *28*, 29, 31
water supplies 8, 10–11, 38, 117, 129, 137, 202
  see also Bawana and Bhalswa, Delhi
Waugh, Morales 58
weapons 108
Web 2.0 171, 181 n7
Weinstein, L. and Ren, X. 22
Wekerle, G.R. 155

Whitzman, C. 49, 53, 189
  community safety planning process 94, 95
Wilson, E. 40, 42
Wolverhampton, UK 147
Women Against Violence campaign 66
Women and Habitat Network 43
Women for Economic Justice 68 n4
Women Friendly City projects, South Korea 91
Women in Cities International (WICI) 13 n1, 19, 44, 75, 76, 88 n3, 96–100, 117, 123, 194, 198 n31, 205
  Together for Women's Safety. Creating Safer Communities for Marginalized Women and Everyone 158 n2
Women of the Dawn 97–100
Women's Action Centre on Urban Safety 13 n3
Women's Convention: Akron, Ohio 153
Women's Design Service 147
Women's Feature Service 124
Women's League of Burma 65, 66, 67, 68
Women's Machinery 88 n5
Women's Night Out event 45
women's police stations 155–6

Women's Safety Audit (WSA) 4, 5, 6, 11, 12, 75, 97, 144–5, 151, 193–4, 207
  Bawana and Bhalswa, Delhi *125*, 126
  Gender Inclusive Cities Programme 78, 80, 202
  gender mainstreaming 146
  public transport 43, 47
Women's Transport Network 44, 49
women's voice/leadership 2, 3, 6
World Bank 38–9, 43, 197 n4
World Charter for the Right to the City (2004-5) 5, 118
World Health Organization (WHO) 6–7, 14 n21, 189–90
World Social Forums 118
World Urban Forum (2006) 20

Yamuna Pushta 25, 27, 122, 124
Young, I.M. 42
YouTube 171
'Y R U Looking at Me' campaign 177, *178*
Yuval-Davis, N. 152, 154, 157

Zakira, Aisha 175
zoning 122
Zukin, Sharon, 'Whose Culture, Whose City?' 167